Ethical Educational Leadership in
Turbulent Times
(Re)Solving Moral Dilemmas

Ethical Educational Leadership in Turbulent Times

(Re)Solving Moral Dilemmas

Joan Poliner Shapiro • Steven Jay Gross

LEA Lawrence Erlbaum Associates
Taylor & Francis Group

New York   London

UNIVERSITY OF CHICHESTER

Lawrence Erlbaum Associates
Taylor & Francis Group
270 Madison Avenue
New York, NY 10016

Lawrence Erlbaum Associates
Taylor & Francis Group
2 Park Square
Milton Park, Abingdon
Oxon OX14 4RN

© 2008 by Taylor & Francis Group, LLC
Lawrence Erlbaum Associates is an imprint of Taylor & Francis Group, an Informa business

Printed in the United States of America on acid-free paper
10 9 8 7 6 5 4 3 2 1

International Standard Book Number-13: 978-0-8058-5600-2 (Softcover)

Library of Congress Cataloging-in-Publication Data

Shapiro, Joan Poliner.
  Ethical educational leadership in turbulent times : (re) solving moral dilemmas / Joan Poliner Shapiro and Steven Jay Gross.
       p. cm.
  Includes bibliographical references.
  ISBN-13: 978-0-8058-5600-2 (alk. paper)
  1. Educational leadership--Moral and ethical aspects. I. Gross, Steven Jay. II. Title.

LB2806.S353 2008
371.2--dc22
                                                                    2007015421

Visit the Taylor & Francis Web site at
http://www.taylorandfrancis.com

For my supportive and humorous husband, Dr. Irving M. Shapiro, who practices consistently the ethic of care, mixed with a bit of the ethic of critique, in just the right amounts.

Joan Poliner Shapiro

For Eric Kenneth Gross, my cousin and wonderful friend.

Steven Jay Gross

In memory of Lisa Marie Waller, a gifted educator and a dedicated doctoral student.

Steven Jay Gross
and
Joan Poliner Shapiro

CONTENTS

PREFACE   *ix*

ACKNOWLEDGMENTS   *xi*

Part One ∼ UNDERSTANDING THE THEORETICAL FRAMEWORK

1   **Overview of the Book**   *3*
    Case contributed by Noelle Jacquelin

2   **The Multiple Ethical Paradigms**   *19*

3   **Turbulence Theory**   *37*

Part Two ∼ (RE)SOLVING ETHICAL DILEMMAS

4   **Security versus Civil Liberties**   *55*
    Cases contributed by Susan H. Shapiro, Kelly D. Harbaugh,
    Mary M. Figura, and Lisa Marie Waller

5   **Power versus Accommodation in Curriculum, Instruction,
    and Assessment**   *67*
    Cases contributed by Stacey L. Aronow, James M. O'Connor,
    Robert J. Murphy, and Corrinne A. Caldwell

6   **Accountability versus Responsibility**   *87*
    Cases contributed by Rita M. Becker, Cynthia L. Renehan,
    Troy L. Wiestling, and Kendall L. Glouner

7   **Community Standards versus Individual Rights**   *103*
    Cases contributed by Melissa Sterba, Christopher J. Lake,
    Shaun Little, and Ellen Henderson Brown

8   **Equality versus Equity**   *119*
     Cases contributed by Albert F. Catarro, Jr., Jamie R. Shuda,
     W. Douglas Zander, and Yvonnette J. Marshall

9   **Personal Vision versus Authority**   *137*
     Cases contributed by Terry M. McDonald, Alison J. Staplin,
     Maureen F. Linton, and Emily L. Gross

10   **Rules, Regulations, and Policies versus Individual Needs and
     Concerns in Student Teaching**   *151*
     Cases contributed by David X. Fitt, Joseph P. DuCette, and
     Sara M. Becker

Part Three ∾ INTRODUCING THE NEW DEEL

11   **Control versus Democracy**   *167*

     REFERENCES   *177*
     AUTHORS   *193*
     CONTRIBUTORS   *195*
     INDEX   *203*

PREFACE

$\mathcal{E}$DUCATIONAL LEADERS HAVE ALWAYS HAD TO MAKE important decisions that affect the studies and lives of the next generation. Now, in this unstable era of war, terrorism, natural disasters, accountability, and high stakes testing, the decision making process can be even more daunting. In this book, there is an attempt to assist educational leaders in making those difficult decisions. For the purposes of this book, educational leadership is defined broadly to encompass not only school and central administrators but also lead teachers and administrators in higher education.

The title of this book was carefully considered. Finding a solution to a complex ethical problem, especially during uncertain times, is far from easy. Because of this, the use of the term "(re)solving" was added to signify that while decision making (hopefully using the theoretical framework presented in this book) will no doubt eventually take place, it might not lead to a permanent solution. It might only resolve the problem. However, this resolution phase should provide enough time to bring down the level of turbulence in a tense situation. Thus, whether the ethical dilemma or case is resolved or solved, the decision has the potential to assist educational leaders in dealing with thorny ethical problems.

Part One of this book introduces two theoretical concepts: Multiple Ethical Paradigms (Shapiro & Stefkovich, 2001, 2005) and Turbulence Theory (Gross, 1998, 2004, 2006). The first chapter provides a brief overview of the two concepts and offers an example of how to use them in making ethical decisions. Chapter 2 and Chapter 3 discuss the Multiple Ethical Paradigms and Turbulence Theory, respectively, in more detail. We believe that the Multiple Ethical Paradigms can assist educators in thinking through decision making in rational ways, while Turbulence Theory enables them to take into account the emotional climate of an organization as they make a final decision. We also believe that this combined framework will help educational leaders make appropriate and wise choices to safeguard, challenge, and truly educate the next generation.

To move from theory to practice, Part Two of the book presents ethical dilemmas. The cases are authentic and cover a range of topics, including race/ethnicity, social class, sexuality/gender, religion, diverse learners, and security issues. A number of the dilemmas tend to cover overlapping topics or categories. The cases were developed by practitioners, the majority of whom are also graduate students, as well as by some faculty members who have been in leadership positions. The questions at the end of each case enable the reader to work through the ethical dilemmas. They tap both the ethics of justice, critique, care, and the profession as well as take the emotional context for decision making into account. In addition to the questions posed, an instructor can ask students to discuss the topics or categories covered in a particular dilemma leading to a discussion—for example, about race/ethnicity or religion.

Part Three of the book will introduce the reader to a growing movement for educational leadership in the United States, Canada, Australia, Taiwan, and the United Kingdom called the "New DEEL" (Democratic Ethical Educational Leadership). This movement embodies the values that undergird the Multiple Ethical Paradigms and Turbulence Theory and has the potential to promulgate a new and much needed emphasis on grassroots organizing and community building to support democracy. Instead of a narrow focus on high stakes testing and a constricted curriculum, the New DEEL supports educating young people for civic responsibility and moral lives in these ethically challenging, turbulent times.

ACKNOWLEDGMENTS

WE WOULD LIKE TO THANK OUR EDITOR, Naomi Silverman, for practicing both the ethics of care and of critique in the development of this book as well as acknowledge Lynn Beck, Martha McCarthy, and an anonymous reviewer for their extremely helpful questions, insights, and comments. We would like to extend our sincere appreciation to Jacqueline Stefkovich, whose excellent ideas permeate this book, especially in Chapter 2, and to Robert (Jerry) Starratt, for creating an extremely useful and creative ethical framework on which we could build. We would also like to acknowledge Paul Begley, who has helped to give our work a forum at conferences held under the auspices of the University Council of Educational Administration (UCEA) Center for the Study of Leadership and Ethics. In addition, we would like to send our appreciation to Michelle Young, executive director of UCEA, for encouraging our work in so many ways. The graduate students and colleagues who contributed their dilemmas to this book from Temple University, New York University, and the University of Vermont truly deserve recognition: Stacey Aronow, Rita Becker, Sara Becker, Corrinne Caldwell, Albert Catarro, Joseph P. DuCette, Mary Figura, David X. Fitt, Kendall Glouner, Emily Gross, Kelly D. Harbaugh, Ellen Henderson Brown, Noelle Jacquelin, Christopher Lake, Maureen Linton, Shaun Little, Yvonnette Marshall, Terry McDonald, Robert Murphy, James M. O'Connor, Cynthia Renehan, Jamie R. Shuda, Susan H. Shapiro, Alison Staplin, Melissa Sterba, Lisa Waller, Troy Wiestling, and Douglas Zander.

In particular, we would like to recognize those scholars and practitioners from the U.S., Canada, Taiwan, and Australia who have been working closely with us on the New DEEL. We want to thank Temple University for helping to make this book a reality by providing each of us with a study leave, enabling us the time and space to read and write on ethics. In addition, we would like to thank Kristina P. Corey Legge, a graduate assistant in educational administration at Temple, who helped to put the finishing touches on this book.

Finally, we cannot leave this section without extending special appreciation to our families. Without their tolerance for our work schedule and their unwavering faith in us, this book would not have been possible.

Part One

UNDERSTANDING THE THEORETICAL FRAMEWORK

*T*HIS FIRST SECTION OF THIS BOOK prepares the reader to work with the Multiple Ethical Paradigms and Turbulence Theory. It presents, in some detail, the theoretical framework for solving or resolving complex ethical dilemmas.

Chapter 1 provides an overview of the two underlying concepts. It offers a brief description of the ethics of justice, critique, care, and the profession, and then introduces the four categories of light, moderate, extreme, and severe turbulence. It also provides an ethical dilemma and resolves it using both the Multiple Ethical Paradigms and Turbulence Theory. Additionally, the designing of a Turbulence Gauge is highlighted.

In Chapter 2, considerable background to the Multiple Ethical Paradigms is offered. Literature emanating from each of the four ethical perspectives is presented. All of the ethics come from rich intellectual traditions, and this chapter highlights appropriate scholars and their work.

Chapter 3 explores Turbulence Theory and includes the evolution of this concept as well as its application in helping to gauge the impact of disturbances in educational settings. Turbulence Theory is also considered in light of its relationship to previous and contemporary scholarship.

1

OVERVIEW OF THE BOOK

Case contributed by Noelle Jacquelin

The answer to fear is not to cower and hide;
It is not to surrender feebly without contest.
The answer is to stand and face it boldly,
look at it, analyze it, and, in the end, act.

Eleanor Roosevelt, 1963

*I*N THE BEGINNING OF THE 21ST CENTURY, in an era of wars, terrorism, hurricanes, financial uncertainty, and high-stakes testing, educational leaders are faced with even more daunting decision-making difficulties than in a more tranquil period. Educational leaders now face profound moral decisions regarding their classrooms, schools, school districts, and higher educational institutions in an ever-changing and challenging world. Beyond the normal ethical decisions they must make, they also need to take into account evacuation plans, psychological assistance, conflict resolutions, and global events and threats that impact their communities. The most difficult decisions to solve are ethical ones that require dealing with paradoxes and complexities. This book is designed to assist educational leaders in the ethical decision-making process. It is especially designed to help them during turbulent times.

Even in the best of times, educational leaders have confronted difficult moral dilemmas each day. Foster (1986, p.33) explained it this way: "Each administrative decision carries with it a restructuring of human life: that is why administration at its heart is the resolution of moral dilemmas." Fullan (2001) speaks of leaders being asked to constantly provide "once-and-for-all answers" to big problems that are "complex, rife with paradoxes and dilemmas" (p.2). Homer-Dixon (2000) carries these ideas further when he states:

> We demand that (leaders) solve, or at least manage, a multitude of inter-connected problems that can develop into crises without warning; we require them to navigate an increasingly turbulent reality that is, in key aspects, literally incomprehensible to the human mind; we buffet them on every side with bolder, more powerful special interests that challenge every innovative policy idea; we submerge them in often unhelpful and distracting information; and we force them to decide and act at an even faster pace. (p.15)

In this complex and challenging era, more and more is being asked of those in charge. Under these circumstances, no longer can central and school administrators do it all alone (Donaldson, 2001; Fullan, 2001). For the purposes of this book, educational leadership is defined broadly to encompass not only administrators but also those who take on decision-making functions through distributive leadership (Elmore, 2000; Guiney, 2001; Hart, 1994a, 1994b; Katzenmeyer & Moller, 2001; Neufeld & Roper, 2003; Poglinco et al., 2003; Spillane, Halverson, & Diamond, 2001). Educational leaders would then include an ever-increasing list of positions and titles, such as teacher leaders, instructional coaches, coordinators, department chairs, and members of crisis management teams. In particular, teacher leaders might serve as heads of charter schools and of learning communities or take on the roles of cooperating teachers and supervisors assisting universities in pre-paring the next generation of educators (Campbell, 2004a; Glickman, 2002; Hansen, 2001; Hostetler, 1997; Strike & Ternasky, 1993).

There is a caveat, however, concerning distributive leadership. In this era of accountability, final decisions are expected to reside with the person who is at the top of the hierarchy. In the United States, public school principals and superintendents, for example, have been singled out in legislation, such as the No Child Left Behind Act of 2001 (NCLB), to make the hard decisions and be held accountable for them. Thus, there is a tension between the appointed leader and those who also should have something to say in the decision-making process. Despite this warning, there will be examples of distributive leadership woven throughout the ethical dilemmas.

In this book, the term *ethics* relates well to values as discussed by Begley (1999), especially when he turned to decision making and problem solving. Begley emphasized that decision making "inevitably involves values to the extent that preferred alternatives are selected and others are rejected" (p.4). Begley also stressed the problems that educational leaders face because of value conflicts.

Some of these conflicts involve articulated values while others deal with core values that have not been made known and that "may be incompatible with organizational or community values" (p. 4). Such value conflicts are described throughout this book within the different ethical dilemmas.

At the theoretical level, this book rests on the concepts of the Multiple Ethical Paradigms of the ethics of justice, critique, care, and the profession (Shapiro & Stefkovich, 2001, 2005) and Turbulence Theory (Gross, 1998, 2004, 2006). These combined ideas form the theoretical framework that is meant to help educational leaders solve dilemmas in an unstable era. It brings together what Goleman (1995) calls the "two minds," the rational and the emotional. This amalgamation attempts to maintain the balance between two distinctly different ways of knowing. Goleman described them well when he wrote:

> These two fundamentally different ways of knowing interact to construct our mental life. One, the rational mind, is the mode of comprehension we are typically conscious of: more prominent in awareness, thoughtful, able to ponder and reflect. But alongside that there is another system of knowing impulsive and powerful, if sometimes illogical—the emotional mind...
>
> The emotional/rational dichotomy approximates the folk distinction between "heart" and "head"; knowing something is right "in your heart" is a different order of conviction—somehow a deeper kind of certainty—than thinking so with your rational mind. (p. 8)

The foci of this book, then, are the following:

1. To present the Multiple Ethical Paradigms of justice, critique, care, and the profession that deals primarily with the rational mind (Chapter 2);
2. To introduce the concept of Turbulence Theory that taps the emotional mind (Chapter 3);
3. To provide authentic ethical dilemmas that will be analyzed using the combination of the Multiple Ethical Paradigms and Turbulence Theory (Chapter 4 through Chapter 10);
4. To assist educational leaders in resolving and sometimes even solving difficult dilemmas in uncertain times;
5. To introduce Democratic Ethical Educational Leadership (New DEEL), a concept for transformative leadership incorporating ethics as well as democratic approaches into professional and even personal lives (Chapter 11).

This particular chapter is meant to provide an overview to the book by offering a brief introduction to the Multiple Ethical Paradigms and to

Turbulence Theory, followed by an authentic ethical dilemma from the field. This dilemma highlights some of the complexities that educational leaders now face in a period of rapid change. Following the dilemma, a discussion of how to use the theoretical framework to help deal with the case is presented. And finally, some questions are offered to demonstrate how this dilemma could be used in a classroom to spark discussion, lead to deep reflection, and help to resolve or solve the dilemma.

A Brief Introduction to the Multiple Ethical Paradigms

The underlying perspectives for helping educational leaders solve dilemmas in turbulent times are provided in a book entitled, *Ethical Leadership and Decision Making in Education: Applying Theoretical Perspectives to Complex Dilemmas*. This work, written by Shapiro and Stefkovich (2001, 2005), takes into account the Multiple Ethical Paradigms of justice, critique, care, and the profession. Starratt (1994a) had brought together the three paradigms of justice, critique, and care in his approach to ethics and schools. This model developed those ethics still further and added a fourth lens or paradigm, the ethic of the profession.

Turning to Shapiro and Stefkovich's Multiple Ethical Paradigm approach for an overview, one of the lenses is the ethic of justice. This model focuses on rights, law, and policies. It is part of a liberal democratic tradition that believes in faith in the legal system and in progress (Delgado, 1995). This paradigm focuses on concepts that include fairness, equality, and individual freedom. This lens leads to questions, such as: Is there a law, right, or policy that would be appropriate for resolving a particular ethical dilemma? Why is this law, right, or policy the correct one for this particular case? How should the law, right, or policy be implemented?

The ethic of critique has been discussed by a number of writers and activists who are not convinced by the analytic and rational approach of the justice paradigm. Some of these scholars find a tension between the ethic of justice—focusing on laws, rights, or policies—and, for example, the concept of democracy. Not only do they force us to rethink important concepts such as democracy but they also ask us to redefine and reframe other concepts such as privilege, power, culture, language, and, in particular, social justice. This ethic asks educators to deal with the difficult questions regarding class, race, gender, and other areas of difference, including: Who makes the laws, rules, or policies? Who benefits from these laws, rules, or policies? Who has the power? And who are the silenced voices?

While the ethic of care has been articulated recently by some male ethicists, for the most part this ethic has been discussed in contemporary times in greater detail by feminist scholars, who have challenged the dominant—and what they consider to be often patriarchal—ethic of justice in our society by turning to the ethic of care for moral decisionmaking. Attention to this ethic can lead to other discussions of concepts such as loyalty, trust, and empowerment. This ethic asks that individuals consider the consequences of their decisions and actions. It asks them to take into account questions, such as: Who will benefit from what I decide? Who will be hurt by my actions? What are the long-term effects of a decision I make today? And if I am helped by someone now, what should I do in the future about giving back to this individual or to society in general?

Finally, the ethic of the profession is best illustrated, for educational leaders, in a 1996 document, "Standards for School Leaders," developed by the Interstate School Leaders Licensure Consortium (ISLLC). Of these, Standard 5 states that, "A school administrator is an educational leader who promotes the success of all students by acting with integrity, fairness, and in an ethical manner" (ISLLC, 1996, p.18). This ethic places the student at the center of the decision-making process. It also takes into account not only the standards of the profession but the ethics of the community, the personal and professional codes of an educational leader, and the professional codes of a number of educational organizations (Shapiro & Stefkovich, 2001, 2005). The ethic of the profession in resolving or solving an ethical dilemma raises questions, including: What is in the best interests of the student? What are the personal and professional codes of an educational leader? What professional organizations' codes of ethics should be considered? What does the community think about this issue? And what is the appropriate way for a professional to act in this particular situation?

What follows is a representation of the Multiple Ethical Paradigms (Figure 1.1).

Figure 1.1 Multiple Ethical Paradigms

A Brief Introduction to Turbulence Theory

In his books, *Staying Centered: Curriculum Leadership in a Turbulent Era* and *Promises Kept: Sustaining School and District Leadership in Turbulent Times*, Gross (1998, 2004) found that sites that had developed curriculum, instructional, and assessment innovations for several years all experienced some degree of turbulence or volatile conditions. Further, he discovered that the degree of turbulence at the ten schools and districts he had studied could be divided into four levels:

Light turbulence includes ongoing issues with the normal functioning of the school. Examples of this include dealing with a disjointed community or geographic isolation of the institution. One school in Gross' study, for instance, responded to its geographic isolation by joining a national reform organization and by hosting an annual statewide conference on innovation at small schools. The key to light turbulence is the fact that it is part of the institution's environment and that it can be handled easily in a way that will, at least, keep the issue in check.

Moderate turbulence is related to specific issues that are widely recognized as important and needing to be solved. The loss of an important support structure would be one example of moderate turbulence. Rapid growth of the student body would be another example of moderate turbulence. Faced with the sudden expansion in students, a school that Gross investigated made this issue the center of in-service meetings just prior to the opening of school. Faculty members were trained in ways to welcome, listen to, and integrate new students. The principal modeled the attitude of acceptance by stating that the new students were not simply joining their institution but had every right to help change the school since that fit their school's philosophy. Moderate turbulence, therefore, is not part of normal operations; it quickly gains nearly everyone's attention and yet it can be responded to with a focused effort.

Severe turbulence is found in cases where the whole enterprise seems threatened. A conflict of community values was at the heart of one instance of severe turbulence in Gross' work. In that case, members of the community were deeply divided in their reaction to specific reforms. School board elections became highly emotional, friendships were ended due to pressure to join one faction or another, and the process of reform was suspended. The district used a four-stage strategy to respond to this dilemma. This included a shift to issues upon which agreement was less controversial, electing a centrist community member to serve as board chair, holding televised meetings of a strategic planning council, and reminding community members that stability and trust rather than disharmony were the district's norms. In severe turbulence, the problems are so serious that normal administrative actions seem inadequate. A coordinated set of strategies is very likely needed while business-as-usual thinking needs to be suspended.

Extreme turbulence would mean serious danger of the destruction of the institution. Gross speculated that this degree of turbulence was possible based on the fact that institutions do, of course, become unraveled. All of the ten sites in the 1998 study were able to respond to their own cases of turbulence, ranging from light to severe, with success. However, a follow-up study (Gross, 2000) did reveal a case of extreme turbulence where a cascading series of pressures caused an end to the entire reform process.

Turbulence Theory, therefore, gives us an enhanced ability to calibrate the severity of the issue at hand. It further aids us in our attempt to contextualize a given problem as we construct strategies to move to less troubled waters.

Table 1.1 is a generic turbulence gauge for assessing the emotional climate for ethical decision making.

Considering Turbulence Theory in the Context of Ethical Decision Making

While much of Gross' early work on Turbulence Theory was used to help explain the behavior of people facing organizational potentials and challenges, working with Shapiro it soon became clear that there was an application in the realm of ethical decision making. Those facing ethical dilemmas in the midst of busy organizational lives need to respond in a deeply reflective, systematic fashion as well as take into account the emotional context of decision making. For these purposes, we have connected the Multiple Ethical Paradigms with Turbulence Theory in our scholarship in working with field

Table 1.1 Definitions of Turbulence

Degree of Turbulence	General Definition
Light	Associated with ongoing issues, little or no disruption in normal work environment, subtle signs of stress
Moderate	Widespread awareness of the issue, specific origins
Severe	Fear for the entire enterprise, possibility of large-scale community demonstrations, a feeling of crisis
Extreme	Structural damage to the institution's normal operation is occurring

practitioners and when advising university and state officials. In this context, the four levels of turbulence, in the form of a gauge, are used early in the process to help illuminate the degree of disruption represented by the dilemma. Positionality of individuals and cascading events enter into the reflections as well at this time.* The Turbulence Gauge previously described is used after this reflection to estimate the level of turbulence. Thereafter, an analysis of the problem through the perspective of the combined ethical lenses takes place, followed by a course of action. At the conclusion of this process, a second estimate of turbulence is conducted, given that course of action as one asks, "If I take this course of action, where might turbulence be as a result, and for whom?"

Although not thought to be a lock-step approach, Figure 1.2 illustrates one cycle we suggest.

According to Glaser and Strauss (1967), theory needs to provide:

• Relevant predictions
• Explanations
• Interpretations
• Applications (p. 3)

Shapiro and Gross contend that Turbulence Theory, used in conjunction with the Multiple Ethical Paradigms, helps those facing ethical dilemmas perform all four of the preceding tasks. As Suskind (2004) observed when critiquing the rigid use of case studies by students in graduate schools of business:

> They discover, often to their surprise, that the world is dynamic, it flows and changes, often for no good reason. The key is flexibility, rather than sticking to your guns in a debate, and constant reassessment of shifting realities. In short, thoughtful second-guessing. (p. 48)

An Example of an Authentic Ethical Dilemma

An ethical dilemma, written by Noelle Jacquelin, a graduate student who was also a school administrator, will be presented. It is provided as an illustration to enable the reader to understand how to begin to use the Multiple Ethical Paradigms of justice, critique, care, and the profession and Turbulence Theory to solve difficult ethical dilemmas in a rapidly changing era.

---

* Please refer to Chapter 3 for an examination of positionality and cascading in the context of Turbulence Theory.

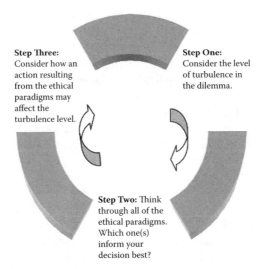

Step Three:
Consider how an
action resulting
from the ethical
paradigms may
affect the
turbulence level.

Step One:
Consider the level
of turbulence in
the dilemma.

Step Two: Think
through all of the
ethical paradigms.
Which one(s)
inform your
decision best?

**Figure 1.2   Using the Multiple Ethical Paradigms and
Turbulence Theory as an integrated system**

A Case: What in God's Name?

The principal hung up the telephone mixed with a tingle of excitement and a feeling of dread. She vividly recalled the woman's voice over the line: "This is most definitely an ACLU case. Here is the New Jersey director's private number. Please call tomorrow as soon as you can. Tell him I referred you."

Ms. Hockel, the thirty-something principal and mother of two, sat on the sofa in her living room smoking and wondering what the "right" action or inaction should be in this case. This was just one of the many ethical dilemmas that she had encountered in her short eight-month tenure in this new district, yet this one really bothered her. It bothered her more than the district's recent financial audit conducted by the state when misappropriations were suspected. She wondered why. Perhaps it was because this dilemma centered more directly on the children and their intellectual, spiritual, and moral development rather than adult error or ethics.

This case was such that she felt the need to discuss it with trusted colleagues outside of her district and with family members. She agonized, "What's right here? Will I go to court? Will I go to Hell? More importantly, what do I do tomorrow?" That very same morning, a man with a drill and a mission had affixed free "In God We Trust" signs to each classroom and office wall with the blessing of the tiny one-school school district's superintendent, Dr. Quinn.

Ms. Hockel promptly removed her sign despite the admonishing remarks and looks from her administrative assistant, who was a devout Catholic.

She had only been in the district a short while. She knew that Dr. Quinn had been certified under New Jersey's alternate route for the superintendent's certification, and she had privately felt that he was lacking in some important foundational administrative knowledge and background, most notably in the areas of law and ethics. Ms. Hockel was not naïve. She realized that if she did not assert her view in this case, there could be some long-term consequences, both personally and professionally. But the superintendent was an intelligent man. He had explained his belief in hanging the signs throughout the school at the last board meeting. Dr. Quinn felt strongly that the children needed direction and that the triumvirate of American morality and citizenship—the home, the church, and the school—had broken down for these particular children. He felt they had no clear direction from the community at large. "Furthermore," he explained, "the motto is our national motto, and it is on our currency." Ms. Hockel thought to herself: Had not the board itself unanimously approved the signs for display? Who was she to argue? What did she know? After all, the school's solicitor, a close friend of the superintendent's, had been present at the meeting. Was she, as the superintendent often jokingly stated, just "too liberal"? She recalled the steady stream of teachers who had secretly poured into her office that afternoon to comment on the plaques. Some were angered because they were not "asked first." Others objected, citing legal reasons. Still others praised the superintendent for making a decision that "could only be positive."

The students hailed from a community fraught with problems. They were poor, and sixty-eight percent of the adults had never finished high school. Additionally, they were viewed by the majority of faculty members as unprepared to parent effectively because most of them had been very young when they had become parents. Many of the teachers, the superintendent, and Ms. Hockel felt the numbers spoke for themselves. Nearly fifty percent of the children were in kinship or regular foster care. The large and numerous "In God We Trust" signs ominously presented Ms. Hockel with a true ethical paradox, and it was tearing her apart. Ms. Hockel assumed the superintendent had a sincere desire to instill "values" in an increasingly "value-less" society. Yet were these the appropriate values for the community and, more importantly, should the school be the one to merge church and state? Additionally, the critique provided by many of the teachers fueled Ms. Hockel's own quiet personal concerns. The signs spurred a philosophical debate among the ethics of critique, justice, care, and the profession. They also provided a real-life dilemma for which she had little time for reflection; she knew she had to analyze this paradox in a timely manner for the sake of all individuals involved, particularly the children. She also knew that she did not want to raise the level of turbulence in the school.

The Multiple Ethical Paradigms Approach

To handle this ethical dilemma, Ms. Hockel should work through the Multiple Ethical Paradigms of justice, critique, care, and the profession. What follows is an analysis of the case, using each of the four ethics.

The Ethic of Justice

In this dilemma, as in all of the cases in this book, it is essential to consider the current law, rights, and policies and how they should be applied, illuminating the ethic of justice. Initially, in this dilemma Ms. Hockel reacted by mentioning the separation of church and state in public schools. However, Dr. Quinn believes that the motto, "In God We Trust," need not be perceived as religious as it is on the national currency. He also believes that the motto offers a values orientation to the community that is in need of ethics. While both individuals have their own points of view, it is important to look at the law, rules, and policies as they now relate to this dilemma.

For example, in this particular instance, there are requirements found in the NCLB that could affect the interpretation of the division between church and state in public schools. In a memo written by Rod Paige (2003), then secretary of education in the George W. Bush administration, information about prayer in public elementary and secondary schools was provided. Paige turned to the guidance section of the implementation of NCLB. He wrote:

> The guidance clarifies the rights of students to pray in public schools. As stated in the guidance, "the First Amendment forbids religious activity that is sponsored by the government but protects religious activity that is initiated by private individuals" such as students. Therefore, "[a]mong other things, students may read their Bibles or other scriptures, say grace before meals, and pray or study religious materials with fellow students during recess, the lunch hour, or other noninstructional time to the same extent that they may engage in nonreligious activities." Public schools should not be hostile to the religious rights of their students and their families.
>
> At the same time, school officials may not "compel students to participate in prayer or other religious activities." Nor may teachers, school administrators and other school employees, when acting in their official capacities as representatives of the state, encourage or discourage prayer, or participate in such activities with students.

Paige went on to say:

> In these challenging times, it is more important than ever to recognize the freedoms we have. I hope that this guidance can contribute to a common understanding of the meaning of the First Amendment in the public school setting. I encourage you to distribute this guidance widely in your community and to discuss its contents and importance with school administrators, teachers, parents, and students. Paige, R. (2003)

As Ms. Hockel read this memo, the division between church and state in public schools became no longer as clear-cut as she had thought. The law had been modified in an ever-changing era. As she reread the memo, she asked herself a number of conflicting questions: Who initiated this hanging of the mottos? Was it the students or their families, or was it a school official? Did the mottos compel students to pray in school? Ms. Hockel decided that she needed to now seek some legal assistance to inquire: What does this guidance or modification of the law mean in this particular situation? How will it be interpreted by a court? Overall, what does it mean if she removes the mottos or keeps them on the walls from a legal perspective?

The Ethic of Critique

With the new interpretation of the law in mind, Ms. Hockel had to review Dr. Quinn's actions with fresh eyes. She asked: Could Dr. Quinn put up such signs in this new era? Would the modifications of the interpretation of the First Amendment enable him to do this? She also needed to ask: Who has modified the law? Why has it been changed? And finally, should she go along with the changes and revise her own views about the divisions of church and state in the public schools or should she maintain her own perspective?

The Ethic of Care

Turning to the paradigm of the ethic of care, Ms. Hockel decided to focus on her students, her teachers and staff, and the local community. She posed a number of questions that highlighted the concept of care, concern, and connectedness over time. She reflected: Will the motto help or hurt the young people in her building? What about her teachers and staff and their morale? Will these signs create a rift in her staff? And how will the parents and others in the local community respond to these signs? Will the well-intentioned mottos create conflict in the population? Or will these signs do what the superintendent hopes and help to create better values for the children and their families?

The Ethic of the Profession

As an educational leader, Ms. Hockel determined that it was important for her to consider her own personal and professional codes. As she thought about her own values and beliefs, she asked: Why did she automatically tear down the sign? How strong is her belief in the division between church and state in the public schools? Where do her beliefs come from—her family, religion, friends, mentors, education? She also thought about the various constituencies and how they must now be taken into consideration as an educational leader. What about the views of her superior, the superintendent? Can she learn to live with his desire to keep the mottos on the walls? Thinking of the educational hierarchy, should she simply go along with his decision?

Turning to the community, she questioned their values. Will they think that the school is forcing its beliefs on their children? Or alternatively, will they be pleased with the new signs and believe that they might positively affect their children? Above all, what will these mottos mean to the children? Are they of value to them? Can they make a positive difference in their lives? Or will they convey another message, that of religion in public schools? And what will that mean to them now and in the future?

Turbulence Level: Moderate

In this era of uncertainty, wars, and changing interpretations of laws, putting up and tearing down "In God We Trust" mottos in a public school become significant acts. This scenario represents a case of moderate turbulence in which normal administrative responses may prove inadequate. By removing the sign in front of her secretary, Ms. Hockel made a statement that met with disapproval. The teachers in the school already have visited the principal, indicating a whole range of emotions and values from approval to anger. Some plan to join community members at the next school board meeting to protest.

Now the principal needs to act. She has a number of choices: Should she continue to tear down the signs knowing that there is a good chance that turbulence might escalate in the short run? Should she confront the superintendent, realizing that this response could be deemed as insubordina-

Table 1.2   Turbulence Gauge for This Ethical Dilemma

Degree of Turbulence	General Definition	Turbulence as It Is Applied to This Situation
Light	Associated with ongoing issues, little or no disruption in normal work environment, subtle signs of stress	The issue is raised and both sides enter into dialogue before a decision is made. A workable agreement is found built upon respect for the values of each side
Moderate	Widespread awareness of the issue, specific origins	The issue reveals a clear division between thoughtful people. Respect exists between the sides, as well. Creative problem solving is still possible but must come soon
Severe	Fear for the entire enterprise, possibility of large-scale community demonstrations, a feeling of crisis	Communication among all parties is constricted, and the sides harden their positions. They plan to battle for advantage
Extreme	Structural damage to the institution's normal operation is occurring	Large-scale demonstrations are held. Deep, long-lived divisions are created. Court battles playing out in the media are common, draining the life out of the system

tion and she might lose her job? Should she discuss the dilemma with her teachers and staff knowing that she opens herself up to direct confrontation and/or support that will also affect turbulence? Should she speak with the parents and open the discussion to the community with the possibilities of support or conflict? Or should she directly appeal to the board and go over the head of the superintendent, knowing full well that this will indeed be treated as insubordination?

Whatever the principal decides to do, she must seek to stabilize this small, potentially volatile school district. It is particularly challenging in a country that is currently affected by common religious and political beliefs in the name of patriotism. Short of thoughtful, engaging, and creative outreach, the whole enterprise may be threatened and move toward severe turbulence.

Table 1.2 is a turbulence gauge appropriate to this case. It demonstrates ways to decrease or increase the volatility of this situation through decision making.

After deep reflection, Ms. Hockel now believes that she is prepared to act. What do you think she will do? To assist Ms. Hockel and you, the reader, a number of key questions are presented related to this dilemma. They tap different ethical perspectives as well as Turbulence Theory and should be helpful in making a final decision.

Questions for Discussion

1. Are there laws, rights, or policies that are appropriate to this case, and if so, should they be followed? If there are no laws, are there guidelines to consider? (Ethic of Justice)

2. If there are laws, rights, policies, or guidelines, who made them and why might they be inappropriate in this situation? If there are no laws, rights, policies, or guidelines, why aren't there any? What concepts should be considered beyond the law, rights, policies, or guidelines? (Ethic of Critique)

3. If Ms. Hockel pulls down the signs, who will she hurt? Who will she help? In the long term, will her decision make a difference in the lives of her students, teachers, or the local community? Discuss. (Ethic of Care)

4. What about the children? What is the best course of action for Ms. Hockel to follow that would place their best interests at the center of the decision-making process? In her role as principal, what would be the best decision for Ms. Hockel to make? Why should she choose this action or inaction? (Ethic of the Profession)

5. Since this is a case of moderate turbulence, can you identify how this dilemma may escalate if handled in merely conventional ways? Can you identify how the turbulence level could be lowered in this case? (Application of Turbulence Theory)

6. How might the administration use this moderate turbulence as a learning experience? Consider ways that the energy brought on by this turbulence can be refocused to energize and enlighten the school and its community. (Application of Turbulence Theory)

Dilemmas in Education in a Time of Turbulence

In an era in which patriotism and religion are very important, the dilemma, "A Case: In God We Trust," became difficult to solve. In another time and place, the separation of church and state would take precedence, and the dilemma might not have even occurred. Additionally, under normal circumstances, if the case emerged it could have been handled swiftly by focusing on the ethic of justice. However, in the current climate in which guidelines, for example, have been developed to interpret laws, lines are no longer so clear. Emotions are running high, and Ms. Hockel has been left with a difficult decision to make.

Pedagogically, one way to give students their own voice—in keeping with the work of Gilligan (1982), Belenky, Clinchy, Goldberger, and Tarule (1986), Noddings (1992), Shapiro and Smith-Rosenberg (1989), Shapiro and Stefkovich (1997, 1998, 2001, 2005), Stefkovich and Shapiro (1994, 2003), Weis and Fine (1993), and others—is through meaningful discussions of ethical dilemmas. The formal presentations of these dilemmas can lead to probing questions and answers by peers and faculty members. Breaking down silence by opening up university classrooms for honest and challenging discussions is a way to begin to prepare educational leaders to cross the borders into their communities to deal with difficult issues and even previously taboo topics. Using student-written ethical dilemmas that describe real-life situations can also be an effective approach to make certain that all students are knowledgeable about a number of current emotional and sometimes painful issues prior to actually confronting them in their work and in their private lives.

In a time of turbulence, it seems essential that the classroom provide the safe space to discuss crisis situations. None of us know how we will react under unusual pressure. Using both Turbulence Theory and the Multiple Ethical Paradigms of justice, critique, care, and the profession, we anticipate that educational leaders will be able to approach the inevitable conflicts with more confidence, taking into account both emotions and reason. By trying out authentic dilemmas, by determining what type of turbulence will be caused by the dilemma and how to deal with it, and by using diverse ethical perspectives to work toward solutions, it is hoped that this combination may be of help to new as well as experienced educational leaders—such as principals, superintendents, teacher leaders, instructional coaches, coordinators, supervisors, cooperating or master teachers, and members of crisis management teams—who must make difficult decisions in chaotic times.

2

THE MULTIPLE ETHICAL PARADIGMS*

Developing the Model

*J*OAN SHAPIRO AND JACQUELINE STEFKOVICH came together as a writing team when they realized that they responded to different ethics and saw the world from dissimilar perspectives (Shapiro, 2006; Stekovich & Shapiro, 1994). This awareness came about through the teaching of ethics. Specifically, it occurred when Stefkovich took over an ethics class that Shapiro had taught. Her approach in teaching an ethical dilemma was so different from Shapiro's that it seemed to be essential for the two of them to come together to discuss their theoretical and pedagogical approaches. As they talked, they realized that in Shapiro's teaching, the ethics of care and critique were often emphasized, while Stefkovich tended to utilize the ethics of justice and the profession when analyzing ethical dilemmas. It turned out that Shapiro's background as a teacher and as a women's studies faculty member and Stefkovich's experiences as a school counselor and as a lawyer accounted for these diverse ways of knowing. The merging of different ethics brought the writing team together—a collaboration that has lasted for well over a decade.

In the course of conversations, Stefkovich and Shapiro began to discuss not only paradigms but also pedagogy and even concrete assignments. They became cognizant that they both liked working through ethical dilemmas with their students. They also became aware that they asked their students to carry out self-reflection via the development of their personal and professional codes of ethics. Ultimately, they both requested students to write their own authentic ethical dilemmas from the field. Their graduate students'

---

* This chapter, comes, in part, from Chapter 2 in Shapiro and Stefkovich's *Ethical Leadership and Decision Making in Education* (2005).

educational experiences were diverse. Some came from K–12 backgrounds, while others were in higher education; a number were urban educators and many were from the suburbs and rural areas. Over time, having written a number of exploratory articles together on pedagogy and paradigms (Shapiro & Stefkovich, 1997, 1998; Stefkovich & Shapiro, 1994, 1998), the team turned to the idea of compiling a case book of ethical dilemmas utilizing some of the ethical dilemmas developed by their graduate students.

The designing of a case book seemed to be a very appropriate format. One reason was that in Stefkovich's law training, cases were often used, while in Shapiro's women's studies course, focusing on ethics, ethical dilemmas were utilized as teaching vehicles. Thus, it came naturally to them both to turn to dilemmas or cases.

While the writing team liked the few case books that were then available, they became aware that something was lacking in most if not all of them. They felt that the practical aspect of the students' training could be met fairly well in the classroom through the use of ethical dilemmas, but they began to notice that theory was missing. In an effort to help their students, they began to read more widely and more deeply in the area of ethics, moving through the backgrounds to the ethics of justice, critique, and care. These three ethics had been developed by Starratt (1994a) in his book, *Building an Ethical School*. The fourth paradigm, the ethic of the profession, was shaped in detail by Shapiro and Stefkovich (2001, 2005); this led to the concept of the Multiple Ethical Paradigms. They used these perspectives as approaches to resolve or solve ethical dilemmas.

In this chapter, one goal is to provide background to the Multiple Ethical Paradigms to help the reader understand these paradigms. Another intention is to assist the reader in responding to some of the questions listed at the end of each of the dilemmas in this book. A number of the questions highlight the ethics of justice, critique, care, and the profession.

To understand the Multiple Ethical Paradigms, it is important to define ethics itself. This concept has had numerous meanings over time. Initially, it came from the Greek word *ethos*, which meant customs or usages, especially belonging to one group as distinguished from another. Later, ethics came to mean disposition or character, customs, and approved ways of acting. Dewey (1902), for example, defined ethics as the science that dealt with conduct insofar as this is considered as right or wrong, good or bad. Although Dewey's characterization of ethics as a science might be disputed, his focus on behavior cannot be in doubt. Reflecting upon these definitions using a critical lens, one might ask: Good or bad by whose standards? Right or wrong according to whom? Or even, approved ways of acting by whom?

In an attempt to answer these and other important questions, the ethics of justice, critique, care, and the profession will be described. These ethics will be shown to be emanating from diverse traditions and sometimes, while emerging from different starting points, even collide with each other. They also will be depicted keeping in mind how they impact school administrators, teacher leaders, and higher educational administrators' decision-making processes in the contemporary world.

The Ethic of Justice

In the past, philosophers such as Aristotle, Rousseau, Hegel, Marx, and Dewey tended to see society as central rather than the individual, and sought to teach individuals how to behave throughout their lives within communities. Within this tradition, justice emerged from "communal understandings" (Starratt, 1994a, p.50). Noddings (1999) added to this idea when she wrote about justice, saying, "in modern times, it (justice) has pointed more directly at a preferred relationship between institutions and human beings" (p. 7).

The ethic of justice deals with laws, rights, and policies and is part of a liberal democratic tradition that, according to Delgado (1995), "is characterized by incrementalism, faith in the legal system, and hope for progress" (p. 1). The liberal part of this tradition is defined as a "commitment to human freedom," and the democratic aspect implies "procedures for making decisions that respect the equal sovereignty of the people" (Strike, 1991, p. 415). Present-day philosophers and writers, coming from a justice perspective, frequently have dealt with issues such as rights and impartiality that are very much a part of distributive justice. In fact, Rawls (1971) defined justice as fairness.

Educators and ethicists from the ethic of justice have profoundly affected approaches associated with education and educational leadership. Modern-day ethical writings in education, using the foundational principle of the ethic of justice, include among others works by Beauchamp and Childress (1984); Goodlad, Soder, and Sirotnik (1990); Kohlberg (1981); Sergiovanni (1992); Strike, Haller, and Soltis (1998); and Yodof, Kirp, and Levin (1992).

Turning to one of those authors, Kohlberg (1981) felt deeply about the ethic of justice. One of the reasons for his passion for this paradigm was that as a young soldier in World War II, he had helped to liberate one of the concentration camps and saw what an unjust society could create. He argued that, "there is a great concern not only to make schools more just—that is, to provide equality of educational opportunity and to allow freedom of belief—but also to educate so that free and just people emerge from schools" (p. 74). For Kohlberg, "justice is not a rule or set of rules, it is a moral principle… a mode of choosing that is universal, a rule of choosing that we want all people to adopt always in all situations" (p. 39). From his point of view, Kohlberg's approach to education could not be "value free." Instead, Kohlberg's model maintained that schools should teach principles; in particular, those of justice, equity, and respect for liberty.

From the late 1960s through the early 1980s, Kohlberg introduced his "just-community" concept to the schools. In institutions as diverse as the comprehensive school Roosevelt High, The Bronx High School of Science, and an alternative high school in Cambridge, Massachusetts, students and teachers managed school discipline and sometimes even dealt with the running of the school together. In a civil and thoughtful manner, students were taught to deal with problems within the school, turning to rules, rights, and laws for guidance (Hersh, Paolitto, & Reimer, 1979).

Not dissimilar to Kohlberg, Sergiovanni (1992) called for moral leadership and especially requested the principle of justice in the designing of his "virtuous schools." Sergiovanni thought of educational leadership as a stewardship and asked educational administrators to create institutions that were just and beneficent. By beneficence, Sergiovanni meant that there should be deep concern for the welfare of the school as a community, a concept that extended beyond the school walls and into the local environment, taking into account not only students, teachers, and administrators but families as well.

Sergiovanni's virtuous schools placed the principle of justice at its heart. He explained, "Accepting this principle meant that every parent, teacher, student, administrator, and other member of the school community must be treated with the same equality, dignity, and fair play." (pp. 105–106)

The ethic of justice, from a contemporary perspective, takes into account a wide variety of issues. Viewing ethical dilemmas from this vantage point, one may raise queries regarding the interpretation of the rule of law as well as deal with the more abstract concepts of fairness, liberty, and responsibility. These may include, but are certainly not limited to, questions related to equality versus equity, moral absolutism versus situational ethics, and the rights of individuals versus the greater good of the community.

Moreover, the ethic of justice frequently has served as the framework for legal principles and ideals, particularly as they affect education. In many instances, courts have been reluctant to impose restrictions on school officials, thus allowing them considerable discretion in making important administrative decisions (*Board of Education v. Pico*, 1981). At the same time, court opinions have frequently reflected the values of the education community and society at large (Stefkovich & Guba, 1998). For example, only in recent years have courts upheld the use of metal detectors in schools to screen for weapons (*People v. Dukes*, 1992). Additionally, what is legal in some places might be considered illegal in others. For example, corporal punishment (Hyman & Snook, 2000) is still legal in some states, and strip-searching is legal in many of the states (Stefkovich & O'Brien, 2000). In those states, it is left up to school officials and the community whether such practices are to be supported or not. Here, ethical issues such as due process and privacy rights are often balanced against the need for civility and the good of the majority.

Broadly framed, then, the ethic of justice takes into account questions such as: Is there a law, right, or policy that relates to a particular case? If there is a law, right, or policy, should it be enforced? Is the law enforced in some places and not in others? Why or why not? And if there is not a law, right, or policy, should there be one?

The Ethic of Critique

Frequently, the ethic of critique opposes or highlights problems inherent in the ethic of justice. Many writers and activists (e.g., Apple, 1988, 2000, 2001, 2003; Astuto, Clark, & Read, 1994; Bakhtin, 1981; Bowles & Gintis, 1988; Foucault, 1983; Freire, 1970; Giroux, 1994, 2000, 2003; Greene, 1988; Larson & Murtadha, 2002; Purpel, 1989, 2004; Shapiro & Purpel, 1993, 1998; Shapiro, 1999; Shapiro, 2006) are not convinced by the analytic and rational approach of the justice paradigm. Some of these scholars find a tension between the ethic of justice, rights, and laws and concepts such as democracy and social justice. In response, they raise difficult questions by critiquing both the laws, rights, and policies themselves and the process used to determine if the laws, rights, and policies are just. They also ask questions related to circumstances when a ruling can be wrong, such as in the case of earlier Jim Crow laws supporting racial segregation (Starratt, 1994c).

Instead of accepting the decisions and values of those in authority, these scholars and activists challenge the status quo by utilizing an ethic that deals with inconsistencies, formulates the hard questions, and debates and challenges the issues. Their intent is to awaken us to our own unstated values and make us realize how frequently our own morals may have been modified and possibly even corrupted over time. Not only do they force us to rethink important concepts such as democracy and social justice, they also ask us to redefine and reframe other concepts such as privilege, power, culture, language, and even justice itself. While deconstructing the accepted concepts, they also provide us with a language of empowerment, transformation, and possibilities.

The ethic of critique is based on critical theory, which has at its center an analysis of social class and its inequities. According to Foster (1986), critical theorists are scholars who have approached social analysis in an investigative and critical manner and who have conducted investigations of social structure from perspectives originating in a modified Marxian analysis (p. 71).

More recently, critical theorists have turned to the intersection of race and gender as well as social class in their analyses. A modern example of the work of critical theorists can be found in their argument that schools reproduce inequities similar to those in society (e.g., Bourdieu, 1977, 2001; Lareau, 1987, 2003). Tracking, for example, can be seen as one way to make certain that working-class girls and boys know their place (Oakes, 1993). To accomplish this end, those who manage schools "[make] decisions about the appropriateness of various topics and skills and, in doing so... [limit]... sharply what some students would learn" (Oakes, 1993, p. 87).

Despite the inequities related to tracking, a paradox does exist. Carnoy and Levin (1985) pointed to this important contradiction when they indicated that schools also represented the major force in the United States for expanding economic opportunity and democratic rights. So on the one hand, schools track students and keep them in their place, while on the other hand, they offer financial and democratic advantages to all. Such inconsistencies are often addressed by those who turn to the ethic of critique.

Along with critical theory, the ethic of critique is also frequently linked to critical pedagogy (Freire, 1970). Giroux (1991) asked educators to understand that their classrooms are political sites as well as educational locations and, as such, ethics is not a matter of individual choice or relativism but a "social discourse grounded in struggles that refuse to accept needless human suffering and exploitation." He went on to say that in this respect, the ethic of critique provided "a discourse for expanding basic human rights" (p. 48) and might serve as a vehicle in the struggle against inequality. In this vein, critical theorists are often concerned with hearing the voices of those who are silenced, particularly students (Giroux, 1988, 2003; Weis & Fine, 1993).

To Giroux (1991, 2000, 2003), Welch (1991), and other educators who work within this tradition, the language of critique is central. However, many of them feel that discourse alone will not suffice. These scholars are frequently activists who believe discourse should be a beginning leading to some type of action, preferably political. For example, Shapiro and Purpel (1993) emphasized empowering people through the discussion of options. Such a dialogue hopefully would provide what Giroux and Aronowitz (1985) called a "language of possibility" that, when applied to educational institutions, might enable them to avoid reproducing the "isms" in society (i.e., classism, racism, sexism, heterosexism).

Turning to educational leadership in particular, Parker and Shapiro (1993) argued that one way to rectify some wrongs in school and in society would be to place more attention upon the analysis of social class in the preparation of principals and superintendents. They believed that social class analysis "is crucial given the growing divisions of wealth and power in the United States, and their impact on inequitable distribution of resources both within and among school districts" (pp. 39–40). Through the critical analysis of social class, there is the possibility that more knowledgeable, moral, and sensitive educational leaders might be prepared.

In her writings in educational leadership, Capper (1993) stressed the need for moral leaders to be concerned with "freedom, equality, and the principles of a democratic society" (p. 14). She provided a useful summary of the roots of and philosophy supporting the ethic of critique as it pertains to educational leaders. She spoke of the Frankfurt school in the United States in the 1920s, at the New School for Social Research in New York City, in which immigrants tried to make sense of the oppression they had endured in Europe. This school provided not only a Marxist critique but took into account psychology and its effect on the individual. Capper wrote:

> Grounded in the work of the Frankfurt school, critical theorists in educational administration are ultimately concerned with suffering and oppression, and critically reflect on current and historical social inequities. They believe in the imperative of leadership and authority and work toward the empowerment and transformation of followers, while grounding decisions in morals and values. (p. 15)

Thus, by demystifying and questioning what is happening in society and in schools, critical theorists may help educators rectify wrongs while identifying key morals and values.

This ethic then asks educators to examine and grapple with those possibilities that could enable all children—whatever their social class, race, or gender—to have opportunities to grow, learn, and achieve. Such a process should lead to the development of options related to important concepts such as oppression, power, privilege, authority, language, voice, and empowerment.

In summary, the ethic of critique, inherent in critical theory and critical pedagogy, is aimed at awakening all of us to inequities in society and, in particular, to injustices within education at all levels. It asks us to deal with the difficult questions regarding social class, race, gender, and other areas of difference, such as: Who makes the laws, rules, and policies? Who benefits from them? Who has the power? Who are silenced?

Once such difficult questions are answered, this ethic then considers: What could make a difference to enable those who have been silenced, ignored, and oppressed to become empowered? What new possibilities could be presented to lead toward social justice and the making of a better society?

Similar to the ethic of critique, the ethic of care is often juxtaposed with the ethic of justice in the Western contemporary world. For example, Strike (1999) created a distinction between the two ethics in this way:

> Justice aims at a society and at personal relationships in which people are treated fairly, where they get what they are due, in which they are respected as equals, and where mutually agreeable conditions of cooperation are respected. Caring aims at a society and at personal relationships in which nurturance and relationships are highly valued. (p. 21)

Roland Martin (1993) continued with the dissimilarity between the ethic of justice and that of care. She created a sharp difference between the male productive and the female reproductive processes and how they are valued in society. She wrote:

> One of the most important findings of contemporary scholarship is that our culture embraces a hierarchy of value that places the productive processes of society and their associated traits above society's reproductive processes and the associated traits of care and nurturance. There is nothing new about this. We are the inheritors of a tradition of Western thought according to which the functions, tasks, and traits associated with females are deemed less valuable than those associated with males. (p. 144)

Some feminist scholars (e.g., Beck, 1994; Belenky, Clinchy, Goldberger, & Tarule, 1986; Gilligan, 1982; Gilligan, Ward, & Taylor, 1988; Ginsberg, Shapiro, & Brown, 2004; Goldberger, Tarule, Clinchy, & Belenky, 1996; Grogan, 1996; Marshall, 1995; Noddings, 1984, 1992, 2002, 2003; Sernak, 1998; Shapiro & Smith-Rosenberg, 1989; Shapiro, Ginsberg, & Brown, 2003) have challenged the dominant—and what they consider to be often patriarchal—ethic of justice and have made the ethic of care more central to moral decision making and to society in general. They have paid special attention to concepts such as loyalty, trust, and empowerment. Similar to critical theorists, these feminist scholars have emphasized social justice as a pivotal concept associated with the ethic of care.

Gilligan (1982), in her classic book, *In a Different Voice*, introduced the ethic of care in the resolutions of moral dilemmas. In her research as a former graduate student of Kohlberg's, she used initially the same types of moral dilemmas as he did in his work. However, Gilligan discovered that unlike Kohlberg's male interviewees, who adopted rights and laws for the solution of moral issues, women and girls frequently turned to another voice of care, concern, and connection in finding answers to ethical cases.

Not content to simply hear the other voice at a private level, Noddings (1992) moved the ethic of care into the public forum, as it relates to education, by creating an educational hierarchy placing "care" at the top. She wrote, "The first job of the schools is to care for our children" (p. xiv). In her discussion, Noddings emphasized that holding on to a competitive edge in achievement has meant that some children may see themselves merely as pawns in a nation of demanding and uncaring adults. For Noddings, "Caring is the very bedrock of all successful education and ... contemporary schooling can be revitalized in its light" (p. 27).

Noddings and Gilligan are not alone in believing the ethic of care is essential in education. In relation to the curriculum, for instance, Roland Martin (1993) wrote of the three C's of caring, concern, and connection. Although she did not ask educators to teach "Compassion 101a" or to offer "Objectivity 101a," she did implore them to broaden the curriculum to include the experiences of both sexes and not just one, and to stop leaving out the ethic of care. For Roland Martin, education should be an "integration of reason and emotion, self and other" (p. 144).

Although the ethic of care most recently has been associated with feminists, men and women alike attest to its importance and relevancy. Beck (1994) made this point when she wrote, "Caring—as a foundational ethic—addresses concerns and needs as expressed by many persons; that it, in a sense, transcends ideological boundaries" (p. 3). Male ethicists and educators, including Buber (1965) and Sergiovanni (1992), have helped to develop this paradigm. These scholars have sought to make education a "human enterprise" (Starratt, 1991, p. 195).

In fact, within the philosophy of utilitarianism, Bentham, Mills, and Hume spoke of an ethic of care that was part of the public sphere (Blackburn, personal communication, 2006). The concept of the greatest happiness of the greatest number, according to Blackburn (2001), moved care into the civic realm. He wrote: "An ethic of care and benevolence, which is essentially what utilitarianism is, gives less scope to a kind of moral philosophy modeled on law, with its hidden and complex structures and formulae known only to the initiates" (p. 93).

The ethic of care is important not only to scholars in the past and in the present but also to educational leaders who are often asked to make moral decisions. If the ethic of care is used to resolve dilemmas, then there is a need to revise how educational leaders are prepared. In the past, they were trained using military and business models. This meant that educational leaders were taught about the importance of the hierarchy and the need to follow those at the top and, at the same time, be in command and in charge of sub-ordinates (Guthrie, 1990). They led by developing "rules, policies, standard operating procedures, information systems... or a variety of more informal techniques" (Bolman & Deal, 1991, p. 48). These techniques and rules may have worked well when the ethic of justice, rights, and laws was the primary basis for leaders making moral decisions; however, they are inadequate when considering other ethical paradigms, such as the ethic of care, that require leaders to consider multiple voices in the decision-making process.

Beck (1994) stressed that it is essential for educational leaders to move away from a top-down, hierarchical model for making moral and other decisions and instead turn to a leadership style that emphasizes relationships and con-nections. Administrators need to "encourage collaborative efforts between faculty, staff, and students... [which would serve] to promote interpersonal interactions, to deemphasize competition, to facilitate a sense of belonging, and to increase individuals' skills as they learn from one another" (p. 85). One could extrapolate from what Beck has written that educational admin-istrators need to distribute leadership not by simply handing over tasks but by making certain that everyone is involved in the process of education and feels as if they are heard and of worth.

When an ethic of care is valued, educational leaders can become what Barth (1990) has called, "head learner(s)" (p. 513). What Barth meant by this term is the making of outstanding leaders and learners who wish to listen to others when preparing to make important moral decisions. Developing these individuals, then, must more heavily focus on the knowledge of cultures and of diversity, with a special emphasis on learning how to listen, observe, and respond to others. For example, Shapiro, Sewell, DuCette, and Myrick (1997), in their study of inner-city youth, identified three different types of caring: attention and support, discipline, and "staying on them," or prodding them over time. As to the latter, although prodding students to complete homework might be viewed as nagging, these researchers discovered that the students they interviewed saw prodding as indicating someone cared about them.

Thus, the ethic of care offers another perspective and another way to respond to complex moral problems facing educational leaders in their daily work. Viewing ethical dilemmas through this paradigm might prompt questions related to how educators could assist young people in meeting their needs and desires and could reflect solutions that show a concern for others as part of decision making. This ethic directs individuals to consider the consequences of their decisions and actions. It asks them to consider questions such as: Who will benefit from what I decide? Who will be hurt by my actions? What are the long-term effects of a decision I make today? And if I am helped by someone now, what should I do in the future about giving back to this individual or to society in general?

The Ethic of the Profession

Shapiro and Stefkovich (2001, 2005) gave considerable attention to the ethic of the profession in their work on the Multiple Ethical Paradigms. They felt that there was a need to bring this ethic to the attention of educational leaders. They were aware that other fields had ethical requirements for their profession (i.e., law, medicine, dentistry, business) and believed that educational leadership needed ethics to play a central role both for the legitimacy of the profession and, in particular, for the students in this field.

However, Stefkovich and Shapiro were not alone in their interest in the ethic of the profession for educational administration. In recent years, there has been increasing attention placed on ethics for educational leaders. A number of writers (e.g., Beck, 1994; Beck & Murphy, 1994a, 1994b; Beck, Murphy, & Associates, 1997; Beckner, 2004; Begley, 1999; Begley & Johansson, 1998, 2003; Burford, 2004; Cambron-McCabe & Foster, 1994; Duke & Grogan, 1997; Goldring & Greenfield, 2002; Greenfield, 1995; Mertz, 1997; Normore, 2004; O'Keefe, 1997; Starratt, 1991, 1994a, 1994b, 1994c, 2003, 2004; Strike, Haller & Soltis, 1998, 2005; Willower, 1999) advocated for prospective school administrators to have some preparation in ethics, and especially in ethical decision making. In the area of teacher leadership, there have been similar calls (Campbell, 2004; Hansen, 2001; Hostetler, 1997; Strike & Ternasky, 1993). Teacher leaders such as those who are heads of charter schools or learning communities, teacher coaches, master or cooperating teachers, and supervisors of intern teachers need to be prepared as ethical professionals.

Greenfield (1993) pointed out that ethical preparation could "enable a prospective principal or superintendent to develop the attitudes, beliefs, knowledge, and skills associated with competence in moral reasoning" (p. 285). Stressing the importance for such preparation, Greenfield offered a stern admonition:

> A failure to provide the opportunity for school administrators to develop such competence constitutes a failure to serve the children we are obligated to serve as public educators. As a profession, educational administration thus has a moral obligation to train prospective administrators to be able to apply the principles, rules, ideals, and virtues associated with the development of ethical schools. (p. 285)

Recognizing this need for the profession of educational leadership, ethics was identified as one of the competencies necessary for school leaders by the Interstate School Leaders Licensure Consortium (ISLLC, 1996). This consortium, working under the auspices of the Council of Chief State School Officers and in collaboration with the National Policy Board for Educational Administration (NPBEA), set forth in its major document, "Standards for School Leaders," six standards for the profession. Of these, Standard 5 stated that: "A school administrator is an educational leader who promotes the success of all students by acting with integrity, fairness, and in an ethical manner" (ISLLC, 1996, p. 18). To meet this standard, an administrator needed to (a) possess a knowledge and understanding of various ethical frameworks and perspectives on ethics; (b) have a knowledge and understanding of professional codes of ethics; (c) believe in, value, and be committed to bringing ethical principles to the decision-making process; and (d) believe in, value, and be committed to developing a caring school community (ISLLC, 1996, p. 18). This standard, with its requirements, officially recognized the importance of ethics in the knowledge base for school administrators. Corresponding with these standards, some states began to require principals to pass examinations measuring competencies that included ethics. After more than a decade, the ISLLC standards are now under review. No doubt some modifications will be made. However, although there will be revisions, it is hoped that the conceptual changes will remain, enabling ethics to continue as an important standard.

In the past, professional ethics has generally been viewed as a subset of the justice paradigm. This is likely the case because professional ethics is often equated with codes, rules, and policies, all of which fit neatly into traditional concepts of justice (Beauchamp & Childress, 1984). Some states have established their own codes or standards. For instance, *The Pennsylvania Code of Professional Practice and Conduct for Educators* (1992) and *Texas' Ethics, Standards, and Practices* (Texas Administrative Code, 1998) focus heavily on the ethics of justice as well as the profession.

In addition, a number of education-related professional organizations have developed their own professional ethical codes. Defined by Beauchamp and Childress (1984) as "an articulated statement of role morality as seen by members of the profession" (p. 41), some of these ethical codes are long-standing, while some are considerably more recent. Examples of these organizations include, but are certainly not limited to, the American Association of School Administrators, the American Association of University Professors, the American Psychological Association, the Association of School Business Officials, the Association for Supervision and Curriculum Development, and the National Education Association. Currently, the University Council of Educational Administration is developing a set of standards for those who prepare educational leaders in research universities. Their hope is to create a code that is meaningful by combining the voices, perspectives, and values of many of those within the field of educational leadership.

However, despite the attempts to make the codes and standards more significant, generally there is a paradox regarding ethical codes set forth by the states and professional associations. On the one hand, they have tended to be limited in their responsiveness in that they are somewhat removed from the day-to-day personal and professional dilemmas educational leaders face. Nash (1996), in his book on professional ethics for educators and human service personnel, recognized these limitations as he observed his students' lack of interest in such codes:

> What are we to make of this almost universal disparagement of professional codes of ethics? What does the nearly total disregard of professional codes mean? For years, I thought it was something in my delivery that evoked such strong, antagonistic responses. For example, whenever I ask students to bring their codes to class, few knew where to locate them, and most get utterly surly when I make such a request. I understand, now, however, that they do not want to be bothered with what they consider a trivial, irrelevant assignment, because they simply do not see a correlation between learning how to make ethical decisions and appealing to a code of ethics. (p. 95)

On the other hand, it should not be forgotten that professional codes of ethics serve as guideposts and aspirations for a field, offering statements about its appearance and character (Lebacqz, 1985). They personify "the highest moral ideals of the profession," thus "presenting an ideal image of the moral character of both the profession and the professional" (Nash, 1996, p. 96). Seen in this light, standardized codes can provide a most valuable function. Thus, it is possible that the problem may not lie as much in the codes themselves but in the fact that sometimes too much is expected from them with regard to moral decision making (Lebacqz, 1985; Nash, 1996).

However, despite a positive approach to standardized codes, Nash (1996) and Shapiro and Stefkovich (2001, 2005) did observe a lack of connection between their students' own personal and professional codes and those set forth by states or professional groups. For the most part, students seemed not to pay attention to the latter codes or, if they were aware, such formalized professional codes affected them very little. The majority of them found it more valuable to create their own codes.

A graduate student, who was also a department chair, pointed out the disparity this way:

> Surprisingly to me, I even enjoyed doing the personal and professional ethics statements. I have been in union meetings where professional ethical codes were discussed. They were so bland and general as to be meaningless. Doing these statements forced me to think about what I do and how I live whereas the previous discussions did not. It was a very positive experience. I also subscribe to the notion that [standardized] professional ethical codes are of limited value. I look to myself to determine what decisions I can live with. Outside attempts at control have little impact on me and what I do. (Shapiro & Stefkovich, 2005, p. 22)

This department chair was not alone in finding the process of developing personal and professional codes of his own enjoyable and meaningful. Overtime, Stefkovich and Shapiro discovered that aspiring educational leaders should be given the opportunity to create their own personal codes of ethics based on life stories and critical incidences as well as their own professional codes based on the work experiences and expectations. Developing these statements necessitated that graduate students reflect upon concepts related to their own moral compasses, their professional behaviors, and their decision-making processes.

Actions by school administrators are likely to be strongly influenced by personal values (Begley, 1999; Begley & Johansson, 1998; Begley & Zaretsky, 2004; Willower & Lacata, 1997), and personal codes of ethics build on these values and experiences (Shapiro & Stefkovich, 1997, 1998; Stefkovich & Shapiro, 1994). It is not always easy to separate professional from personal ethical codes. The observations of this superintendent of a large rural district aptly sum up the experiences and the sentiments of many of practitioner-students:

> A professional ethical code cannot be established without linkage and reference to one's personal code of ethics and thereby acknowledges such influencing factors. In retrospect, and as a result of [developing my own ethical codes]… I can see the influence professional responsibilities have upon my personal values, priorities, and behavior. It seems there is an unmistakable "co-influence" of the two codes. One cannot be completely independent of the other. (Shapiro & Stefkovich, 1998, p. 137)

Other factors that should play roles in the development of individual professional codes include not only considerations of personal codes but also of formal codes of ethics established by professional associations and written standards of the profession (e.g., ISLLC). In addition, an awareness and understanding of community standards, including both the professional community and the community in which the leader works, require attention and recognition.

As educational leaders or students in training develop their professional (and personal) codes, they consider various ethical models, either focusing on specific paradigms or, optimally, integrating the ethics of justice, care, and critique. This filtering process provides the basis for professional judgments and professional ethical decision making; it may also result in clashes among codes.

The development of professional ethics is far from a clear process and often presents pitfalls. In fact, Shapiro and Stefkovich (1998, 2005) identified four possible clashes that affected the creation of one's own professional ethical codes. Some of these problems have already been mentioned in this section. First, there may be clashes between an individual's personal and professional codes of ethics. Second, there may be clashes within the professional code itself. This may occur when an individual's personal ethical code conflicts with an ethical code set forth by the profession or when the individual has been prepared in two or more professions. In this latter case, codes of one profession may be different from another. Hence, a code that serves an individual well in one career may not in a new field. Third, there may be clashes of professional codes among educational leaders; what one administrator sees as ethical, another may not. Fourth, there may be clashes between a leader's personal and professional code of ethics and customs and practices set forth by the community (i.e., either the professional community, the school community, or the community in which the educational leader works). For example, behavior that may be considered unethical in one community might, in even a neighboring community, merely be seen as a matter of personal preference.

Furman (Furman-Brown, 2002; Furman, 2003a, 2003b, 2004) expanded on what she characterized as a separate ethic of the community. In her writings, she challenged educational leaders to move away from heroic (solo) managerial decisions and turn toward community involvement in the decision-making process. Her definition of community appeared to be a comprehensive and participatory process. It also seemed to dovetail well with a distributive model in which the work and the decisions expected of the educational leader are shared with appropriate others (Elmore, 2000; Katzenmyer & Moller, 2001; Neufeld & Roper, 2003; Poglinco et al., 2003; Spillane, Haverson, & Diamond, 2001).

To deal with the four clashes previously discussed, and professional ethics in general, it is important to ground the decision-making process in something meaningful. Greenfield (1993) contended that schools, particularly public schools, should be the central sites for "preparing children to assume the roles and responsibilities of citizenship in a democratic society" (p. 268). Gross and Shapiro (2005) also spoke of the importance of fostering the development of young people moving them forward to become critical and moral citizens.

Not all those who write about the importance of the study of ethics in educational leadership discuss the needs of children; nonetheless, this focus on students is clearly consistent with the backbone of the profession. Other professions often have one basic principle driving the profession. In medicine, it is "First, do no harm." In law, it is the assertion that all clients deserve "zealous representation." In education, Shapiro and Stefkovich (2001, 2005) believed that if there was a moral imperative for the profession, it was to serve the best interests of the student. Consequently, they believed that this ideal must lie at the heart of any professional paradigm for educational leaders from pre-K–16 and beyond.

This focus on the best interests of the student is reflected in most educational professional association codes. For example, the American Association of School Administrators' *Statement of Ethics for School Administrators* (American Association of School Administrators, 1981) begins with the assertion: "The educational administrator... makes the well-being of students the fundamental value of all decision making and actions." Serving the best interests of the student is also consistent with the ISLLC's standards for the profession, each of which opens with the words: "A school administrator is an educational leader who promotes the success of all students by..." (ISLLC, 1996). This emphasis on a student's best interests is also in concert with Noddings' (1992, 2003) ethic of care that places students at the top of the educational hierarchy, as well as is reflective of the concerns of many critical theorists who believe that students' voices and concerns are too often silenced (Giroux, 1988, 2003; Weis & Fine, 1993).

Frequent confrontations with moral dilemmas become even more complex as cases increasingly involve a variety of student populations, parents, and communities comprising diversity in broad terms that extend well beyond categories of race and ethnicity. In this respect, differences—encompassing cultural categories of race and ethnicity, religion, social class, gender, disability, and sexual orientation as well as individual differences that may take into account learning styles, exceptionalities, and age—often cannot be ignored (Banks, 2001; Cushner, McClelland, & Safford, 1992; Gollnick & Chinn, 1998; Shapiro, Sewell, & DuCette, 2002; Shapiro, 1999; Sleeter & Grant, 2003; Tooms & Alston, 2005).

The literature does not define "best interests of the student" (Stefkovich, O'Brien, & Moore, 2002). In the absence of such clarification, school leaders have often referred to a student's best interests to justify adults' interests (Walker, 1998). Recent attempts have been made, however, to fill this gap (Stefkovich, 2006; Stefkovich & O'Brien, 2004; Walker, 1995, 1998).

Stefkovich (2006) conceptualizes decisions related to a student's best interests as those incorporating individual rights, accepting and teaching students to accept responsibility for their actions, and respecting students. These three Rs—rights, responsibility, and respect—are key, according to Stefkovich, to making ethical decisions that are in a student's best interests and, in turn, to fulfilling one's professional obligations as educational leaders.

In this chapter, a paradigm for the profession has been described that expects educational leaders to formulate and examine their own professional codes of ethics in light of individual personal codes of ethics, as well as standards set forth by the profession, and then calls on them to place students at the center of the ethical decision-making process. It also asks them to take into account the wishes of the community.

The ethic of the profession then goes beyond the ethics of justice, critique, and care to inquire: What would the profession ask me to do? What do various communities expect me to accomplish? What about clashes of codes—does this exist, and is there a problem? And what should I take into account to consider the best interests of the students, who may be diverse in their composition and their needs?

3

TURBULENCE THEORY

It Started on a New Year's Eve Flight

S TEVE GROSS WAS A GOOD FLYER. From the time of his first flight in 1956 from Idyllwild Airport in New York (later to be renamed in honor of President Kennedy) to Nassau in the Bahamas and throughout his teenage years, getting on an airplane was nothing short of a dream trip in a modified spaceship. Even as a small child, he always held fast to the idea that no matter how cloudy, rainy, or snowy the surface conditions, a few minutes after take-off and a few thousand feet of altitude, the sun was shining and he would be able to look down on a vista of earth unimaginable only a hundred years earlier.

This enthusiasm came naturally enough. Gross' grandfather had the same perspective and was one of the first builders of biplanes when he worked for the Glenn Curtiss Company, an early competitor to the Wright brothers. Later, during World War I he joined the navy and was sent to southern France to assemble early naval aircraft, where his unit entertained then assistant secretary of the Navy, Franklin Delano Roosevelt during a tour of the front. A generation later during World War II, his father left the infantry to join the precursor to today's Air Force, the Army Air Corps. Showing an inherent ability with multi-engine airplanes and leading a crew, he became a pilot in the 8th Air Force, flying 30 missions over occupied Europe, including the D-Day invasion in a B-17 named *Wolf Pack*. Among his many medals at the end of the war was the Distinguished Flying Cross. To add to this list of airborne enthusiasts closely connected to Gross is the case of his father-in-law—a graduate of the Chinese Air Academy, a national hero for his daring fighter-pilot exploits against the Japanese in World War II, a general in the Republic of China's Air Force, and later commandant of that nation's air academy.

With this background and with scores of beautiful flights behind him, he anticipated a lifelong love of flying. That was an illusion, and it was with that illusion fully intact that he cheerfully boarded a jet bound from Miami to Philadelphia on New Year's Eve 1970. Sitting next to Gross was a retired couple who seemed nervous. "Oh, please don't pay much attention to us," said the woman. "It's just that this is our first airplane ride and we're a little on edge." It was not hubris but a sense of community that inspired Gross to reply. "Look, I have been on airplanes since I was six years old, here and around the world. You're never going to be safer than you are right now. The ride to the airport was by far the most dangerous part of the trip." Reflecting on his little speech now, he sounded like a brainwashed lobbyist for the airlines, but this was a genuine enthusiasm and proved correct until dinner was served (please remember, it was a different era and hot meals were still the norm, even on two-hour flights). There were the passengers with hot turkey, mashed potatoes, and brilliant green peas steaming in front of them. Gross and his new friends were enjoying the meal, and he even got the husband to wink at his wife as he was teased about his recent angst. Then with the suddenness of a runaway rollercoaster careening down a vertical drop, the plane fell. Turkey, mashed potatoes, and peas became airborne, quickly decorating the passengers' clothing. Screams and panicked cries foreshadowing gruesome deaths spread throughout the cabin, and the elderly man sitting next to him, his dentures rocking wildly in a half-spilled glass of water in front of him, started to cry.

A quality that later helped Gross to become a caring teacher took over. As the plane steadied itself, he tried to keep a calming dialogue (that ended up being nothing more than a monologue) going. "Oh, that was terrible, but it was only an air pocket. It happens now and again and is nothing serious. We'll be there soon, and all we've had was a scare and a little dinner spread over our clothing." It was useless. The man's crying did slow but Gross could see by the couple's nervous frowns that their brittle confidence in flying and in his advice was shattered. His counsel to them was really his own way of dealing with the fissures now evident in his idealistic image of flight. By the time he reached his parents' home and started to mix into their New Year's Eve party, he knew the damage was done. Gross felt traumatized and would look at flying now as a risky business. In truth, he had had his first experience with severe turbulence.

For years, Gross was a white-knuckled flyer, not ceasing flight altogether but dreading it. As in other cases of trauma, even a small stimulus like the report of thunderstorms en route, let alone a small amount of bumpiness on board, was enough to re-awaken his fears and unleash squadrons of menacing butterflies in his stomach. He became so focused on the fear of turbulence that he once asked his father if he shared his concern when he was flying missions over Nazi Germany. With an amused, kindly, but ironic expression his father replied, "Actually, Steve, compared to flak and enemy aircraft, turbulence was not exactly high on my list of worries."

Steve Gross had fear but no context for the next 25 years. All of that changed at a place called The World's Biggest Bookstore in Toronto, Canada. He was in town doing research on a book about initiating serious innovation in public schools and, frankly, he was in a bit of a funk. The high school he was studying seemed to match an emerging and disturbing pattern. No matter how thoughtful the change in curriculum, instruction, and assessment, and no matter how carefully and sensitively the plans were constructed with the surrounding community, there always seemed to be a strong level of disturbance associated with significant change. Why? Gross felt that it was somehow unfair for these considerate, talented educators to have to face angry groups of parents as they unveiled their designs for school reform.

Certainly, he understood that change always brought with it opposition. He had enough theory and philosophy to see that Hegel's dialectic (Hegel, 1892) applied, and that these new concepts could easily be labeled as today's antithesis resulting from the current thesis, leading to some new synthesis that in turn would attract a new antithesis. That, however, was little comfort as he tried to frame the world of educational innovation. What Gross needed was a way of understanding four looming questions:

- How might the levels of disturbance facing innovating schools be described so that different degrees of challenge could be compared?
- How might the emotional strength of that disturbance be more thoroughly understood?
- How might the school look at its own disturbance in a measured way so that reasoned action could be more likely?
- Might there be a positive aspect to the disturbances facing schools that decide to innovate? Or was turbulence always a detrimental force, always to be avoided or at least diminished?

Gross had come to this mother of all bookstores simply to wander in a comfortable space. Aimlessly browsing among countless aisles filled with books was like a balm and freed him to let his mind float. It was nearly closing time when he happened on the how-to section of the store and spotted a manual for beginning pilots. Given his attitude about flight, he had no idea why his hands reached for it so automatically. He rapidly turned the pages to the section on turbulence and there it was: a pilot's set of definitions for turbulence. Of course, there were times when there seemed to be no movement at all during flight, the book stated; this was known as "smooth-as-glass" flying. But normally, there were four levels of turbulence, including light, moderate, severe, and extreme. The text went on to describe each of the four levels:

- Light: little or no movement of the craft
- Moderate: very noticeable waves
- Severe: strong gusts that threaten control of the craft
- Extreme: forces so great that control is lost and structural damage to the craft occurs

Even in texts dedicated to the study of turbulence under many conditions, these four basic levels were fundamental (Lester, 1994).

The more Gross thought about it, the more these categories started to have meaning for the problems facing innovating schools. Continuing his research trips to schools in North America, he began to apply the four levels of turbulence to conditions that he witnessed.

During that year of investigations, Gross found clear examples of three turbulence levels. For example, one elementary school found it difficult to engage all families since they came from two disjointed communities, one upper-middle class living near the campus and the other a working-class community residing miles away. This was a concern to school leaders and the local PTA because it meant that one group of parents would have access to the school and be able to influence it while the second might feel disenfranchised. While no immediate crisis existed, the issue of a disjointed community led to a series of responses and regular monitoring. In this way, it was much like the light turbulence level since there was little disturbance but attention needed to be paid.

A high school in the study seemed to face a more concentrated challenge. While this school was doing well and following through on its innovative ideas, it suddenly had to absorb students from a sister school in the same district that was forced to close. This issue was hardly a case of light turbulence since the consequences of not accommodating the new students and their families would be serious for the school and its reform agenda. Responding to this challenge, school leaders made welcoming new students their highest priority and took the position that the new students had the right to influence their new school as much as they had the obligation to be influenced by it. A pre-semester in-service for the school's professional staff led to specific responses, including an orientation for new students, inclusion of the school's student advisory program, and a "buddy" system linking new to current students. This school faced and responded to moderate turbulence. The influx of many new students represented a noticeable wave to the school. This was not a case of business as usual but a specific issue requiring focused attention. It is useful to note that cases of moderate turbulence compel action, sensitivity, and creativity. Often, existing committee structures called to action in time and given clear focus can respond to this level of turbulence.

A Midwest district faced a qualitatively different challenge. This district was known for its high performance, including its solid results in state-sponsored tests. School and district leaders worked for several years to infuse new curriculum and instructional practices into their programs. While many community members supported the new set of learning objectives, another group found these too close to the principles of outcomes-based education, or OBE (Spady, 1988). Since OBE had become a politically charged issue, it was not long before the two camps saw each other as diametrically opposed. Soon, names were hurled across the growing divide, tempers flared, and long-time friendships withered in the heat of acrimonious debate. Neither light nor moderate turbulence could describe this condition since the shockwaves of this crisis threatened the entire reform program of the district and its schools.

It was clear that short of an intense effort to regain control, the district was headed for disaster. Fortunately, district and community leaders did rally. A highly respected community member, not identified with either side, became board chairperson. Another community member with professional group facilitation skills organized and conducted a series of forums, including all sides in the debate. These meetings were taped and broadcast over the local cable access channel. After weeks of intensive listening and sharing, the community saw that their common interests outweighed their differences. Compromises and a modified direction were found. The community and its school district experienced an episode of severe turbulence. The entire enterprise was at risk in much the same way as severe turbulence threatens the aircraft with total loss of control. In the air, extraordinary maneuvers may be required to recover from this level of turbulence. This applies to reforming schools as well. No existing organizational structure was used to get this district back on its reformed flight path; new leaders inventing new responses were needed.

The original study making up *Staying Centered: Curriculum Leadership in a Turbulent Era* (Gross, 1998) did not uncover an example of extreme turbulence. This was not surprising because extreme turbulence would mean the destruction of the reform program, and he was only studying ongoing innovations. His speculation on the existence of extreme turbulence kept the place open for such a possibility, and he was certain that eventually he would find such a case because, regrettably, educational reform often missed its mark (Sarason, 1990).

It was not long before an example did reveal itself (Gross, 2000). On Gross' initial visit to this school, he found a smoothly working reform that had a well-organized curriculum, strong parental support, solid teacher participation, well-coordinated after-school programs, and positive relations with the area superintendent. Given the challenges of high levels of poverty in the families the school served, their success was even more remarkable. What a contrast his next visit turned out to be, only two years later. Gone was the relationship with the district after the departure of the supportive area superintendent. On top of that, the school was compelled to grow too rapidly in size and in grade level. Instead of a small K–5 elementary school, the building now accommodated grades K–8 in much larger numbers. This growth led to hiring many new teachers, some of whom did not seem to support the original reform agenda. Adding to the stress was the problem that one of the grades had not performed adequately on a state test, thereby placing the entire school on a need-to-improve list. Finally, the foundation that financed the original reform was ending its support because the funding cycle was at its end.

When Gross arrived, he found that the gifted principal who initiated the reform was preparing to retire. With a degree of regret, Gross concluded that he had found an example of extreme turbulence, leading to the destruction of the reform itself. Like extreme turbulence in an airplane, this condition does more than grab attention; it creates a crisis to which even the inventiveness of talented school and community leaders may not be equal.

With the example of extreme turbulence, the metaphor seemed complete. Each level of turbulence had an equivalent from the data on innovating schools. Just as important, there were responses to each of the first three levels (light, moderate, and severe) that seemed instructive to academics and practitioners. Answers to three of Gross' four questions were starting to emerge. With turbulence, he could now describe different degrees of challenge facing innovating school. Likewise, he could speak to the relative emotional strength of disturbances. By using the four levels of turbulence, schools could reflect upon their issues in measured ways and pursue responses that reflected their current condition. While all metaphors are limited (Morgan, 1997), the metaphor of turbulence seemed to fit three of his questions well and he gained a new vocabulary to share with fellow educators.

The Positive Aspects of Turbulence

Giving a paper on Turbulence Theory and its relationship to ethical decision making at a University Council of Educational Administration (UCEA) conference with his co-author, Joan Shapiro (Shapiro & Gross, 2002), led to a question that pushed his thinking further. A colleague in the audience challenged the idea of turbulence being simply a negative force that leaders needed to defend against. "Steve, isn't turbulence also the force that opens up new possibilities for the organization?" He was immediately struck by two aspects of this question. First, it seemed quite credible. Why would turbulence merely be a problem? Weren't the very innovations that attracted my initial research a type of turbulence, compared to the traditions that they sought to replace? In fact, the concept of turbulence being a positive force had recently been described in the literature on business management (Gryskiewicz, 1999). He also recalled Lewin's (1947) pioneering work in action research involved unfreezing, change, and refreezing in organizations. This can also be seen as the purposeful escalation of turbulence in an organization aimed at positive change.*

Almost at once, Gross saw that at the micro-level, turbulence was needed for flight to occur in the first place. Lift simply could not occur in a vacuum. Molecules of air, moving faster over the top of the wing than the bottom, are required (Braybrook, 1985). It also became obvious that even modern aircraft take off and land facing the wind. The turbulence of that air movement is needed to send airplanes aloft and help them to land safely. Out of control, turbulence could lead to disaster, but well understood and monitored, it was an essential element of life in the air.

Further thought caused him to see where he had limited his perspective. Gross' own traumatic experience caused him to color his attitude toward disturbances. Until challenged by this question, he had created categories that made turbulence a problem for innovators to avoid or handle, just as he hoped that radar and good piloting skills would help aircraft avoid or handle turbulence. Now, he realized that this was important but not the complete story.

Steve Gross needed to deepen his understanding of the nature of turbulence, and so he opened himself up to considering its different manifestations that might add new dimensions to the existing metaphor beyond air movement and airplanes. He expanded his explorations as soon as the 2002–2003

---

* Yet the concept of positive change resulting from turbulence is relative. Traditionalists in that same organization may see the action research process as an unwelcome interference with the normal life of the group.

academic year ended, and he had the opportunity to literally go into the field back home in Vermont. At first, he tried to simply look at air movement closer to the ground and spent time watching the impact of even small bursts of wind on plants and trees. Although he did learn a great deal from these observations, such as the uneven impact of barely perceptible breezes, he was not satisfied with this tack. Hiking in the Green Mountains National Forest one morning, he heard the sound of a brook and stopped to simply enjoy it. While he had walked past this small body of water scores of times, on that day it had an unanticipated attraction. What he saw was a complex swirling of water, first moving rapidly, then slowing, taking twigs and leaves along, only to treat these differently as its motion shifted. Gross spent weeks observing creeks, rivers, waterfalls, and small streams throughout that summer. He recorded everything that he could possibly see each day, waiting until much later to attempt to analyze his observations. He allowed the flowing bodies of water to show new aspects of this type of turbulence. In the spirit of Grounded Theory (Glaser & Strauss, 1967), he allowed insights gained from one day's field work to inform his perspective on the following day's work.

Positionality

One new element of Turbulence Theory emerging from expanding the metaphor to include the behavior of flowing water was *positionality*. Gross noticed that a moving river did not have the same impact on twigs and leaves at its center as it did on those similar objects at its edges. In fact, careful examinations caused him to see that the impact of the water's flow had many varying levels of impact, all depending upon the position of the object relative to the center of the stream or its banks. Leaves at the center of the flow moved rapidly, while leaves the same size on the sides might move much slower, get caught on the banks, or become trapped in small whirlpools.

Position mattered in bodies of moving water, and he soon found parallels in organizational turbulence. Turbulence might seem uniform viewed from far away but at the level of the specific case, where one was in relation to the organization, seemed very meaningful. Reflecting on his earlier work on turbulence in the air, it was clear to him that his own sense of concern when the seat belt sign was illuminated was likely far greater than that of the pilot. In schools, the case of severe turbulence described above meant different things to the superintendent, the high school principal, the parents, and area business leaders.

Defining Positionality in Turbulence Theory

This variety of movement in the same stream with objects the same size seemed very much like the concept of positionality theory (Alcoff, 1991; Hauser, 1997; Kezar, 2000; Maher & Tetreault, 1993, 1994) and standpoint theory (Collins, 1997) used in social science.

Recent scholarship has revealed a debate between these two perspectives. Defending Standpoint Theory, Collins (1997) states:

> First, the notion of Standpoint Theory refers to historically shared, group experiences. Groups have a degree of permanence over time such that group realities transcend individual experiences. For instance, African-Americans as a stigmatized racial group existed long before I was born and will probably continue long after I die. While my individual experiences with institutionalized racism will be unique, the types of opportunities and constraints that I encounter on a daily basis will resemble those confronting African-Americans as a group. (p. 375)

Countering this claim for the utility of Standpoint Theory, Kezar (2000) describes the utility of Positionality Theory:

> Positionality Theory acknowledges that people have multiple, overlapping identities, and thus make meaning from various aspects of their identity, including social class, professional standing, and so forth. Therefore, it is more complex and dynamic than Standpoint Theory while retaining its epistemological concerns. Positionality Theory assumes that power relationships can change and that social categories are fluid, dynamic, affected by history and social changes. (p. 725)

The type of positionality Gross suggests for Turbulence Theory combines elements of both of these perspectives. When thinking of positionality as developed in Turbulence Theory, it is important to understand the relative situation of individuals in the organization in a multidimensional fashion. In the case of educational institutions, this means not only attempting to be empathetic to the turbulence as students might experience it, for example, but also acknowledging that groups of students (as organized by gender, race, age, socioeconomic status (SES), or years in the community, for instance) may experience it differently. Equally, it means seeing individuals in each of their group affiliations and, simultaneously, as separate beings. This is not a linear, easily nested process.

While this sounds perplexing at first, the result can become a systematic process in which those facing a dilemma can ask a series of questions leading to a richer understanding of the authentic positions and perspectives of others without condescending, or as Alcoff (1991) describes it, speaking for others. A reasonable sequence of questions to illuminate positionality during turbulence might be:

> What different groups exist in our organization—younger students, older students, staff, faculty, administration, parents? How might the current turbulence affect each of them?
>
> What different demographics exist in our organization—gender, race, social class, neighborhood, English as a second language, Special Education? Within each group? What might their perspectives be?
>
> What do we know about individual situations? How might this alter the way this turbulence is perceived?

While light or moderate levels of turbulence might allow for detailed speculation, data gathering, and analysis as a means of working through the problem, severe or the threat of extreme turbulence likely offer no such opportunity since the need for a rapid, well-considered response is too acute. Therefore, a deep, ongoing understanding of this type of positionality within our organizations is highly recommended.

Cascading

The second addition to Turbulence Theory coming from Gross' examinations of flowing water was *cascading*. Anyone who has seen even a small river or creek is familiar with the nature of water as it tumbles over a series of small rocks. While he had experienced this all of his life, it was not until he took the time to think about this phenomenon as a metaphor that he saw its meaning for the study of organizations and the people in them. Water picks up speed as it cascades. The turbulence of the water is easily increased as it moves from one downturn to the next.

The effect of cascading had its parallel in organizations facing turbulence. In the case of extreme turbulence described earlier in this chapter, none of the destabilizing blows facing the innovating school—rapid growth, disappointing test results, withdrawal of superintendent support, loss of foundation funds, and departure of the founding principal—were isolated. Each in turn escalated the level of turbulence facing the school, just as a series of vertical drops amplifies the speed of water at it cascades. The same phenomena can be seen in the horrifying firestorms created by massive bombing in World War II in cities like Dresden (McKee, 1982). Each explosion intensified city fires, thereby raising the air temperature. Hot air rising sucked cool air from the ground into the fire, thereby fueling fires and causing them to grow, thereby magnifying the intensity of the fire. The combined forces led to ground winds with such power that people were literally hurled into an inferno. A third example of multiple forces assembled to heighten turbulence through cascading is the case of massive student protests in France during 1968 (Kurlansky, 2004):

> In chemistry, it is found that some very stable elements placed in proximity to other seemingly moribund elements can spontaneously produce explosions. Hidden within this bored, overstuffed, complacent society were barely noticeable elements—a radicalized youth with a hopelessly old-fashioned geriatric leader, overpopulated universities, angry workers, a sudden consumerism enthralling some and sickening others, sharp differences between generations, and perhaps even boredom itself—that when put together could be explosive. (p. 218)

With these examples in mind,* the concept of cascading, like positionality, became a new addition to Turbulence Theory that helped Gross understand dynamic forces within organizations in a richer context. For those experiencing turbulence even at the light level, it is important to consider forces in the environment that may propel that turbulence to higher levels. Community concern over a new social studies curriculum in isolation may represent a moderate level of turbulence. However, that same issue in the wake of a badly handled labor dispute, a rise in property taxes, and a report of failure in standardized tests is a quite another matter. Therefore, understanding cascading is a matter of understanding context and the force of a series of turbulent conditions. By using Turbulence Theory and carefully measuring the degree of turbulence represented by each issue, it is possible for educational leaders to prioritize their response.

Turbulence Theory's Relationship to Chaos Theory

While it is beyond the scope of this chapter to enter into a detailed comparison and contrast between Turbulence Theory and related concepts, some brief mention at the chapter's close seems useful. Following, Gross describes his perspective on Turbulence Theory's connection to and distinction from

---

* Cases of cascading during turbulence are connected to the process of positive feedback loops in organizational theory (Senge, 1990) wherein trends seem to reinforce and increase one another's impact. This is the case of the firestorm because it only grows more deadly due to its own cycle, as described previously. In an earlier study, Gross (2004) found that avoiding just such a positive feedback loop was a crucial adjustment for reforming schools to make if they hoped to sustain innovations over time.

Chaos Theory, as well as reflecting on Turbulence Theory's strengths and limits as a metaphor.

Gross is often asked to describe the differences between Turbulence Theory and Chaos Theory, and usually begins his answer by sharing some of the similarities that he sees. Both focus upon the combined importance of seemingly small changes, thereby asking us to remember that detail and pattern matter, especially in complex systems. Both make us think about the ebb and flow of life from seeming instability to renewed and transformed models of stability. Both seem to be elements in the natural world with strong parallels in our organizational lives.

Yet key differences also exist between Turbulence Theory and Chaos Theory. Though inspired by natural phenomena,* Turbulence Theory is designed to help us better understand life in micro and macro human organizations. Further, Turbulence Theory's use of a turbulence gauge (described in Chapter 1) and its combination with rich concepts such as Multiple Ethical Paradigms make it operational for people in organizations to employ it when they wish to observe, plan, and act. Turbulence Theory recognizes complexity but is constructed to provide useful tools to help those employing it to flow with rapidly evolving change, thereby taking advantage of its benefits and minimizing its potential for harm.

Besides pointing to the similarities and differences between Turbulence Theory and Chaos Theory, it is useful to explain that the two theories can be combined with potentially beneficial results. For example, we might consider an escalating pattern of turbulence as an episode of an organization being stuck on one side of a Lorenz Attractor (a type of swirling figure eight wherein each side behaves like a powerful whirlpool). Further consideration of the benefits of combining these theoretical lenses seems worthwhile since, in their application to organizations, they are each metaphors with strengths and limits.

Turbulence Theory as a Metaphor

Morgan (1997) describes the use of metaphors in understanding organizational life in rich, flexible ways:

---

* While illustrations supporting Turbulence Theory may derive from the movement of small particles, such as the turbulent flow of water droplets in a stream or the dynamics of molecules on an airplane wing, we may learn just as much about turbulence from examples in architecture. One illustrative case is of the Tacoma Narrows suspension bridge, nicknamed "Galloping Gertie" that fell apart in a graphic demonstration of extreme turbulence (Levy & Salvadori, 2002).

Metaphor is often regarded just as a device for embellishing discourse, but its significance is much greater than this. The use of metaphor implies *a way of thinking* (original emphasis) and *a way of seeing* (original emphasis) that pervade how we understand our world generally. (p. 4)

Noting the limits of any given theory, Morgan cautions:

In recognizing theory as metaphor, we quickly appreciate that no single theory will ever give us a perfect or all-purpose point of view. We realize that the challenge is to become skilled in the art of using metaphor: to find fresh ways of seeing, understanding, and shaping situations that we want to organize and manage. (pp. 5–6)

In this context, Turbulence Theory is a metaphor for both the episodic and continuing forces that we live with each day in our organizations. As Morgan observes, each successful metaphor—each well-considered theory—illuminates an aspect of realty. Coinciding with this illumination, however, each metaphor simultaneously obscures something of reality. Turbulence Theory illuminates levels of change in our organizations and helps us frame them. This chapter describes some of the ways in which it can be used to gain a deeper understanding of these forces. However, Turbulence Theory is not intended to be, in Morgan's words, an all-purpose point of view. The careful application of Turbulence Theory is intended to add a new dimension to our understanding of organizational life and, in the context of this book, to our understanding of the forces surrounding ethical dilemmas.

Guidance for the Application of Turbulence Theory

While not intending to impose a formulaic approach to using Turbulence Theory, some guidance is in order. As the earlier parts of this chapter indicate, there are key variables to consider when using Turbulence Theory. These include contextual forces, positionality, the degree of turbulence in any given situation, and the possible consequences of a changed level of turbulence. Each of these variables in turn is made up of several elements that are described below. The key variables to consider in Turbulence Theory are discussed in an order that most closely resembles the stages that Gross and Shapiro's graduate students have used when thinking through levels of turbulence and possible responses to it in their own ethical dilemmas. At the conclusion of each of the key variables, a summary dialogue among those working on the issue is suggested as a way of pulling the main threads together. Similarly, a summary dialogue is suggested after considering all of the key variables so that a greater appreciation of the inter-relationship among the variables may be achieved.

Contextual Forces

Early on, it is important to explore contextual variables surrounding any given situation. In Turbulence Theory, the relevant issues of context include cascading, relationships among key individuals, and the current stability or volatility of the organization. When examining cascading, it is useful to collect data on the forces that are at play in the current situation. If a school is facing an ethical dilemma over a controversial new curriculum, for instance, other seemingly unrelated events might contribute to turbulence, such as a teacher strike, budget defeat, poor test scores, or a combination of all three. What is the relationship among them? How have they emerged in the recent past? What does this particular organization's history tell us about the potential for cascading to have a serious impact on turbulence? Seeing relationships between key individuals in context causes us to ask similar questions. What past history exists, both constructive and combative, between these individuals that bears on this situation? Remembering the architectural example of Galloping Gertie, we come to the issue of the current stability or volatility of the organization itself. This requires considering its recent history from an internal and external perspective. One way of viewing this contextual variable is to ask the question: Is the current turbulence an exception or part of a larger pattern of disruption?

Positionality

Once the contextual forces have been explored in some detail, a series of questions about positionality will further illuminate turbulence as different individuals and groups within the organization may be experiencing it. The purpose of the discussion on positionality earlier in this chapter was designed to define that term as it applies to Turbulence Theory. Clearly, one's position in an organization during turbulence is also a key variable, and one that deserves examination from multiple perspectives suggested in the questions raised earlier. As those questions imply, there are three places to begin to explore positionality as it relates to turbulence. First, there is the job of defining the functional groups involved in the issue. In schools, functional groups typically include younger and older students, faculty, staff, administration, parents, board members, and the wider community. What does the dilemma look like from each of these perspectives? While this is crucial information, stopping at this point risks over-generalizing about individuals within these functional groups and assuming that every teacher, for instance, will feel similarly about a given turbulent issue. Therefore, the next lens of positionality is one of demographics. This includes categories that are obvious such as gender, age, ethnicity, race, religion, sexual orientation, level of formal education, and socio-economic status. It also includes perspectives not so commonly considered, such as years living in a given community. Judgment needs to be exercised in this phase of analysis because an individual's multiple demographic affiliations are complex. Larger patterns that relate to the specific turbulent condition are what matters most. Finally, there is the position of the individual. Does this turbulence mean something of particular significance to one or more of the key actors in the current situation?

Establishing the Current Level of Turbulence

After the forces of context and positionality are considered, it is more likely that a reasonable estimate of the level of turbulence may be made. The turbulence gauge depicted in Chapter 1 is offered as a guide in this process. Having thought through contextual and positionality variables, it is now time to look at the four levels of turbulence (light, moderate, severe, and extreme) found in the first column, as well as the corresponding general definitions found in the second column, and select the closest fit. Those working through the problem may then describe their situation in the appropriate cell of the second column entitled "Turbulence as It Is Applied to This Situation." The turbulence gauge is completed when all of the cells in the second column are filled. This is normally done by estimating the conditions one would find if turbulence was either higher or lower than the current level. Because establishing a level of turbulence is the result of complex conceptual analysis, it is highly useful for individuals to compare their findings at this point and explore their insights through dialogue. This will allow divergent views to be aired and may lead to greater confidence in the current level of turbulence.

Possible Consequences of Changing Levels of Turbulence

Context, positionality, and the current level of turbulence are obviously key variables whose qualities and interactions merit early analysis. However, because Turbulence Theory is not a static construction, change in turbulence level is an additional variable requiring attention. Individuals or groups working through turbulence would be wise to explore questions such as these: What is likely to happen to the current level of turbulence if no attention is paid to the situation in the short- and medium-term (raising the issue of cascading)? Would more turbulence help or harm the organization's pursuit of its goals (reflecting the potential for positive results from turbulence)? How might contemplated actions reduce the level of turbulence (when that level is considered too high and, consequently, harmful)? This exercise will help formulate relevant predictions of turbulence.

By carefully examining the key variables (contextual forces, positionality, the current level of turbulence, and consequences of changing levels of turbulence) in this order, relationships between pairs and among groups typically emerge, leading to a richer understanding of the flow of turbulence in a given situation. Using Turbulence Theory in this way fulfills four of the relevant requirements that Glaser and Strauss (1967) make for theories described in Chapter 1. Contextual forces and positionality help to explain and interpret turbulence in multidimensional ways that capture the dynamic flow of volatile conditions in our schools. Determining the current level of turbulence and possible changes in turbulence helps scholars and practitioners make relevant predictions that can guide decision making. In so doing, Turbulence Theory has become a useful tool applied to dynamic, challenging conditions that abound in the schools of our era.

Conclusion

That evening long ago when Steve Gross experienced a few moments of severe turbulence in flight thrust him into a new way of looking at the world. He may have been just a bit ahead of things because today, it seems that nearly everyone accepts that we live under turbulent conditions of some kind. Events like September 11, 2001 and its aftermath are easy to spot. So are natural crises like Hurricane Katrina in 2005 and the Indian Ocean tsunamis that killed over 300,000 people in December 2004. The fast pace of change, represented by the post-industrial information economy and its dislocations, seems to fit this metaphor as well. The purpose of Turbulence Theory transcends the need to describe these sudden and sometimes wrenching changes; it is meant to help us gain perspective on this movement, see potential benefits, and retain needed flexibility. The hope of Turbulence Theory is that it may help us work with the conditions of our era.

Part Two

(RE)SOLVING ETHICAL DILEMMAS

*I*N THE NEXT SEVEN CHAPTERS, ethical dilemmas are presented. They cover a range of challenges and focus on problems that develop in an unstable and sometimes even in a fairly stable world. The paradoxes that will be discussed include: security versus civil liberties; power versus accommodation in curriculum, instruction, and assessment; accountability versus responsibility; community standards versus individual rights; equality versus equity; personal vision versus authority; and rules, regulations, and policies versus individual needs and concerns in student teaching.

The ethical dilemmas in each chapter are written by graduate students and colleagues in education. The dilemmas cover issues in K–12 as well as include some cases in higher education. The ethical dilemmas should ring true, as most are based on authentic field experiences.

Each of the seven chapters contains an introduction to a highlighted paradox that serves as a title and is appropriate for a particular group of ethical dilemmas; individual dilemmas then follow. At the end of each dilemma or case, key questions that tap aspects of the Multiple Ethical Paradigms and Turbulence Theory are provided. The plan is to have the reader work her or his way through each case and then, by answering the questions, find ways to resolve or solve the ethical dilemma. The overarching intent is to help prepare educational leaders, in advance, for some of the difficult ethical problems that they will have to face in the future, enabling them to work on these challenging situations in the relatively safe spaces of the classroom or even in their home.

4

SECURITY VERSUS CIVIL LIBERTIES

Cases contributed by Susan H. Shapiro, Kelly D. Harbaugh,
Mary M. Figura, and Lisa Marie Waller

*I*N AN UNSTABLE WORLD RIDDLED WITH TERRORISM, violence, and environmental disasters, there is a strong need for security. Under demanding
circumstances, leaders are expected to protect their citizenry. One way to
keep them safe is to seek control. Purpel (1989) believed that because of this
desire for control, in our bureaucratized, computerized culture we value
"work, productivity, efficiency and uniformity over play, flexibility, diversity
and freedom" (p. 48). To establish control—especially at a time of chaos—he
pointed out that frequently there is a need for new rules and regulations.

Some of these rules exist only during a crisis, while others tend to endure.
For example, in the United States there are now color codes that are put into
effect if a city or state is facing a potentially threatening situation. These codes
are generally—although not always—short-term interventions. However,
there has also been longer-term legislation, such as the USA PATRIOT
Act, that has existed to enable the government to deal with those who are
suspected of terrorism swiftly without providing due process.

Despite external and internal dangers, most democratic countries pride
themselves on providing civil liberties to their people. Free speech, trial by
jury, freedom of religion, and other rights offered to citizens in constitu-
tions are thought to be essential in a free society. Self-determination and
autonomy are inherent concepts that citizens in many democracies believe
that they are entitled to receive.

Purpel (1989) spoke of how bureaucracy "sharply conflicts with our dedication to democratic principles which stress self-determination and a process
for both sustaining autonomy and adjusting conflicts" (p. 49). He went on to
speak of John Dewey's conceptualization of the school as a "'laboratory' of

democracy where students and teachers could wrestle with the challenges of the democratic experience" (p. 49).

Despite the current trend towards security and control, there is a counter-trend that takes the development of civil liberties into account in schools. For example, there is at least an increasing cry for more service education (Keith, 1999, 2005). Service learning does ask students to go beyond the school and help organizations within society. In addition, there are a number of scholars (Boyd, 2000; Gross & Shapiro, 2005; Gutmann, 1999; Gutmann & Thompson, 2004; Shapiro & Purpel, 2004) who strongly believe that students should have an excellent civics education to be prepared to play important roles in the democratic process.

Schools, like nations, are dealing with the same inconsistencies inherent in the paradox of shielding people who are in danger versus protecting their individual rights. On the one hand, there is a need to provide safe schools in any and all emergencies. Under such circumstances, educational leaders often have to function *in loco parentis*. In addition, they are expected to perform roles to protect their students and staff that they have never been prepared for in their studies nor ever experienced before in their lives.

Despite the dangers, on the other hand, educators know that it is important to give young people the opportunity to not only learn about democracy but also take part in it. Students need to understand and use their rights to enable them to become good citizens. School leaders also must take into consideration the civil rights of the students' parents as well as of members of the local community. Even during a crisis, there is a need for educational leaders to take into account the law and be able to explain the rationales for what they are doing when they change or modify policies to deal with emergencies.

This chapter deals with difficult dilemmas that educational leaders now face. These cases place school administrators and teacher leaders in circumstances in which they face terror or violence and have to act. The need to protect their students becomes salient; but also the awareness of what they are doing in terms of laws and rights becomes essential.

In the first ethical dilemma, "Protecting Young Children in Terrifying Times," Susan H. Shapiro describes the problems faced by a preschool director in evacuating her school that is close to the World Trade Center on September 11, 2001. The little children within the school need to be cared for and kept calm. But also, the rights of the teachers and those of the parents have to be taken into consideration. This ethical dilemma deals with issues that school leaders should never have to face, but these are concerns that must now be taken very seriously.

Kelly D. Harbaugh's case, "Bomb Threat: Real or Hoax/React or Ignore," focuses on a rookie principal who must decide whether to ignore or respond to a bomb threat. Ethics weigh on her shoulders. On one shoulder is piled thoughts about disregarding the threat; on the other are considerations regarding a response. To ignore the threat might be justified as the administrator spares the school from disruption and fear. Conversely, her reaction to control the situation could be justified to secure the school and the safety of her students and staff. Her decision is to react or ignore.

In "Disciplinarian or Intimidator?," Mary M. Figura describes a confrontation between a lead teacher of a small learning community and an eighth-grade student in the school's hallway. The confrontation escalates into a physical altercation because of aggressive behaviors on both sides. The dilemma focuses on the teacher leader's professional ethical behavior and his disciplinary tactics when dealing with violent students. It also deals with the student's responses to the lead teacher. Discipline and violence in schools are significant issues that receive widespread public attention, and in many schools—including this one—a zero-tolerance policy has become the norm.

Finally, in "Lady, You Can't Lay the Law Down to the Law!," Lisa Marie Waller describes a scene in which an intruder enters a high school and assaults a student. The intruder runs; a student chases the intruder, mobilizing other students. The intruder leaves and the assistant principal requests that the assaulted student remain in a room. She then asks the security resource officer to assist her by holding the student in the classroom while she "cleans" the halls. Instead of responding to her request, the officer lets the student go and the events that follow spiral out of control.

Protecting Young Children in Terrifying Times

It was a Tuesday morning, September 11, 2001. Aida Rodriguez was a daycare director of a private preschool in lower Manhattan. It was a new teacher's first day. The staff was having a welcome breakfast for her. They ordered bagels and coffee and invited the parents to come to the room. It was a bright and sunny day, and only a few parents had shown up for breakfast. Aida and the staff were joking around about how no one wanted to welcome the new teacher and they all wanted to soak up the sunshine instead.

That's when it began. Two teachers ran into the room crying. They said a plane had hit the World Trade Center (WTC). At first, Aida thought that it must be an accident. She even felt a little annoyed that these teachers were being so unprofessional. It was obviously some terrible accident but nothing that required such emotional behavior. Aida turned on the radio and the announcer said that another plane had hit the WTC. By then, everyone realized that this was no accident. Some of the parents in the room decided to go out and see. Aida said that they should go ahead because she knew she needed to stay in the school, as she was in charge. Aida tried to keep things as normal as possible.

Then the first of the parents started coming in covered in soot. One parent appeared at the door and looked like he was in shock. He walked into the classroom and silently took his child away. One of the parents suggested that Aida go see what was going on outside. She went and saw the two large buildings on fire. It started to dawn on her that they were under attack. While she watched the buildings burn, she could see things, small shapes pouring down from the top floors. Those on the street said they were people falling. At that point, Aida knew it was not business as usual. She felt that she had to get back into the school and protect the children.

When Aida returned, it was chaos. Parents were crying and lined up to use the phones. Children were hysterical. Aida then walked into the baby room where they were all listening to the radio. There were reports that the White House and the Pentagon were hit. She suddenly thought, "Oh my God, we are all going to die." At that time, she made a decision that if she was going to die, she was going to make it as calm as she could for the children and her staff. She felt it essential to reassure everyone it was all going to be O.K.

Aida got back to work. She called one representative from each classroom into her office. She told them to turn off all the radios except for the one in the baby room. She told them she would keep them informed as she found out information. She told them to tell the children that they were safe and something bad was happening but it was a grown-up problem. She told them that if the children asked questions, they should make the answers as simple and as truthful as possible. Aida also let the teachers know if they had to cry, they should leave the room and come into her office or the kitchen. Armed with new directives, the teachers went back to their rooms.

Throughout the day, decisions were made and carried out by Aida Rodriguez and her staff. Together they managed to reach almost all the parents by phone and let them know that they should pick up their children, as the school and the city were closing.

The parents kept arriving, hysterical. In their panic, some of the parents insisted that Aida release their children immediately. In response, Aida took one parent after another into her office and tried to calm them down before they took their children. She said, "My grandparents lived through two world wars and they survived, and so will we." She did not believe what she was saying but she told them to take their children home before it was impossible to get home. Throughout, she thought she was sending them home to die with their children. Every time she said it, she felt a little sicker. "What should we do?" they all asked. "Take them home. Be with your children."

People started running past the school, screaming. They said the buildings had fallen. It was panic outside. Aida and her staff could hear the fighter planes in the air. It sounded like there were hundreds of them. Interestingly enough, everyone felt a little safer. However, they could not be sure if they were the "good guys" or the "bad guys."

The bridges and tunnels began to close and it seemed as if they were locked on the island. Aida began sending staff home. She started with the ones who needed to get to their loved ones first and those who lived the farthest away. She kept just a few teachers in the building as the amount of children began to dwindle. Parents were crying; so were some of the staff.

She made a policy for herself that she wouldn't release a child until she felt the parents were calm enough to hold him or her. Aida wasn't going to have any dropped babies on her watch. She began to make plans. If the children or staff couldn't get home, the school would be kept open. All could sleep in the school. She began to wonder what would happen if no one came to pick up a child. What if both of the parents were dead? She began to scan the children's files for the World Trade Center. Several folders had that business address listed.

In some ways, Aida felt exhilarated; in other ways, she just wanted to run. But deep down inside, she knew she could handle this. She could work until the end. She knew she was doing the best job she had ever done in her life. If necessary, she would die making children feel safe and loved. If it had to be, they would die without the terror that she was feeling.

Toward the end of the school day, Aida gathered what was left of her staff and children, placed them in one room, and showed a movie. It was *The Lion King*, probably not the best choice. Aida did not think anyone really watched it. By this time, the children were frightened and so were the adults.

Eventually, just a few children were left with the new teacher who had started the day with a party. Aida tried to send her home, but she didn't want to leave. Finally, Aida insisted, as she would have to walk up to 90th Street, far, far away. The last of the children, one whose mother worked in a blood bank and another whose mother was an ER nurse, were picked up. Every child had someone, at least one parent, left alive.

Questions for Discussion

1. The law states that parents must have access to their children at all times. Was the director correct when she refused to let the parents have their children until they had calmed down? Discuss.

2. Was it caring to keep the teachers on duty who felt that they needed to be with their family during the attacks? Were the needs of the school community more important than the needs of the teachers?
3. Was it right to explain what was happening to the children? Was the director correct when she said children's questions should be answered as simply and as truthfully as possible?
4. Being a director is a job, isn't it? Is facing death what is expected of a school leader today? How far does the ethic of the profession go? Was this situation handled professionally?
5. How did the director and staff keep the level of turbulence moderate for the children? Was positionality a factor in this case? Explain.
6. How could the director and staff have increased the level of turbulence for the children and their families? Could the director and staff have decreased the level of turbulence any further? Discuss.

Bomb Threat: Real or Hoax/React or Ignore

It was a clear, crisp February morning as Principal Bellini parked her car outside of Dew Valley High School. Although her first year in this administrative position had its share of grueling challenges, the days seemed to pass swiftly. She was energized by the rapid pace and daily chaos of operating a high school with over 900 students, 70 professional staff, and 15 support staff. The suburban community was united behind its schools, and Ms. Bellini was supported by students, parents, and staff. She was the third principal of Dew Valley in as many years, and the school community was looking forward to a fair and consistent leader who would remain with the district for more than one year. Ms. Bellini was passionate about her new position and described herself as a student advocate, first and foremost. She genuinely cared about all students and utilized several means in order to get to know as many of them as possible. As an instructional leader, she strived to raise the academic bar through improved delivery of the curriculum. She realized this would be possible through a united team approach with the staff. In summary, her motto was a quote by John C. Maxwell: "You can love people without leading them, but you can't lead people without loving them."

The day began as usual. By 9:00 a.m., Ms. Bellini was doing her second walk through the building. Classes were in session and the halls were empty. As she rounded a corner, she noticed a piece of notebook paper on the floor. She casually stooped over to pick up the paper and dispose of it in a nearby trash can. Just by chance, she glanced down at the paper and noticed scribbling that appeared to be words. Upon closer inspection, she read, "There is a bomb in the building. It's gonna blow and people will die. You deserve it."

Ms. Bellini hastily folded the piece of paper and headed for her office. Once in her office, she closed the door and reread the note. She responded out loud by saying, "What do I do now?" She had absolutely no experience with this type of situation. Butterflies began to swarm in her stomach. She took a deep breath and told herself to remain calm and composed. As her thought process began, it was as if there were two massive weights on her shoulders. The weight on the right shoulder represented the following thoughts: "Did anyone else see this note? If not, this can be easy—no one has to know that I saw the note. Therefore, I don't need to take any further steps but to throw away the note and carry on with the tasks of the day. If someone does report seeing the note, I can still say I never saw it. Because they would not be able to present the note, the situation could be treated as hearsay or rumor. Again, no additional action would be required. Chances are this is just a prank by some class clown, and I'm not going to waste my time on it."

On the left shoulder was an equally heavy weight, which amassed the following thoughts: "Even if I am the first person besides the true author to view this note, I cannot take the chance of it being a hoax. If something did happen, regardless of how minor, I could never justify to myself or anyone else the decision to ignore the note. I have no professional basis from which to conclude whether the note is real or a prank. Therefore, there is only one correct decision. I should notify the superintendent to discuss our plan of action according to our Crisis Management Plan."

The right shoulder bore down once again and made Ms. Bellini contemplate the effects of reacting to a prank. She thought: "The author of the note will be given control. The normal flow of the day will be interrupted, if not halted. Students and staff may become angered or scared and the outcome of any plan of action may be disastrous. The media will surely appear and distort everything. Parents will panic and flood the premises. All of these combined would lead to widespread criticism of me and my possible demise."

The left shoulder countered with: "Chaos, confusion, and fear can be avoided through clear, succinct, and composed communications. Regardless of who I am dealing with, I have to be confident and levelheaded. Students and staff will mirror my reactions. All decisions from this point forward must be based upon the school community's safety and mental well-being. The media sharks can be kept at bay and fed innocuous tidbits of information until the situation is in our control, and then the media can be my ally. Parents will be informed of the safety and welfare of the students as readily as possible. Teachers and staff have practiced possible plans of actions for bomb threats. These plans are comprehensive and realistic. There will be a team approach throughout the handling of the situation. I will not have to attempt to think of everything or deal with everything on my own. As a school family, we will prevail regardless of whether this note is real or a hoax."

The weight of the left shoulder began to morph into a force as the weight of the right shoulder began to shrink. However, she could not help but continue to have doubts: ignore or react?

Questions for Discussion

1. In this dilemma, Principal Bellini views the ethic of justice as being secondary to the other three paradigms. Do you agree? Why?
2. Which of the four paradigms—justice, critique, care, or the profession—is the most applicable to this dilemma? Why?
3. Which of the four paradigms can be utilized to determine the best response to the threat?
4. Could Ms. Bellini exercise ethical leadership by ignoring the threat? Please explain.
5. How could Ms. Bellini bring the turbulence level down in this case? And how could she manage to increase it? Discuss.
6. How does Ms. Bellini relate her level of turbulence to that of students and staff (positionality)?

Disciplinarian or Intimidator?

Ralph Leaving was an assistant principal at Independence Middle School in the Liberty School District, a suburban middle-class district. Mr. Leaving had been having disciplinary problems with an eighth-grade student, Leon Milton. Leon had been trouble since he arrived at Independence three years ago as a sixth-grade student. He was referred to the office on a weekly basis for bullying, fighting, theft, defiance, and most recently, harassment of a teacher. He had previously been truant and suspended from school.

Mr. Leaving suspected that Leon needed special education services; however, his mother never agreed to the testing. When Mr. Leaving contacted home, he found that Leon had little or no supervision and a lack of support from his mother, with whom he lived. One illustration of this neglect was although Leon's home was in a rough neighborhood, he was allowed to "hang out" with older teenagers and he did not have a curfew. The guidance counselor told Mr. Leaving that Leon "does not like being told what to do" after the last time he was sent to the office.

Leon had been causing trouble all week, and Mr. Leaving began to feel aggravated that he was taking up so much of his time. While walking in the hall, Mr. Leaving noticed the student running down the hallway without a pass. When Mr. Leaving stopped Leon, he became rude, disruptive, and argumentative. Cornering him, Mr. Leaving argued with him in the hallway. When Leon tried to remove himself from the situation, the assistant principal grabbed his arm. At this point, Leon turned to Mr. Leaving in a confrontational manner and punched him in the stomach. Mr. Leaving retaliated by punching Leon and wrestling him to the floor. The physical confrontation ended when three male teachers intervened to separate the two. As he was being escorted to the office, Mr. Leaving told the teachers he had fought back in self-defense.

Since he was hired, Mr. Leaving had done a satisfactory job as an assistant principal. Although he was not a compassionate person, he had been fair to his students. Mrs. Dugan, the principal, would not have hired Mr. Leaving except that she was required to hire within the school district if anyone applied for an opening. The previous superintendent, Robert Wilson, felt that hiring administrators from a teacher pool of applicants was the "right thing" to do for the school district. Mrs. Dugan did not feel that way, but her suggestions to look at other candidates fell on deaf ears. Mr. Wilson wanted administrators hired from within the school district, no matter what the cost. It was during her search for a new administrator that Mrs. Dugan was introduced to Mr. Leaving, who turned out to be a personal friend of Mr. Wilson's.

Since Mr. Leaving's hiring, a new superintendent was hired by the board. The school board went against Mr. Wilson's recommendation to hire from within and hired a well-qualified superintendent from another district who did not support the hiring system and was quite vocal about changing the system in order to hire the best administrators for the district. The new superintendent was not fond of Mr. Leaving's style of discipline and had told Mrs. Dugan her concerns.

When Mrs. Dugan informed the new superintendent of the incident, she wanted a full investigation. Mrs. Dugan requested Mr. Leaving's personnel file from the district office and was astounded at what she saw. Included in his file were disciplinary letters from past administrators regarding his behavior as a teacher. Almost two years before he was hired, Mr. Leaving had to take a leave of absence because he had been involved in several physical confrontations with staff members and students. One confrontation even manifested itself into a lawsuit, which had been settled out of court. The dossier showed that he had taken anger management classes and was then reinstated to another position in a middle school.

As Mrs. Dugan sat, staring at the information in the file, she had to remind herself that she was not aware of the previous problems when she hired Mr. Leaving, since Mr. Wilson wrote Mr. Leaving's letter of recommendation and he supported his hiring. However, in the past three months Mrs. Dugan had reprimanded Mr. Leaving several times for his short temper and his recent uncontrollable, angry outbursts at staff members, parents, and students. Mrs. Dugan did not write letters for his file but did have the dates that she had spoken to Mr. Leaving documented with her secretary.

Although she had read the information in his file, she knew she had to review the incident from the security tape that she had taken from the VCR in her office. While the tape was of poor quality, she could see that Mr. Leaving could have removed himself from the situation. She now had to decide if the incident was a physical confrontation or self-defense, as the assistant principal had claimed. The overarching question for Mrs. Dugan seemed to be: Was Mr. Leaving a disciplinarian or an intimidator in this situation?

Questions for Discussion

1. To what extent should Leon be held responsible for the incident? Mr. Leaving? Leon's mother? Mr. Wilson? Mrs. Dugan? What course of action should Mrs. Dugan take that would be in the best interest of Leon? The best interest of Mr. Leaving?
2. What needs to be done legally? Should Leon be expelled from school? Should charges be filed against Mr. Leaving? Because Leon was suspected to be a student who could receive special education services, what legal rights does Leon have? Could this incident be a manifestation of his disability?
3. Who is responsible for the incident? Who benefits from the zero-tolerance policy? Who had the control and the power to prevent this situation? Discuss.
4. What educational outcome is fair for Leon? What professional outcome is fair for Mr. Leaving? Should past behavior be a reason not to hire someone? What hiring practices should be changed in the Liberty

School District? What disciplinary conclusion will be shared with the superintendent?

5. What is the level of turbulence in this dilemma for Mrs. Dugan? Mr Leaving? Leon? How could it be decreased? How could it be increased?

Lady, You Can't Lay the Law Down to the Law!

Buttonwood High School is situated in an urban district located in Mullen County. The school is home to over 1500 students, 130 teachers, a head principal, three assistant principals, and two school resource officers (SRO). The school district is on the state empowerment list; over half of the students scored at the basic and/or below basic level on the Buttonwood Proficiency Exam (BPE). However, in an effort to avoid a "takeover," the local mayor stepped in to help the ailing school system.

In October 2002, Ms. Howard, the head principal, was out of the building visiting a partner school. During her absence, Ms. Lee and Mr. Brown, two assistant principals, were responsible for the building. Mr. Jacob, the third assistant principal, was out of the building for the day as well. A male intruder entered Buttonwood High School. He made his way to the gymnasium area to "call [a student] out" (request a fight). Evidently, the student was picking on his girlfriend. The intruder assaulted the student, pulled off his $300 gold chain, and proceeded to run out of the building.

Ms. Lee received word that there was an intruder in the building. She proceeded to the first level, calling for help from an SRO. Meanwhile, the student began to chase the intruder, mobilizing other students as he ran throughout the building. The assaulted student was very upset and bleeding around his neck from the theft of his gold chain. Ms. Lee's goal was to take him to the nurse, but she had to remove students from the hall first. She managed to get him into a secure location. Ms. Lee distinctly remembered asking the SRO—who was also a captain on the local police force—to detain the student until she "cleaned the hall." The SRO confirmed the detention of the student. Ms. Lee proceeded to clean the hall while Mr. Brown, the other assistant principal, called for a building lockdown.

After clearing the halls, Ms. Lee proceeded to the room with the SRO and the student. She was shocked to find that the student was not in his care. She inquired into the whereabouts of the student and was told that he had let him go. Ms. Lee thought, "Who do you think you are, Moses?" She could not believe it! The SRO stated that he assessed the situation and had no legal right to detain the student. His job was to "catch" the intruder. Ms. Lee commented on his lack of judgment and experience with high school students. Mr. Brown could not find the assaulted student.

News of the incident traveled quickly throughout the school and beyond. Ms. Lee received phone calls from the superintendent, the mayor's office, the chief of police, and the head principal in the midst of the violence. However, her goal was to locate the assaulted student. Mr. Brown found him sitting in an assembly. Ms. Lee asked the SRO a second time for assistance. The captain told Ms. Lee to leave the student alone, and that he was fine and everything would die down. However, her intuition and experience told her that the SRO was wrong. She asked him again to remove the student from the assembly; he said, "No."

The student refused to leave the auditorium with Mr. Brown. Now, it was clear that there was a need to call in police from the outside. The assembly ended and all hell broke loose. Students were engaged in four fights at one time at Buttonwood High School. The scene was chaotic. The assaulted student's girlfriend located the girlfriend of the intruder. The intruder's girlfriend declared, "The student deserved to be assaulted!" The other fights were a direct result of the incident. In the end, over ten students were suspended, and Ms. Lee and Mr. Brown were in the hot seat.

Questions for Discussion

1. Should the SRO have kept the student in his custody? What is the law in this situation?
2. If there is a law regarding this incident, should it have been followed? Was it appropriate?
3. What about the care of the students? Was Ms. Lee right to focus on the injured student? What about the other students in the school? How could they have been cared for?
4. What responsibility does Ms. Lee have to the head principal? What responsibility does Ms. Lee have to the community and the students? Did the students deserve a suspension?
5. During the incident, what was the level of turbulence? Did the level modify throughout the dilemma?
6. How was the turbulence level raised in this case? How did one turbulent situation contribute to greater incidents of turbulence (cascading) in this case? And how could it have been decreased?

5

POWER VERSUS ACCOMMODATION
IN CURRICULUM, INSTRUCTION,
AND ASSESSMENT

*Cases contributed by Stacey L. Aronow, James M. O'Connor,
Robert J. Murphy, and Corrinne A. Caldwell*

*I*T CAN BE ARGUED THAT CURRICULUM, instruction, and assessment are
at the heart of the educational enterprise and, therefore, at the center of
many controversial questions, such as: Who sets the learning agenda? Who
determines what gets included in a new canon, or that there needs to be
a unitary set of ideas learned by all? Whose values are elevated and at the
cost of what other person or group? These challenging queries have been
at the heart of educational debate since the first schools were organized in
North America, and have continued to our time. What has been called,
"The Struggle for the American Curriculum" (Kliebard, 1987), reflects this
dynamic tension. The American experience includes calls for a curriculum
that emphasizes liberal studies for all students, but it also includes calls for
a curriculum that demands students be educated in ways relevant to their
likely goals and needs. Others insist on a close connection between school
and democratic life in the larger society (Dewey, 1916), only to be countered
by those insisting on rigid learning standards, hierarchically imposed, vigor-
ously tested, and undergirded through by sanctions and rewards. For every
plea to honor the learning priorities of individual students, there is an equal
and opposite outcry for a common curriculum if we are to preserve a thread
of national identity and equity. These are not mere theoretical issues reserved
for polite debating societies. These curriculum shifts represent deeply held
values and are typically expressed with passion because so much is at stake.

To round out the picture, this is not only a question of considering the
curriculum alone, since it does not exist in isolation. In *Staying Centered:*

Curriculum Leadership in a Turbulent Era (1998), Gross described the curriculum as the learning agenda, instruction as the way the agenda is shared with students, and assessment as the means by which we determine the extent to which students have grasped that agenda. Gross's research went on to show that curriculum, instruction, and assessment worked together as a dynamic C (curriculum), I (instruction), A (assessment) triangle. When one element was changed, such as is the case in curriculum reform, there is an impact on instruction and assessment. In the current era of high-stakes testing, the change is in assessment with the predictable demand for a curriculum that matches the test and instruction that covers only those items on the test.

Not only are curriculum and instruction dynamically related, they are also intertwined with issues of power and accommodation. In the context of curriculum, instruction, and assessment, power and accommodation need definition. For our purposes, power refers to the ability to impose values, content, processes, rewards, and sanctions in setting the learning agenda (curriculum), sharing that agenda (instruction), and measuring what may be called progress in relation to that agenda (assessment). Thus, power is the ability to fashion a coordinated Curriculum–Instruction–Assessment (CIA) triangle reflecting a particular set of values. In a time of No Child Left Behind (NCLB) legislation, for instance, power refers to a typically standardized curriculum, taught in a uniform fashion and measured in standardized, commercially purchased tests. The sanctions associated with NCLB are a key element in this movement's power since they are an official enforcement dimension of the law. The very fact that NCLB is a national law tied to federal funding illustrates the use of power in curriculum, instruction, and assessment, and is only the latest example of the use of such power in the direction of the accountability movement. But NCLB is only one example of power in curriculum, instruction, and assessment. The cases in this chapter illustrate other ways in which power is used to influence decisions at the institution and classroom levels.

On the other side of the paradox is the concept of accommodation. If power enables the creation of a CIA triangle that can be imposed upon a school, district, state, or nation, accommodation demands flexibility and adaptation to the needs of individuals and groups so that their aspirations can be included. For our purposes, accommodation in the context of curriculum-instruction-assessment refers to the forces that confront and alter the givens in any CIA triangle to make it more responsive and a better fit to the dynamic and diverse qualities and beliefs within a school or school system setting. Whereas power is reminiscent of the machine metaphor (Morgan, 1997) with its command and control system of rules, accommodation is more closely allied to the metaphor of organizations as brains using concepts of double-loop learning that question the givens of heretofore underexamined truths.

Accommodation is connected for many to special education laws that require changes in classroom structures (physical and pedagogic) and approaches so that a whole class of learners can be included in school settings instead of being segregated. Special education has changed instruction most clearly, but changes in assessment are also evident with extensions to the length of time some students are allowed to take in examinations.

Instructional innovations such as multiple intelligence approaches (Gardner, 1993) are another example of accommodation in the classroom. Instead of claiming intelligence to be monolithic, Gardner has identified eight types of intelligences and, along with other writers in the field, suggests methods of instruction that allow access to learning for students with a variety of diverse learning strengths.

Clearly, accommodation in curriculum (the learning agenda) has been part of the American educational experience for over 100 years (Kliebard, 1987; Vallance, 1973). When we ask questions about including sex education in the high school curriculum, for instance, we are pursuing an issue of accommodation. Will we accommodate the current structure of classroom topics to include a subject that some feel crucial to the needs of adolescent learners, even if it means dropping something else? In recent years, questions of accommodating the traditional canon of English and American literature to include writers from the African-American, Latino, Native American, or gay and lesbian communities have become familiar to school leaders and policy analysts.

Finally, accommodation in assessment is also relevant to our era. Moving from the basics movement of the 1970s and 1980s, local, district, and state leaders began to consider assessment techniques that were more flexible than standardized tests. From the mid-1980s to the mid-1990s, criticisms of filling in the bubbles with a Number 2 pencil on a computer-scored test became familiar, while alternative approaches to assessment became common. In this decade of assessment accommodation, concepts such as student writing portfolios began to carry as much weight as standardized assessments in states such as Vermont. School report cards likewise became more flexible and started to allow teachers to record growth over time in content areas in descriptive language. These changes in assessment, in turn, have come under fire in the past decade as school systems witnessed the revival of standardized testing regimes. Accommodations that allowed diverse types of students the chance to document their learning in flexible ways have atrophied, giving room in policy and practice to the power of an imposed assessment system.

Thus, power and accommodation live in dynamic tension. If power completely overwhelms accommodation, the system becomes hidebound and loses its ability to adapt to changing circumstances. In a heterogeneous, complex, dynamic, and turbulent world, the oppressive qualities of such a system seem unfair, undemocratic, and out of touch with reality. Yet social critics and historians (Schlesinger, 1991) warn us against the balkanizing effect of too much accommodation, especially in the curriculum. They wonder how a diverse society can survive without compelling, common learning experiences. Without such commonalities in the learning agenda, for what does an American (or for that matter, a Chinese, Jordanian, or South African) education stand? What will bind us together as a society? Considered in this light, it is not surprising that power on one hand and accommodation on the other place educators in the center of difficult ethical dilemmas.

Because so much is at stake and because curriculum, instruction, and assessment are such charged concepts, this chapter's title seems timely and apt. Each of the authors has examined a particular aspect of this conflict.

In "Who Should Teach the Classes No One Wants to Teach?," Stacey L. Aronow raises the question of accommodation to new teachers, veteran teachers, and especially students with diverse needs when the time comes to make teaching assignments. Can power and accommodation be balanced? What happens when sharp disagreements erupt?

James M. O'Connor's dilemma, "Authentic Education or a Threat to the Organization?," takes us further into a new teacher's world. Will Danny, a recently hired faculty member, continue to employ a successful student-centered approach to social studies or will he conform to the pressures to cover the official curriculum? How will he decide between his goal of accommodation to student needs and interests and the power of the imposed curriculum?

The question of power and accommodation in curriculum and instruction is examined from a different angle by Robert J. Murphy in his dilemma, "Achieving a Culturally Sensitive Teaching Approach." Cultural misunderstandings boil over when an American graduate program is "exported" to an East Asian setting. Are these students merely unresponsive to the values of their American instructors or are these instructors simply culturally insensitive? How might the American instructors modify their power to accommodate the needs of students coming from a different set of values?

A new dean is thrust into a curriculum controversy in Corrinne A. Caldwell's dilemma. Set in a rural branch campus of a major university, "A Harvard Curriculum Versus a Useful Curriculum" pits the competing values of local student needs with the demands for a rigorous liberal arts curriculum. How can this local leader protect her desire to accommodate the needs of students at the branch campus when key faculty groups and leaders from the main campus oppose this idea?

Who Should Teach the Classes No One Wants to Teach?

Hope Smythe sighed deeply and massaged her now throbbing temple as she read the latest e-mail from Principal Janet Healey. As head of the science department at Whiningham High School, Hope had just received a friendly reminder that the first draft of next year's department teacher schedule would be due on Thursday. Although it was not the official responsibility of department heads to generate teacher schedules, it was their responsibility to follow their boss' directives. It was entirely understandable to Hope why the principal would want to divest herself of the job of determining teacher schedules. After last year's turbulent unrest in the science department, Hope would rather grade inaccurate lab reports until the cows came home than experience a repeat episode.

Last year, the board had voted to change the high school's bell schedule from a nine-period traditional schedule to a four-period block schedule. Recognizing that even the most experienced of teachers would be expending great energy preparing for class each day—as most were new to the block format—Principal Healey had told her department heads that in sketching out the next year's schedule, they should base their decisions on two criteria. First, all attempts should be made to give teachers as few course preparations (or "preps," as they were called) as possible; and second, teachers should be given courses they had previously taught. The principal believed that by making these objectives a priority, it would create schedules that would lessen the potential stress level of her faculty once it began teaching in the block.

And so, Hope had set out to create the master teaching schedule for her department. Before beginning to sketch out the schedule, she had asked each member of the department to complete a form that solicited their course preferences. She was determined to generate a schedule that would offer maximum satisfaction among department members. Once the schedule had been tentatively planned, the principal approved it before Hope took it to the department.

After looking at the schedule, of the 15 members in the department, 14 were fairly satisfied with what they saw. Not everyone had received everything that they wanted but most had received schedules with some bright spots despite a few dimmer ones. Hope's attempt at producing a schedule that offered teachers few preps and courses that they had already taught appeared to have been successful. Several teachers had been assigned only one prep and most had no more than two. If they had more than two, more than likely they would be teaching only two during a given semester. The consensus was that next year's assignment wouldn't be too terrible.

The one teacher who had not been as pleased with his schedule was the department's newest member, Bob Semple, a half-time teacher moving to a full-time position the next year. Hope had scheduled Bob with four career-level classes and two advanced placement (AP) chemistry classes. At Whiningham High School, career courses were for students who had no intention of going to college. The career-level curriculum desired to give students a balanced view of chemistry by exploring how it would serve them in the "real world" in which they lived. Most career students were unruly at best. Effective classroom management was at the core of any teacher's relative success as a teacher of career-level classes. No one ever jumped at the opportunity to teach career-level classes, and thus they were the most dreaded courses to teach. However, at Whiningham it was a necessary evil and some teachers simply had to do it.

Bob's previous position had been at a vocational technical school where he had experience teaching career-level students. This experience played a key role in the decision to hire him. Hope had reasoned that with the relatively little effort needed in terms of lesson planning and grading involved when one teaches career-level classes, she knew she could also give him a plum and intellectually stimulating course, AP Chemistry, filled with the high school's very best upperclassmen. While the grading load for AP Chemistry would be daunting, coupling it with career-level classes would make it a more reasonable burden. Bob, a newlywed, had a baby on the way and was currently pursuing his masters. With this in mind, Hope believed that she had made Bob's first full-time teaching schedule at Whiningham a fair one.

Unfortunately, another member of the department, 15-year veteran Ivan Mullet (a rather ornery fellow), had decided to oppose what he considered a vicious injustice in giving the newest member of the department four career-level classes classes, often thought to be the worst classes to teach. At his own request, Ivan had taught these very same career-level classes the past two years. He acknowledged that he had asked for these courses because of the light paper load but adamantly refused teaching them a third year. After making it clear that he would no longer teach career-level classes, Hope had scheduled Ivan with only the classes he requested—three honors and three college-preparatory. Despite his own schedule satisfaction, using Bob's schedule and a healthy dose of self-righteous indignation he had begun campaigning for a change in the schedule Hope had drafted.

At first, he had accused more experienced teachers of being selfish for not teaching the career-level classes and leaving them to the newest member. He berated members of the department, suggesting that the only reason they did not want to teach these classes was because they themselves were inept as educators and could not handle such students. He suggested that the department had a history of dumping the unwanted classes on new teachers, which could drive them from the profession. Ivan even generated an alternate schedule, which, while it scattered the career classes so that almost every teacher had at least one, it had completely disregarded the two objectives originally set up by the principal.

It became obvious to many members of the department that Ivan's alternate schedule attacked some teachers in the department while leaving others alone. When his verbal wailings went unheeded, in frustration he had written what was now known as "The Manifesto," condemning the department for acting as poor educators who were willing to let one of their members hang out to dry. He had named individual names and alluded to several others, attacking their integrity. He had made 15 photocopies and placed a copy of the letter in each member's mailbox.

Department outcry as a result of the letter had been fast and furious. Several members were in tears as a result of the accusations, others were enraged, and the majority had felt decidedly insulted. Those in the department who had felt maligned by Ivan's accusatory letter contended that Ivan had jumped to some unfair conclusions. It was true that most of the department believed that, as more experienced teachers with seniority, they had already had their share of career-level classes and did not take kindly to the possibility of teaching them again. They felt that their years at the high school should count for something. Giving the new teachers the less-favored classes might not be ideal but it certainly was not because the veteran teachers were inept educators. Some members argued that the special electives they taught along with some of the extracurricular activities they advised demanded an exorbitant amount of time and effort to do well. Giving them career-level classes to teach—something they had not taught before—would be unfair, especially when others in the department did not participate in any school-related activities outside the official school day.

At wit's end, Hope decided that with such an exhibition of unprofessional behavior, Ivan had overstepped his bounds. That afternoon, with "The Manifesto" in hand, Hope had spoken with Principal Healey. After reading the letter and listening to Hope's assessment of the situation, Principal Healey chose to officially reprimand Ivan, placing a letter in his file. The principal had demanded that Ivan write a letter of apology to the department and personally apologize to those mentioned in the letter. Ivan had done so bitterly and with a complete lack of sincerity, at one point practically throwing the apology letter at those to which it was intended.

Even now, a year after the fact, Ivan still argues that he is the one wronged because his letter was only supposed to have been seen by the department. He still accuses Hope of behaving inappropriately by showing the principal the document and "airing the department's dirty laundry." Thus, while he had apologized because he was "told to do so," he had done so using words that dripped with sarcasm and false pretense.

Despite Ivan's expressed opposition, the schedule as originally approved by the principal had remained intact. The department, which had previously been running smoothly with some mild turbulence, was caught in a patch of severe turbulence. Some of the teachers—especially those alluded to in the letter—were angry. They had felt betrayed, insulted, and senselessly attacked. A few teachers had told Hope they could not bear to even look at Ivan. The school year ended two months later with gaping wounds that were far from healed.

And now, it was time for Hope to schedule once again. Hope obliged herself a quick shudder. True, a couple of months away from each other had allowed the most festering of wounds to heal somewhat. Since the beginning of the school year, department members had been able to exchange pleasantries over lunch and put their collective efforts into other issues, such as a successful transition to the block schedule. The severity of last year's turbulence had settled down, and the department was currently operating on a more moderate track.

However, two months before scheduling became a priority, Ivan had demanded that the department develop a teacher scheduling philosophy indicative of how members would like scheduling to run in the future. And so at a recent department meeting, Hope had asked members to agree or disagree with a number of philosophical statements that she created. She also asked department members for any other statements to add to the list. She figured that if she could get direct consensus on a statement, it could become part of the department's philosophy. Some of the statements included: tenured teachers have paid their dues; experience in teaching a course counts; schedules should be created for the optimal benefit to students; one prep is ideal and the fewer the preps the better; first-year teachers should get preference in scheduling; a priority in scheduling should be the rotation of career classes; and teachers, as professionals, should have a voice in their schedules.

After reviewing the results, she discovered she only had consensus when it came to teachers having a say in their schedules and work being scheduled for optimal benefit to students. She could have predicted that outcome without all the effort. Meanwhile, she still had 14 rather demanding teachers to please, each ready to beat down her classroom door if they found themselves unsatisfied with the scheduling results.

Questions for Discussion

1. What is the level of turbulence in this situation? Explain. How should Hope handle the situation to lower the level of turbulence? What decision could Hope make that would increase the level of turbulence?
2. Given their seniority, what scheduling expectations are appropriate for tenured teachers to have? What is the fairest way to distribute courses throughout the department so that all members are satisfied? How do equity and equality play a role in this scenario?
3. To what extent should Hope be responsible to new teachers in terms of scheduling? What type of teacher schedule will best suit the needs of students?
4. Should a philosophical policy be created for the assigning of future teacher schedules? If no one can agree on what the policy should say, how should the policy be created? Should the policy change when a new teacher is hired?
5. Whose responsibility should it be to create teacher schedules? How acceptable is it for the principal to pass the duty on to department heads even though it isn't "officially" a responsibility of the position?

Authentic Education or a Threat to the Organization?

It had been a trying year for Danny Fledgling, and now he had this to ponder: After a disturbing comment made by his principal, Danny was not sure that he would survive in this environment. Could he make his brand of education work in a district that did not look favorably on the new and different?

Danny was nearing the end of his first year as a social studies teacher in Status Valley School District. He had come to this district because it was the only place that had offered a permanent position. In fact, he had come from out of the state to take the position. If the previous teacher had not left two weeks prior to the start of school, Danny felt sure that the position would have gone to a local person. When he looked at the staff, over half of the faculty had graduated from this high school. The principal and both assistants had either grown up in this town or lived here for most of their careers.

The Status Valley School District was in the central "bible belt" of this state. While near enough to larger metropolitan areas to appear attractive to outsiders, it had managed to remain isolated. The town was in decline from its heyday in the 1950s, yet the locals still circulated as if it was the center of the universe. The surrounding farmlands remain essentially unchanged since the time of the early pioneers. Dairy cows outnumbered humans.

By contrast, Danny came from a background that emphasized change. His father held a career that kept the family on the move. Danny lived in many parts of the country and managed to visit at least four foreign countries before the age of 18. Danny had gone to an urban university that never lost its liberalism of the 1960s. When Danny wasn't in social studies classes that emphasized debate and student involvement, he was involved in student activities that did the same. Danny had been a student senator in Student Council. He had written for the school newspaper and enjoyed the excitement that came with controversial causes. And Danny had been greatly influenced by an education professor who seemed to descend directly from John Dewey. Involving students with a hands-on approach had seemed to Danny like the Holy Grail of education. How better to care for the needs of students than to raise a generation that questioned and enjoyed change? Too bad he had not lived during the 1960s. If he couldn't live in that time, as a teacher of history he could inspire his students to question the status quo and look for alternatives.

Early in Danny's first year, he sensed that not all of his colleagues were happy with his teaching style. He frequently took a historical issue and attempted to place his students directly in that era. He provided them with the facts and feelings needed to understand the era, then arranged them in roles designed to stimulate debate. He always ended each lesson asking students two questions: How can we apply the lessons learned during the studied era to problems occurring today? What ideas from that era could be used to improve today's world?

But this method of teaching often created turbulence within the organization. To an outsider, the loud debates and strongly developed opinions of the students gave the appearance of chaos. Danny called it "organized chaos" but to colleagues walking by, it appeared as an uncontrolled classroom. One older faculty member got to the point of just shaking his head whenever he walked by Danny's classroom.

Word had gotten out that Danny wasn't following the textbook. While his topics followed the historical periods of the curriculum, Danny's emphasis on debate and experiential learning ate up classroom time and required him to skip many parts of the curriculum. Since Danny used many materials from other sources, he felt no need for the textbook. When another social studies teacher bemoaned the shortage of textbooks, Danny announced that he could borrow as many as he wanted from his classroom. "I don't believe in textbooks," said Danny. "They tend to force every student to think in the same frame of mind."

Many students left Danny's classroom excited about the stances they took in the classroom debates. They went into their next classes and later to home articulating those views. The debates about whether or not the United States should have entered World War I left many students openly questioning the current War on Terror. At another time, girls in the class, empowered by a discussion of the suffragettes, organized a demonstration in favor of abortion rights. Many of those students' parents belonged to the local church that had organized demonstrations against those same abortion rights.

Because this was Danny's first year, he spent extensive hours developing the materials for his course. Consequently, he failed to build bonds between himself and his colleagues. He also failed to notice the grumblings of more senior staff members. In fact, he became so wrapped up in the excitement generated by his students that hints of trouble passed right over Danny's head.

> The confrontation emerged in a post-observation conference with the principal. When Danny had been asked for a suitable observation lesson, he had invited the principal to observe an experiential teaching exercise. Similar to a computer game, students drew scenarios from a pile of index cards. Based on the scenario, they would make decisions, act out roles, and interact with other students as if they were characters from history. Danny called it "interactive learning." The principal, seeing students moving about the room noisily interacting and reacting to stimuli, called it chaos. During the conference, the principal realized that there was a massive chasm between his beliefs and those of Danny. He had finally resorted to the basic question, "Danny, what do you wish as an outcome for your students?" Responding as if this was a college classroom philosophical debate, Danny stated that he wanted his students to question everything.
>
> As Danny spoke about the learning that occurs when students question, he became more visibly excited. The principal finally interrupted Danny. He said, "But when you teach them to question, they may question why they have to learn what they are studying. They may question the rules in your classroom. You may be smart enough to answer those questions. But then they will begin to question why I am here and why I have the rules I do for this school. And at that point, it will have gone too far. So from now on, I want no more of this style of teaching. I want no debates. I want no encouragement to questioning. I want the curriculum taught in the correct and complete order. I want the students to be able to tell when things occurred and what were the facts. I want an end to these parent calls and staff member complaints about what you are teaching."

Danny left his office knowing that if he were to remain at Status Valley, he had to review and revise his whole philosophy of teaching. What should he do?

Questions for Discussion

1. What would you consider the level of turbulence when posited from Danny's point of view? How can Danny reduce the level of turbulence? What action of Danny's would raise the level of turbulence?
2. What would you consider the level of turbulence when posited from the school's point of view? What would reduce the level of turbulence? What action would be expected to raise the level of turbulence?
3. What is the ethic of justice in this case as viewed through the lens of the organization? Is it different when viewed through the lens of an individual student?
4. How does the curriculum and teaching style of Danny express an ethic of care? Does the principal exhibit an ethic of care in ordering Danny to change his teaching method?
5. What would the ethic of profession indicate for Danny's decision regarding whether or not to continue with his teaching style? Is the principal adhering to an ethic of profession in his decision? Is Danny or the principal placing the best interests of students at the center of their thinking?
6. Is Danny the only one being silenced in this case? Whose power is the principal representing?

Achieving a Culturally Sensitive Teaching Approach

Southfield University has a nationally recognized graduate program in health care administration. Located in the western part of the United States, Southfield wished to pursue marketing opportunities to penetrate markets in Eastern Asian countries such as Taiwan, Mainland China, Singapore, and Indonesia. The university prided itself in promoting diversity and academic free expression in its faculty recruitment and scholarship.

The graduate program in health care administration had been innovative in online instruction, introducing Southfield's first online degree program in 1991. E-learning was particularly appealing to the working clinician or administrative professional who needed both flexibility and academic rigor.

A distinguishing characteristic of the Southfield program was the diverse background of its faculty. While the main emphasis of the program was to prepare graduate degree candidates for senior and mid-level leadership positions in health care organizations, there was a strong philosophical focus on social justice and ethical awareness in business decision making. The faculty was a balanced mix of working professionals as adjunct faculty and career academicians in full-time tenure track positions. Sixty percent of the faculty was female, of which 20% were African-American, 30% Hispanic, 5% Middle Eastern, 5% East Asian, and 40% Euro-Caucasian.

Within the past five years, one of the emerging business models in medicine was the globalization of health care delivery. Professional physician billing and medical record abstract coding for American hospitals is a burgeoning business in India. A prototype delivery model currently operates outside New Dehli, India, where open-heart surgery patients are flown in from the United States and other western countries and skilled surgeons perform complex cardiac procedures at a greatly reduced cost. Postoperatively, patients are quickly returned to their home countries for local recuperation. Asian medical educators and governments had become increasingly interested in developing administrative leadership talent to operate these nascent, fast-growing opportunities.

In 2002, Southfield University was approached by the business department of a prominent Far East university to establish an extension campus offering the equivalent of an American graduate degree in health care administration management. Learning would be delivered through a combination of teaching modalities including on-site teaching by native business faculty, visiting professors from the United States, and online course offerings taught by the Southfield Health Administrative Services Department. The initial cohort of course offerings began in the fall of 2003.

The pedagogical framework of the collective faculty teaching approach of the department was well grounded in the traditional Aristotelian philosophy, valuing the supremacy of the rights of individuals. In the United States, their program had attracted numerous Asian students, who performed quite well in class discussions and online collaborative projects. The health care administrative curricular model was largely patterned on the Harvard Business School method, where learning was implemented through student analysis and discussion of case studies. The Southfield faculty modified this approach by presenting a significant number of cases studies using social justice and bioethical dilemmas. They were training business leaders to be change agents and to initiate the organizational structure and policy changes needed for their entities to meet new competitive challenges. However, much to their disappointment, the department found the native Asian students minimally "engaged" in questioning the relevance or validity of the lesson material. The students were quick to accept the instructor's position with little inquisition and no criticism of the merit of the arguments. At first, the faculty thought that the online environment may not be fully adaptable to the "cultural" needs of the students. But during an on-site summer course in 2004, Dr. Fred Wilson, who taught the health care economics course, admittedly became a bit unprofessional in his in-class dialogue with the students when he made a not so subtle reference to their herd mentality in accepting his discourse verbatim. "I just can't get comfortable with these students," he lamented. "We're just not connecting. I couldn't wait to end the lecture and take a taxi back to my hotel."

The Health Administration Services Department chairperson, Janet Epstein, was growing increasingly concerned that their catalyst program was not performing to expectations. She pondered: "Are we missing the cultural nuances of the Asian students, or are they simply afraid to ask questions because they are being intimidated by somebody? Is this a political issue?"

> Dr. Epstein's thoughts were interrupted on a Friday afternoon in late July when she received a phone call from Southfield's president, Mark Redmond. He said: "Your HR adjunct has precipitated an incident! She screamed at the class that they lacked the care and compassion to be effective managers. She then told them it was a waste of her time to teach if they did not become more involved in classroom discussions. At the end of her tirade, she walked out of the classroom in disgust. This is the third week of a six-week course. They don't know if she will show up for the next class! The students are devastated. We need some damage control—fast!"

Dr. Redmond was, of course, referring to her department's most outspoken feminist and human resources management instructor, Phyllis Regane. Ironically, Regane was teaching an on-site six-week summer course in conflict management at the Asian campus. Regane was an ACLU attorney who had been an adjunct instructor at Southfield for seven years. Her student evaluation scores had been consistently in the top 25th percentile of all business school faculty. In 2000, she was the recipient of the prestigious Lindback Award for outstanding teaching.

> Dr. Epstein explained to Dr. Redmond: "Phyllis is always fighting for women's equality, no matter in what part of the world the issue may lie. With a diverse student population in this country, she was never at a loss to engage in a lively debate with the students about feminist issues both in the United States and abroad."

The chair went on to elaborate that she had cautioned Regane to tone down her rhetoric because it may not be fully appreciated in a collectivist culture. They were there to play a positive, collaborative role in training the next generation of Asian health care leaders of both sexes. Janet Epstein said that she told Phyllis Regane the following: "We're not going to solve their equality problems overnight, Phyllis. The Asian faculty members are like all the rest. They talk a good line but they set higher admission standards for women than men applicants to get accepted into this program! I know that lately, East Asian women have been making better progress in getting jobs, especially in medicine. But they are only making about 72% of what a man makes, and only occupy about 12% of the business and government leadership positions. That's not good enough, and I think we have to get the students motivated to do something about it!"

Dr. Redmond listened carefully to Janet Epstein's explanation, but then he warned her: "I know Phyllis is a great teacher, but she has to fit over there. We can't have her walk out of a class and then have her return the next time and act if nothing has happened. Several students have petitioned their president, complaining that Regane's actions brought shame and criticism to the school. They do not seem to know what is expected of them. Her radical methods may challenge and inspire students in the States to do better, but it is not working over there. Janet, I am afraid the students will not trust us anymore. Your faculty will have to be very careful. I don't want to dampen their enthusiasm but we have to strike a balance between academic freedom and cultural sensitivities. Review their teaching methods. Make sure they know what the consequences are if they screw up. I need to get back to their president with an apology from Regane and a corrective action plan for our program. If Regane can't control herself, I can't afford to have her teach at Southfield."

Now, Janet knew she was dealing with something much more serious than a few culturally insensitive comments. The strength of the Southfield Health Administration program was its focused ethical approach to teaching business practices and the encouragement of their faculty toward being creative and outspoken. Their goal was to promote critical thinking in their graduate students so they could become more effective leaders. Faculty passion for social justice causes related to health care issues was a hallmark of their program. Checking each faculty member's lesson plan would be tantamount to censorship. Yet, as Dr. Redmond said, entering new educational markets required the need to balance academic freedom and student cultural practices. Years of successful building of trust between the faculty and department chairperson could be lost if this situation was not handled properly. In the context of the American culture, the collective faculty approach to cultural sensitivity appeared to work well. In the context of the East Asian socio-political culture, there was a major disconnection. The faculty needed to re-assess their teaching strategies. Of course, there was also Phyllis Regane to deal with. Janet knew that Phyllis had strong convictions about freedom of expression and promoting issues of social justice. She was afraid that she would not be amenable to a give-and-take discussion to alter her teaching approach. If Phyllis did not yield, Janet would probably be placed in a horrific situation of being pressured by the president not to renew her adjunct contract. The other faculty members would be deeply divided over this decision. It could destroy the program.

Dr. Janet Epstein took a deep breath as she reached for the faculty home telephone list to set up an emergency meeting. The last person on the call list would be Phyllis Regane.

Questions for Discussion

1. What would be the effect on the current turbulence within the program if Dr. Epstein issued a mild rebuke to the faculty and told them to be careful with future classes? How would turbulence be affected if she fired Regane on the spot? What level of turbulence are the students feeling? What level of turbulence is Phyllis Regane likely feeling?
2. What type of faculty preparation may have reduced the level of turbulence in the classroom prior to the start of the extension program?
3. In whose interests is the power over instruction being controlled?
4. Do American university-based international curriculums have both a moral and professional responsibility not to imply the superiority of Western culture in their pedagogy? What is in the best interests of non-Western students?
5. In what way may Phyllis Regane be demonstrating care for her students?
6. Can there be a code of conduct created to help faculty avoid such conflicts? Is this even possible? Is it desirable? How might this conflict represent a positive kind of turbulence?

An Elite Curriculum versus an Appropriate Curriculum

Dr. Gaines had just been appointed dean of Jefferson Campus, a two-year branch campus of a large mid-Atlantic university. Located in a hamlet of 750 people, isolated from even the neighboring small towns, the campus served 850 students, largely enrolled in the liberal arts and one technical program, which had provided the original rationale for establishing the campus in 1902. The entire county ranked near the bottom of all of the statewide socioeconomic measures and was especially low in the percentage of high school graduates who went directly to higher education—at that time, 29%. The campus had 300 residential students, about 200 who lived in off-campus housing, and the rest were commuters.

Dr. Gaines, armed with much enthusiasm and a recent PhD in higher education, had spent the last 11 years in two community colleges, one rural and one inner-city. She was an unusual choice for a branch campus of a research university who, even at this distant outpost, tended to denigrate a community college background. The campus had been working hard on a strategic plan for the past year. Dr. Gaines' heart sank when she read their vision for the future described in the opening sections of the strategic plan, essentially: "We see ourselves as becoming a rigorous liberal arts enclave in this community with a strong focus on transferring students to the main campus." This plan was often referred to as "Harvard in the Mountains."

At the time she was hired, the main campus officers had impressed on Dr. Gaines the need for increasing enrollment and establishing a financially stable operating budget. She was also required to raise money to renovate, replace, and add to the very old physical plant. Her office was located in a log house dating from the mid-1700s. Their instructions did not include any particular preference for curricular direction as long as she did not break any of the main campus' many curricular rules, which were college- and school-based. The local community and a very elderly alumni base provided the only fundraising pool. Even county leaders did not have very much knowledge and very few opinions about the campus. Their children did not attend this campus. The best fundraising year to date had produced $25,000.

Her professional preparation and indeed her interview speech had included many references to her commitment to a participatory planning system. However, right from the start she realized that grassroots participation had produced a plan with a very limited potential for success. The main campus was expecting quick results, both in fundraising and enrollment. Her background and values favored developing community-based two-year associate degree curricula. She felt strongly that the only way to achieve this goal was to reject—politely but firmly—the present campus strategic plan and move aggressively to develop new curricula responsive to the local community. However, she also knew that if she lost campus support right at the beginning of her tenure that she was unlikely to accomplish very much. Achieving acceptable evaluations for her job would depend on positive feedback from the faculty.

As the first year evolved, the librarian, Ms. Staley, a strong proponent of the liberal arts, worked to undermine any prospect of the faculty happily accepting an expanded community-based curriculum. Socially, Dr. Gaines and Ms. Staley became friends. However, even this friendship could not make Ms. Staley into an ally on the curricular front. As the prospect of Dr. Gaines prevailing became more real to the faculty, tensions arose in other areas as well. Even some relatively straightforward committees became contentious—most notably the technology committee, which had the power to recommend spending the very few available unfixed resources. These tense feelings were magnified on this little campus. Increasingly, she could clearly see that implementing a major fundraising campaign and new curricula might require decisive, largely unilateral, and most likely unpopular action.

Eventually, Dr. Gaines recommended two more allied health curricula and gained initial support from the main campus. As these curricula were in the implementation stages, Dr. Gaines was scheduled for a regular administrative review, a very rigorous process in which all campus constituents have an opportunity to participate. She expected the worst. The policy called for faculty members to lead the evaluation committee. The chair, who the faculty appointed, was a curricular opponent and a personally difficult colleague. The campus was buzzing with gossip, and the factions were lining up for their personal appointments with the evaluation team. Dr. Gaines began to have second thoughts—not about the curricula choices but about her decision to confront the opposition head-on, eschewing a more collegial and participative decision making process.

A bad review would almost certainly cause her to be terminated; there was considerable precedence for this action at the university. Two colleagues had abruptly left the previous year following their negative reviews. On the other hand, backing down now would leave the campus and the community without the programs both needed for economic viability. She did have the support of the Campus Advisory Board and, by now, a much more involved larger community. Fortunately, from her perspective advisory boards were influential participants in the administrative evaluation process. Should she hope that their support would carry the day and continue to act on her own values and experience and push her plan, or should she make amends and amendments before it was too late?

As Dr. Gaines pondered the matter quietly in her rustic office, her cell phone rang. On the other end was university provost Spillings. The provost said: "Dr. Gaines, I'm afraid that we are hearing some disturbing news from your campus. Despite some early support for your curriculum ideas over here, we're now convinced that much of your faculty feels betrayed and is about to tear itself apart. On top of that, your present course makes a positive personnel review of your work unlikely. The fallout is simply too great."

Shock is too mild a word to describe Dr. Gaines' reaction to these words. She had a decision to make and little time in which to make it. Would she follow her vision through and defy the power of the faculty faction, as well as Provost Spillings? Or would she quit the contest and acquiesce to a plan for an elite curriculum that she felt unwise and unworkable?

Questions for Discussion

1. How might Dr. Gaines reduce the level of turbulence in this curriculum dispute and still retain her self-respect? Is there any way that she can use the heightened turbulence brought about by this crisis to the advantage of her ideals?
2. If both sides believe that they are working in the best interest of students in this situation, how can we determine who is doing so most sincerely?
3. To what degree has Dr. Gaines shown care to those on the campus with whom she does not agree? What are the consequences?
4. Why shouldn't students at this rural branch campus receive a high status curriculum? In whose interest is it to deny them?
5. If there were a university-wide curriculum policy, how might this dilemma have played out differently?

6

ACCOUNTABILITY VERSUS RESPONSIBILITY

Cases contributed by Rita M. Becker, Cynthia L. Renehan,
Troy L. Wiestling, and Kendall L. Glouner

CURRENTLY, WE ARE IN THE AGE OF ACCOUNTABILITY in education (Leithwood, 2001). In the United States, this era has endured for a long time. It harkens as far back as 1978 with the passage of Proposition 13, when taxpayers in California no longer wanted to pay for public education (Shapiro, 1979). Since that time, the overarching concept of *accountability* that came from the bottom line of an accountant's ledger has served as the cornerstone of national reports that include: A Nation at Risk: The Imperative for Educational Reform (National Commission on Excellence in Education, 1983); America 2000: An Education Strategy (1991), Goals 2000: Educate America Act (1993) and No Child Left Behind (NCLB) (2002). In Goals 2000, for example, the centrality of accountability is noticeable as the term is mentioned 23 times, which is approximately once per page (Sewell, DuCette, & Shapiro, 1998, p. 317), while NCLB has demanded even stronger accountability measures than previously required in past reports.

Although all the national reports included accountability, it is important to understand how complex the concept really has become over time. Moving from a stress on the budget, it has "morphed" into at least ten different forms. They include political, legal, bureaucratic, professional, and market accountabilities (Darling-Hammond & Snyder, 1992). Added to these are parent, student, fiscal, and personal forms of accountability (Gross, Shaw, & Shapiro, 2003). Most recently, public accountability (Gold & Simon, 2004) was introduced, bringing the total to ten.

Despite the diversity inherent in the term, many positive arguments are made regarding the overarching concept of accountability (Scheurich, Skrla, & Johnson, 2000; Skrla, Schewich & Johnson, 2000). Frequently, the term is perceived to be a significant factor in school improvement. For instance, it has been credited with the enhancement of teacher quality, school climate, graduation rates, and resource equity. Traditional accountability is also mentioned for keeping budgets transparent and in check, meeting the approval of many taxpayers. In addition, accountability is also alluded to for the maintenance of high-stakes testing, providing numbers and percentages to indicate successes or failures of students and of their schools.

While accountability is frequently associated with school improvement, it is also often thought to be a concept that attributes culpability (Lithwood, 2001). By turning to numbers alone on standardized tests, taxpayers, legislators, and the nation believe that they are able to determine how students are doing, and many are ready to place sometimes praise—but all too often, blame—on schools. Currently, schools receive report cards based on their ranking on standardized tests, and they are publicly evaluated in newspapers focused on primarily one major factor—the test scores. Unfortunately, all too often other key indicators—such as poverty, drugs, environmental pollutants, and crime—with their negative effects on learning, tend to be ignored. The standardized test in the United States has indeed become the "coin of the realm in public education" (Haladyna, Nolen, & Haas, 1991, p. 2).

Related to testing, accountability has brought with it many regulations. Implementing NCLB in schools, for example, leads to considerable additional work and expenses. Specialists need to be hired to assist students in achieving on standardized tests and adequate secretarial staff is essential to deal with the ever-increasing paperwork to meet the rules and standards within this act.

Attendance policies are another part of the accountability movement in schools. While generally quite transparent, these rules tend to be very rigid and intricate, requiring more paperwork. Of late, special education is also associated with accountability as it is considered essential that all children must reach certain educational standards. To meet the additional demands, it is expected that special education students will have the extra physical and psychological assistance that they require to achieve the necessary learning objectives. It is also assumed by the public that all educational leaders and teachers know how to work with students who have varying needs.

While accountability is the traditional term given to attaining academic standards in schools, there is another term that is not used enough in regard to education. This concept is *responsibility* (Gross & Shapiro, 2002). Responsibility, while similar to accountability, can be perceived of as more inclusive by placing the onus for success or failure of students' achievement on society as a whole and not just on schools. Society includes taxpayers, legislators, parents, teachers, and administrators as well as the students themselves. This term is an ethical one. It is not associated with blame or the budget. Instead, is expects everyone to share in and care about educating the next generation.

In this chapter, Rita M. Becker's dilemma, "Rhetoric versus Reality: School Accountability and the NCLB Act," deals with some of the requirements that public schools now face to annually test their students in grades three through eight. It especially focuses on the media and politicians who have been the primary source of transferring information about schools' test scores to parents. The case deals with the consequences created when the media publishes local rankings based on the results of standardized test scores. In this particular instance, effective administrators and teachers are questioned regarding their educational practices. Because the concern with school accountability is broader in scope than the state, this dilemma discusses national issues as well.

In "Competence versus Ineptitude in an Age of Accountability," Cynthia L. Renehan describes a building principal who is prepared to attend the district personnel meeting armed with a proposal to acquire an additional professional staff member and change a support staff contract from ten to twelve months. The principal believes that he has built a defensible argument based on the requirements of NCLB, and feels confident of his proposal. At the meeting, however, the human resources director makes an unexpected suggestion, which receives support from the superintendent. Dr. Smith is profoundly disturbed by what has occurred as he knows that the school will suffer from the decision. Returning to the building, Dr. Smith must decide how to handle this unexpected decision by somehow managing the human resources he needs to meet the accountability expectations of mandatory legislation.

"Balancing Responsibility: Monitoring Attendance at School and/or Being an Advocate for the Children," written by Troy L. Weistling, deals with a guidance counselor trying to balance what the law requires in terms of attendance with the health, safety, and the well-being of students. In particular, in this dilemma conflict exists regarding educators participating in the total lives of their students or maintaining a balance of involvement by having their responsibility end at the schoolhouse door or at the end of the school day. In this case, mandatory reporting requirements regarding attendance do provide necessary assistance to differentiate between what knowledge and circumstances must be reported, but they do not necessarily deal with the humanistic and nurturing concerns that often become a part of an educator's day.

Kendall L. Glouner's case, "Should I Stay or Should I Go?: Leadership Turnover and Its Effects on Schools," involves making a professional career decision of a lateral move in leadership after only one year in a principal's position. In particular, the principal feels a strong sense of responsibility towards special education students in her present school as well as toward her current district that has offered her support for further education and preparation for higher district leadership positions. The new post would bring with it many positive benefits that would impact her home life as well as her career development. She is torn by what she should do both professionally and personally.

Rhetoric versus Reality: School Accountability and the NCLB Act

At the beginning of the school year, both Courtney Schwartz, the director of elementary education in Thompson School District, and Juan Ortiz, the principal of Happy Valley Elementary School, had anticipated that the large number of students who had transferred after third grade from an urban school to this particular building would probably alter the overall assessment results. In the past, the elementary schools in this district had performed well above the state average every year. In fact, the five elementary schools in this district were most often ranked as five of the top six schools in the county. Because of these successes, the district had allotted most of their resources earmarked for remediation to early intervention, meaning that there were no remedial teachers beyond second grade.

In an effort to prepare for the new student population that would arrive after second grade, when remedial services were no longer offered to the general population, Dr. Schwartz and Mr. Ortiz, along with other administrators in the district, gave their teachers intensive staff development preparation on differentiated instruction and flexible grouping. They, as well as the elementary teachers, were pleased with the progress this group of students had made over the course of several months.

Despite the gains, one of the five elementary schools in the Thompson School District performed slightly below where they had in previous years. It came as no surprise that Happy Valley Elementary moved from fourth in the county to eighth (out of 36 school districts). Dr. Schwartz and Mr. Ortiz suspected that the decrease in scores would correlate with the student transfers. Once they identified all of the students who performed at BASIC and BELOW BASIC levels, they determined that 75% of those students transferred into the school after second grade. Though the ranking had declined from previous years, Dr. Schwartz and Mr. Ortiz were pleased that Happy Valley Elementary scores were still in the top 20% of the county. They were satisfied with their foresight to prepare the teachers to meet the needs of these transient students. They planned to request that remedial teachers be hired to work with intermediate students the following year.

Dr. Schwartz and Mr. Ortiz knew they had work to do to attend to these transfer students; however, nothing prepared them for the public consequences of the drop in their ranking. The local newspaper printed an article insinuating that the principal and teachers had not taught to the curriculum and state standards that year. Immediately after the article appeared in the newspaper, several parents from Happy Valley sent around a petition to suggest that the school board hold the principal and teachers accountable for "not teaching" their children. In response, the school board requested that Dr. Schwartz and Mr. Ortiz determine the reason for the decline in ranking and submit a report with a plan for returning to a more acceptable level of performance.

The director and the principal were challenged with an ethical dilemma. They both feared that defending themselves against being identified as incompetent based on a ranking from a single standardized test score would become customary. They also resented the fact that they had been valued and praised in the past for being strong instructional leaders and were now being questioned as to whether they were sufficiently qualified for their positions. They felt bitter about the unfairness of the legislators and media who, in essence, created one dominant way for parents and school board members to interpret assessment scores and place blame. They were also concerned about the false sense of precision in percentile rankings, which suggested that readers could rely on the numbers as rigorous, objective facts. Above all, their concern was that reliance on centrally calculated statistics in accountability systems would begin to override local, independent administrative judgment of schools.

As they spoke, they realized that their explanations would go well beyond simply submitting a written explanation to the school board regarding the actual reason for the decline in ranking in one elementary building. They felt that their true professional concerns were not temporary. Instead, they were permanent and far more than local. They also knew that they must determine the correct course of action and be relentless about it because their experiences would undoubtedly be presented to colleagues in neighboring school districts if accountability, measured by standardized testing, remained the law.

Questions for Discussion

1. What do you consider to be the level of turbulence for the Thompson School District? For the nation at large? What differences might exist between the level of turbulence for the administrators and local parents (positionality)? In your opinion, did the newspaper purposely raise the level of turbulence in order to increase sales?

2. What actions can Dr. Schwartz and Mr. Ortiz take to lower the turbulence level in the short term and in the long term on both the local and national level?

3. How do policies based on statistics shape practice? How does legislation based on statistics shape future public policy debates?

4. In whose best interest do you think the law has been created? Do you think the law will benefit those it was created to benefit? How and why?

5. Do you think that Dr. Schwartz and Mr. Ortiz care about the students in the Thompson School District? How do you think they felt when they were accused of not attending to the needs of the students? How can the transition students be helped?

6. Do you think public schools should be held accountable for ensuring that all students achieve academic success? What is the best way to hold public schools accountable?

7. Given the climate described, what might happen to the turbulence level if one small piece of bad news about the school came to light at this time (cascading)?

Competence versus Ineptitude in the Age of Accountability

Dr. Smith stood frozen in disbelief, his outstretched hand gripping the door handle. His building seemed foreign to him now, no longer his domain. His mind replayed the events of past few hours: the dreaded personnel meeting. The personnel meetings in the Lafayette School District were historically disturbing, with each building set in fierce competition against the others, in an attempt to provide adequate staffing to meet the continued demands of the No Child Left Behind legislation. At last year's personnel meeting, Dr. Smith received one additional position, a second reading specialist. According to the third quarter district assessments, the scores showed significant improvement when compared with the same-student data from the previous year's third quarter assessments. Confident that the scores would show marked improvement on the state assessment, Dr. Smith planned to request a math specialist to target mathematics instruction by employing the successful reading specialist model. The only other request he planned to make was to change the building clerk to a proper secretary by extending her contract from ten months to twelve so that the paperwork from the current legislation as well as the other office needs could be done well. Dr. Smith shuddered when he recalled the scene that ensued in the summer.

The woman who assisted him during that period, Mrs. Martin, had been a superintendent's secretary during a previous administration. When Mrs. Martin was unable to make the transition from typewriters to computers, her classification was changed to teacher's aide and she was reassigned to Dr. Smith's building. Mrs. Martin retained the twelve-month contract and assisted Dr. Smith during the summer. She tried her best but was unfamiliar with current office routines and procedures, all performed by computer. After an exponential number of mistakes requiring several weeks for the building clerk to untangle upon her return in August, Dr. Smith made up his mind—never again! He created a defensible basis for his secretarial request, focusing on the need for considerable paperwork due to NCLB. He felt confident in his two personnel recommendations.

At the personnel meeting, Dr. Smith patiently awaited his turn, listening to the endless requests from the other principals. Finally, he proposed the math specialist position, which was very easily accepted and put on the docket to be reviewed by the Board of Education. Encouraged, Dr. Smith requested that the building clerk post be changed to the position of a secretary. He was totally unprepared for what was to follow.

An immediate response exploded from the human resources director, Mrs. Wilson. She questioned Dr. Smith about his current situation, reminding him that there was already a person assigned to assist him during the summer. She stated that if he wanted the twelve-month position for the building clerk, he would have to reassign Mrs. Martin and retrieve the existing contract. Mrs. Wilson went on to say that by shifting the two part-time office aides—currently sharing one position—Dr. Smith could place Mrs. Martin in the office effective, say, tomorrow. Dr. Smith would then alter one aide's hours, switching her from morning to afternoon, send the other to another building, and place Mrs. Martin in the office during the busy morning hours. Mrs. Wilson indicated that when she was unable to keep up with the office demands, Mrs. Martin would fail, providing Dr. Smith with all the documentation necessary to dismiss her and transfer the twelve-month contract to the building clerk. After all, she concluded, the move was long overdue. Mrs. Wilson sat back in triumph, as a huge smile spread across her face.

Dr. Smith's jaw dropped. The superintendent agreed with Mrs. Wilson's plan, and he requested that Dr. Smith make the adjustments immediately. He indicated that there would be no further discussion on the subject. The meeting continued around Dr. Smith, as he sat in stunned silence.

He returned to his building, pausing at the door to try to figure out how he would break the news to the office staff. He knew that his office currently operated like a well-oiled machine. The intrusion of untrained Mrs. Martin during the middle of the school year would likely cause a severe disruption to the educational program of students, upset parents who were used to having needs met immediately, and frustrate teachers who benefited from the smoothly operating office. Then he considered the countless hours of paperwork, required by No Child Left Behind, done badly and the review that he would need to carry out to document Mrs. Martin's inadequacies.

Still deep in thought, Dr. Smith was startled back to reality by the movement of the door. Out bustled a flustered Mrs. Martin on her way to lunch. "Oh, Dr. Smith," she whimpered, "my son-in-law just lost his job. My daughter and her children are moving back home with me. I'm so worried. I may have to take a few days off. I just knew you'd understand." Off she went, handkerchief pressed tightly to her face.

Questions for Discussion

1. What is the current level of turbulence in this case for Dr. Smith? Mrs. Wilson? Mrs. Martin? Provide evidence to support your response.
2. How could the principal, Dr. Smith, create more turbulence in this case? In what ways would increasing the level of turbulence change the outcome of the dilemma?
3. Could a creative solution be employed that would lower the level of turbulence? How would lowering the level of turbulence assist in this situation?
4. What ethical lens should Dr. Smith use to solve his dilemma? Why would that lens provide the most assistance in his decision-making process? Would more than one lens assist him in making the most effective decision in this case? If so, which other lens? If not, why not?
5. Through which ethics do Mrs. Wilson and the superintendent appear to be operating? What evidence do you have to support that claim?
6. Could the ethic of critique assist Dr. Smith in approaching his dilemma? How would this paradigm provide support for his decision?
7. Where does the ethic of the profession fit into this dilemma? How will this ethic provide assistance for Dr. Smith during the decision-making process? Are Mrs. Wilson and the superintendent exhibiting the ethic of the profession? How about Mrs. Martin and the building clerk? In what ways do they or do they not express this ethic?

Balancing Responsibility: Monitoring Attendance at
School and/or Being an Advocate for the Children

Mrs. O'Hara, a guidance counselor working at Sloan Elementary School, was just closing her Items of Interest/Signature Needed folder, a morning ritual she performed daily, when the school's secretary, Mrs. Ling, popped in and asked, "Guess who is absent again today?" Mrs. O'Hara had a very strong feeling she knew. Sure enough, Lydia and Jake, siblings who had transferred to Sloan Elementary at the start of the school year, were absent again. Mrs. O'Hara asked Mrs. Ling to provide the most current attendance report for both children and directed her to make her routine telephone call to the home to inquire about the children's absence. Both students were experiencing an extensive number of absences, and the school was currently proceeding with the requirements of the school board's attendance policy. This attendance policy was complex: It expected communication from the school to the parents, reminded them of the district's policy and the state's requirements for compulsory attendance, and included the tardy-to-school letters that were sent after five absences to demonstrate the school's concern as well as medical requirement letters for both students.

After Mrs. Ling replaced her telephone receiver, she came to Mrs. O'Hara's office doorway with a frustrated look on her face. Mrs. Ling reported that she had spoken to the children's mother, Mrs. Bass, who stated that they were absent because they had overslept and that her car was not working. In addition, because of the car problems Mrs. Bass said that her other daughter, Becky, would not be coming to school in the afternoon. This child was new to the school, as she was a kindergarten student.

Similar to her siblings, Becky was experiencing an overwhelming number of absences this school year. In her case, variations of the attendance procedures had been implemented because attendance in a kindergarten program was not mandated by the state. However, despite the lack of clear guidance, Becky's absences were of such a high number that she was in jeopardy of being removed from the school's kindergarten roster.

Distressed with the information just provided, Mrs. O'Hara sat perplexed and contemplated what steps she needed to pursue next. Concerns had been mounting since the beginning of the school year when the family transferred into the county. Routinely, Mrs. O'Hara reviewed the records of all newly enrolled students. As she was going over Lydia, Jake, and Becky's forms, she found them to be incomplete and that they contained some information of concern. It appeared that the parents shared the same last name; however, each child had a different last name and only one of the parents in the household was a biological parent of all the children.

Because of this concern, Mrs. O'Hara, with assistance from Mrs. Ling, performed an extensive investigation of the children's forwarded academic records to ensure their proper placement and to verify that all years of academic placement, including schools attended and grade placement, were taken into account. Several documents received informed them that the children and family were still under the supervision of the Children and Youth Services agency from their prior county. They also had been told that Lydia and Jake were only recently returned to this household as a result of a court decision.

Mrs. O'Hara did not receive the official court adjudication in the student packet, verifying the accuracy of this placement. Therefore, she contacted the parents, the prior schools that the children attended, and the Children and Youth Service agency to obtain the documentation. She was determined to verify that they were legally living in the household assigned; in fact, the principal and she had decided that the students would not be officially enrolled until proper documentation arrived. Eventually, the school received the necessary information and the children were enrolled in the school.

Despite the official clearance, as the year progressed a number of concerns began to surface in regard to the family and the children. Several adults in the school mentioned problems related to their home environment, their clothes, their nutrition, their academic performance and behavior, and school attendance.

Mrs. O'Hara had a decision to make. Today's absence would become the fourth unlawful absence for both Lydia and Jake. Mr. and Mrs. Bass had already been informed of the children's three unlawful absences when they received the First Notice Letter. That letter also informed them that any additional unlawful absences could result in a citation. District attendance policy provided directions that a completed citation should be forwarded to the associate superintendent, who would then deliver it to the district magistrate's office for processing. Past experiences with attendance also gave Mrs. O'Hara some discretion as to whether or not a citation would be processed with the fourth unlawful absence alone. Certainly, she had always considered the impact that a decision like this would have on the children's lives. She knew that the noncompliance of the attendance policy was not a direct result of the children's behavior.

Mrs. O'Hara was faced with the dilemma of deciding whether to advise the principal to process the citation or not. She knew that this action would then require that the family and school district officials come in for an attendance hearing with the local district magistrate. Mrs. O'Hara also had to decide about contacting the Children and Youth Services caseworkers assigned to this family and to inform them that she would be forwarding them copies of all of the attendance records for both Lydia and Jake, including the citation notice. If she did contact them, she knew she should report that while Jake regularly came to school, he also frequently told the school nurse that he had not eaten breakfast. Before taking action and advising the principal strongly about what to do, Mrs. O'Hara questioned whether she was overreacting to this situation. Perhaps it was not as bad as she thought. The more she pondered this situation, the more she felt very strongly that these parents had to be held responsible for their children.

As if things were not complicated enough, Mrs. O'Hara's thoughts were disturbed by the school secretary who said that Becky's natural father, Mr. Shuey, was on the phone asking to speak to his daughter's kindergarten teacher. Before transferring Mr. Shuey to the teacher's classroom, Mrs. Ling thought that Mrs. O'Hara might be interested in speaking with him and, indeed, she was right. The guidance counselor took the call and informed Mr. Shuey that Becky's mother had phoned and reported that she would not be coming to school that afternoon, and she asked if he were aware of today's absence. As the conversation continued, Mr. Shuey began to discuss other concerns that he and his wife had been experiencing with Becky's natural mother and the other children. In addition to his displeasure with Becky's lack of attendance, he stated that Jake had been telling him that he did not eat breakfast. Mr. Shuey also stated that Mrs. Bass frequently asked him for money and told him that she and the children were out of food.

Mrs. O'Hara encouraged Mr. Shuey to contact the county's Children and Youth Services agency to inform them of his worries. However, he explained that he was reluctant to do this because he knew that if Mrs. Bass found out he reported them, it could jeopardize his visitation arrangements with Becky. Mrs. O'Hara was dumbfounded by the man's seeming lack of caring and concern for the other children—even his own—and that he chose to protect his visitation rights over their nutritional needs. Mrs. O'Hara hung up the telephone and rested her face in her hands trying to calm herself down to make a rational decision as to what advice to give to the principal.

Questions for Discussion

1. What is the level of turbulence in this case? How could Mrs. O'Hara increase the level of turbulence? What should she and the principal do to lower the turbulence level?

2. What laws are applicable to this dilemma? Who is obligated to follow these laws? Whose best interest is represented with the laws?
3. What impact has the ethic of care in this dilemma? Has Mrs. O'Hara allowed the ethic of care to obscure her responsibilities? Should care eventually drive her final decision, or might she lose the empathy needed in this situation to her frustration and dismay?
4. Critique the laws that apply to this dilemma. What critical questions could you ask of the Children and Youth Services caseworkers' previous involvement with the family? What do you feel should be Mr. Shuey's actions regarding his daughter?
5. How should Mrs. O'Hara fulfill her professional responsibilities?

Should I Stay or Should I Go? Leadership Turnover and its Effect on Schools

Amy Kozlowski accepted a position of principal in Belleview Elementary School. She followed an educational leader who had been in charge for 14 years and had reached retirement. She heard that he had grown increasingly tired over the last few years from the amount of energy expended supervising a classroom with emotional support students. His frustration caused him to end his career as principal and seek other opportunities.

The staff was apprehensive about having a new principal who was so different from the last. A young woman at the beginning of her administrative career, following a male at the end of his, created an interesting dynamic in the building. Some were eager for the change and some were resistant to what "the new person" would bring to already established rituals and routines.

Surprisingly, the transition was relatively smooth. There were meetings and discussions to gauge philosophies and learn how to understand one another. It seemed that parents, staff, and students were willing to accept Ms. Kozlowski as the new principal.

She liked her new position and her new school. However, one downside was the commute of 45 minutes (minimum) to work and anywhere from 45 minutes to hours to get home, depending on the traffic. There was no way to go home between the end of the school day and evening commitments; what this meant was that she was leaving home at 6:00 a.m. and not returning until at least 9:00 p.m. one or more days per week. Without a family of her own worrying about her and working hard to establish herself as a leader, she chose to ignore the tiresome drive.

As the first semester progressed, what were now two classrooms with emotional support students—instead of one in the building the previous year—continued to become more and more challenging. The special education department had staffed both classrooms with underqualified personnel. One teacher was a "guest teacher" and emergency certified, and the other teacher was right out of college with no experience in public school or with these children. Many of the students were diagnosed with conditions such as bipolar disorder, oppositional defiant disorder, mood disorder, and post-traumatic stress disorder. All of the students in the emotional support program were hospitalized at least once in their short lives for mental health rehabilitation. The nature of working with students with emotional instability was taking its toll on everyone, including regular education classroom teachers, specialists, and the school guidance counselor, as well as the principal. While the principal remained focused and solution-oriented, she also felt her hands were often tied by regulations and budgetary issues that were out of her control. In fact, much to her amazement, she was beginning to relate to the previous principal's discouragement with the situation.

Thankfully, Ms. Kozlowski had experience with students with similar problems in her previous school. She had training and techniques to de-escalate volatile situations and also knew how to safely physically restrain children to keep them from hurting themselves or others when out of control. She had been through enough difficult situations to remain calm and get assistance. One staff member commented, "You're doing a great job with the emotional support students. Thanks for making such a difference here." Another stated, "You really take care of us."

On the one hand, the principal knew that she was making positive changes in the building as evidenced by the encouraging reactions and interactions she was having with students, staff, parents, and other district employees. On the other hand, the increased intensity of handling these students' cases, the addressing of the needs of the other staff and remaining 400 students, the long drive, graduate classes two hours away, and the internship she was involved in with the assistant superintendent, all created a heavy load to carry. She began to think that she was losing the balance between work and personal life that she had tried so hard to preserve in the past.

As she dug deeper into the issue of the emotional support students, she discovered an ongoing battle between the special education department, at the central level, and the educational leader's role in the school. Incidences involving these students were increasing daily and in many cases, it was becoming obvious that several of the children had mental health issues that required intensive therapy, medication, and intervention that were well beyond what a public school could supply. The staff members in the building were not equipped to manage the violent outbursts and quick, unpredictable actions of a few students, but the special education department insisted that it was the responsibility of the principal and the staff to ensure the safety of all as well as provide a quality education.

There was a philosophical debate at hand: How could she continue to justify the benefit of one or two to the detriment of many? How could this be fair? The staff was starting to question whether she was as concerned about the threat these students were having on the climate of the building. From her perspective, the staff did not understand that she could not get past the regulations and guidelines the special education department were imposing to make significant changes in the children's programming.

There were many times when Ms. Kozlowski believed that interpreting the laws that protect the students with an Individualized Education Plan (IEP) could have been better applied by putting more responsibility upon their parents to obtain outside help before the placement in the building could be considered appropriate. However, the special education department would then have to find an alternative placement for the student if it were determined that he or she could not reenter the school. The bottom line was money. The cost to keep the children in the building was far, far less than finding alternative placements, although the latter were frequently the more appropriate route. Actions from these students that would have dictated harsh consequences were minimized by the special education department in an effort to keep the days of suspensions under the 15 maximum as dictated by law before a change in placement was required. Ms. Kozlowski was becoming increasingly tired of focusing on the budget and doing what they thought was the "right" thing. To her, this seemed to be consistent with what she felt was very "wrong."

Three months into her new position, Ms. Kozlowski became engaged to be married. Although not a complete surprise, she had not anticipated the immediate impact this new turn in her personal life would have on all her future decisions, the first of which was to consider applying for a principal position much closer to home that had just become available. It was especially hard to consider applying for the post as her current district was reimbursing her for graduate study and the assistant superintendent was assigning her to some challenging work at the central office level. She was also making changes in the building and extending planning into the following year to help create a vision for the staff, students, and parents. How could she possibly consider leaving a position she had barely even started? What impact would her decision have on others?

She started to weigh the pros and cons. On the one hand, she was driving a long distance to work while the new position would be just ten minutes from home. But the current building had 400 students whereas the new building had 600 students with no assistant principal. The new position was in a district with an outstanding reputation, while her current district was taking a beating because of budgetary constraints that were imposing some significant changes for reconfiguration of grade levels in schools that she did not agree with philosophically. The new position did not include the challenge of working with emotional support students, despite the fact that this was an obligation she felt deeply, enabling her skills to work with special-needs youngsters to be fully utilized. Finally, the new position was ten months compared to her current twelve-month contract. Ten months meant more flexibility and time off to spend at home. She agonized that her duty as an educator was to help all students, understand their special needs, and care for them, wasn't it? However, she also had to consider the draining of her emotional energy and her home life, didn't she? Was the trade-off sufficient?

After considering all the factors, she decided to apply for the new position. It was worth exploring; after all, applying didn't mean she would get the job. She interviewed and was called back a second time. Within two weeks, she was offered the position. A question, whose answer would affect many people, entered Ms. Kozlowski's mind: "Should I stay or should I go?"

Questions for Discussion

1. What is the current level of turbulence at Belleview Elementary School? What actions on the part of the principal would cause the turbulence level to go up or down?
2. Do the special education laws take into account their effect on regular education students? Should suspension regulations be different for students with an IEP from those students who do not have an IEP? Why or why not?
3. Is it ethical to make decisions for the good of one student that ultimately cause the disruption of several other students and staff members? Where does one draw the line in relation to providing an education for one student when it impedes the progress of so many others?
4. When mental health issues are present, where should public schools draw the line with regard to their responsibility to provide an education for students who are mentally unstable and are or are not receiving care outside of the school system? Explain your reasoning.

5. If the principal decided to leave and go to Happy Valley Elementary School, explain who would benefit from the decision? Discuss all parties involved. If the principal decided to stay at Belleview Elementary School, who would likely benefit from this decision? Which decision benefits the greatest number of people given the information that was presented?

6. Is it unethical to leave a district that has reimbursed an employee for graduate courses that does not reap the benefits of the professional growth of the individual?

7. Does a change in leadership in school organizations differ from a change in leadership in other fields? Why or why not? Apply the ethic of care from the district's point of view. Apply the ethic of care from the principal's point of view.

7

COMMUNITY STANDARDS
VERSUS INDIVIDUAL RIGHTS

*Cases contributed by Melissa Sterba, Christopher J. Lake,
Shaun Little, and Ellen Henderson Brown*

*I*N A DEMOCRACY, THERE IS PERHAPS NO TENSION more dynamic than
that between the community and the individual. Society, by definition,
is a complex community, yet without individual rights there is no possibility
of democracy. Where do the rights of the individual end? At what point does
the community move from being an embracing home to being a smothering
prison? Albert Camus (1956) taught us that one's rights ended where the
other person's nose began. In other words, we have no absolute right to
behave in the way we may desire. This is because we don't live in a vacuum.
Yet, Orwell's *1984* (1992) and other dystopian works of literature make the
same point about community. Without boundaries, the community itself
can become criminal. The tragic side of human history continues to make
this point. Ha Jin (2002) reminds us of the oppressive quality of government
through the ironically insightful ravings of a professor in his recent novel,
The Crazed. Reflecting on a career seemingly spent on the analysis of classical
Chinese literature, Professor Yang concluded that he had become little more
than a clerk for the established order. His scholarship, indeed, his life were
wasted because they changed nothing in the larger world. He was merely
kept busy tinkering on his small part of the leviathan.

Responding to the tension between community standards and individual
rights, writers have sought to find equilibrium. Kept in balance, the forces
of community standards and individual rights can complement one another
and make a relatively free society feasible. Humane concepts of community
and individual rights come from widely divergent sources, including world
leaders such as South African Archbishop Desmond Tutu. In his book,

God Has a Dream (2004), Tutu explains the community concept of *ubuntu* in this way: "In the end, our purpose is social and communal harmony and well-being. *Ubuntu* does not say, 'I think, therefore I am.' It says rather, 'I am human because I belong. I participate. I share'" (p. 27). The same pursuit of harmony between community and the individual can be found in the history of education.

In the early 1900s, Ella Flagg Young, the first woman to become superintendent of a major American school system, helped to balance the competing demands of community and individual rights by creating teacher councils that she charged with investigations into important issues of the Chicago school system that she led. Young taught this process to John Dewey, and her example of empowering individual teachers to have influence into their school communities spread throughout the United States in the first quarter of the last century.

John and Evelyn Dewey (1962) depict examples of schools around the United States that demonstrate progressive education in action. Throughout their book, *Schools of Tomorrow*, the Deweys provide specific examples of children learning to grow into community life through the hands-on work of learning in their school. In Chicago, school children learned plant biology through the creation of neighborhood gardens. But individual learning in this example was inextricably linked to community wellbeing. John and Evelyn Dewey stated:

> The work is given a civic turn; that is to say, the value of the gardens to the child and to the neighborhood is demonstrated: to the child as a means of making money or helping his family by supplying them with vegetables, to the community in showing how gardens are a means of cleaning up and beautifying the neighborhood. (p. 70)

The concept of community building has also been the subject of recent scholarly consideration. Furman (2003b) developed the ethic of the community wherein the concept of community itself is transformed to community as processes. She wrote:

> In its simplest terms, an ethic of the community means that administrators, teachers, school staffs, students, parents, and other community members commit to the processes of community; in other words, they feel that they are morally responsible to engage in communal processes as they pursue the moral purposes of schooling and address the ongoing challenges of daily life and work in schools. (p. 4)

In the United States, the schools themselves have acted as a means of forming a community out of a widely diverse national population. William Wraga (2006) makes this point by referencing an observation by Lawrence Cremin:

> Only in a school where children of all economic classes, religious creeds, and political persuasions could meet on a free and equal basis did these leaders see the amelioration of divisive influences which threatened the social cohesion so necessary to the new Republic. (p. 428)

In this way, the American school becomes a kind of community creator since no more comprehensive instrument of social influence then existed. By constructing community, the school in this ideal vision makes common ground out of what is otherwise the chaotic, contested space of individuals and antithetical groups pursuing conflicting visions.

Unfortunately, the harmonious balance between community standards and individual rights, described by Tutu and demonstrated by the Progressives and writers like Furman, has not always prevailed. Until the *Brown v. Board of Education* decision, for example, community standards in many parts of the United States undermined the rights of African-American students to attend the same schools as their white counterparts. Today, the re-segregation of American schools represents an equally insidious and, perhaps, more intractable problem.

The organization of instruction and the attitude schools take toward students is also subject to debate. For instance, Friere (1970) criticized the banking system of education wherein learners are considered passive recipients of information. Ginsberg, Shapiro, and Brown (2004) explore this ground by posing critical questions to teachers:

> What kinds of materials (sources) might you be leaving out? What kinds of questions are you posing and what point of view or perspective is being privileged by those questions? Which students are responding? Which are not? (p. 64)

Herbert Kohl's *I Won't Learn from You!* (1991) depicts the other side of this coin by illustrating the role of student assent in learning. Simply put, Kohl asserts that individual students not only have the right not to learn (one clear community standard in schools), they must actively assent to engage in the process if it is to take place at all.

Clearly, the territory between one's rights and the community standards in school is a space filled with negotiation, judgment, and dilemmas for students, teachers, and administrators. Writers in this chapter have used their dilemmas to highlight the subtleties of the tensions between individual rights and community standards.

In Melissa Sterba's dilemma, "The Trouble with Joe: Joker or Terrorist?", a troublemaking but brilliant student becomes intrigued with computer programming and joins an after-school technology club. At the same time, the student (Joe) misses regular classes and is forced to withdraw from the club in order to attend to his traditional studies. In frustration, Joe creates a web page that includes threatening illustrations directed to faculty, thus precipitating a three-day suspension from school. The cycle continues and leads to parents demanding that Joe be excluded from school altogether. Where do Joe's rights to express his feelings end and the rights of the community to be protected from perceived or real threats begin?

Christopher J. Lake's case, "Sift or Shift: A Moral Dilemma to Censor a Student Newspaper or Change Discipline Implementation," explores the possible limits of student freedom of speech in a school-sponsored publication. When students attempt to print a story that criticizes unequal disciplinary treatment between young men and young women in the school newspaper, the principal intervenes. Determining that such a story would disrupt normal learning at the school, the principal refers to case law giving him the right to quash the story before anyone reads it. Yet is this simply a matter of law, or are other issues—such as fairness in the school—also needing to be considered? Is this story or the underlying conditions that inspired it more likely to upend the quality of learning at this school?

"The Interrupted Party," by Shaun Little, illuminates the question of school community boundaries as it affects teachers. Meeting with fellow faculty members at a local pub on one Friday evening, Mr. Green seems especially troubled. Though a gifted young teacher, he has been given an unsatisfactory review by his principal. What happens when, after several drinks, he is greeted by some of his own middle-grade students and their families? Shocked to see a faculty member obviously intoxicated, parents demand that Mr. Green be fired. The principal faces a dilemma as he prepares to meet with Mr. Green and his colleagues. Is a teacher ever off-duty? What determines acceptable private behavior for teachers? Where does the community have a right to insist on a standard of faculty conduct, and when do they go too far?

The intensively pressured world of university sports is the focus of Ellen Henderson Brown's dilemma, "Coaching in Intercollegiate Athletics: The Pressure to Win versus Personal and Professional Moral Codes." Kevin Givens, head basketball coach at the university in question, is well liked by the administration but needs to produce a winning season in order to keep his job. In the final game of the season, Kevin erupts in a dispute with a referee and is ejected from the game. Facing the anger of students, the press and the alumnae boosters, what is the president of the university to do? Was Kevin merely guilty of overexuberant personal behavior on behalf of his team, or did he violate a clear community norm by losing his temper?

The Trouble with Joe: Joker or Terrorist?

Joe Schien is West High School's most notorious troublemaker. He has a folder filled with pink slips documenting his poor—and sometimes hostile—behavior. Specifically, Joe is known for his temper, his willingness to initiate fights with students, and his continual intimidation of staff. As his folder indicates, Joe has called teachers names, verbally threatened Vice Principal McGuiness, and yelled obscenities in the hallways in the past. He is avoided by many students, being viewed as a bully, and feared by certain teachers as volatile and unpredictable. Yet there is no doubt that Joe is bright. He is particularly interested in computers and spends considerable time participating in an after-school technology club. He possesses demonstrable programming skills and a mastery of the Internet. Unfortunately, these are the very skills that got Joe in trouble.

Like many of Joe's teachers, Ms. Ambrose believed that Joe had potential. As his geometry teacher, she set high standards—never accepting late work, demanding complete proofs and a neat work product. She challenged him, even when he talked back or appeared angry. But at the close of the semester, Joe's behavior began to escalate, causing Ms. Ambrose much concern. Joe missed five consecutive class periods and, as such, failed an in-class examination and several assignments. He was in jeopardy of failing the class. Ms. Ambrose confronted him, telling him that if he didn't make up the work satisfactorily, she would fail him. Moreover, he would be forced to quit the Technology Club as a result of a failing grade. Joe became visibly upset and stormed out of Ms. Ambrose's classroom. His anger did not dissipate immediately. Instead, he used his frustration to create a webpage at home, on his own time, that criticized the district's policy of requiring students to maintain passing grades to participate in extracurricular activities. He lambasted Principal Seaver for administering unfair punishments and complained of favoritism. He created a "hit list" of teachers and students who he called "unfair, unjust, or just plain dumb." Most menacing, however, were the threats he made toward Ms. Ambrose. He called for her resignation. He then urged students to unite and take action "by bullet," if necessary. In fact, he even downloaded Ms. Ambrose's picture and placed a target symbol across her forehead.

Joe shared his website with his closest friend, Andrew. Andrew found it humorous and during his tech class the next day, provided the web address to several classmates. Eventually, students investigated and Mrs. Finelli, the tech teacher, caught a glimpse of Joe's work. Given the visual representation of violence as well as the overt threats made at Ms. Ambrose, Mrs. Finelli contacted Principal Seaver at once. Principal Seaver took immediate, unilateral action. He suspended Joe, even though the webpage was created at home, on Joe's own time, and according to Joe, was "just a joke." As Joe was suspended for three days, he was placed in academic jeopardy in several of his classes. Additionally, he was ordered to "take down the webpage" prior to returning to school and was barred from the Technology Club.

Despite Principal Seaver's action, the staff and community of West High School remained upset. Ms. Ambrose continued to fear Joe's return to school and, given his reputation, petitioned to have his schedule changed. Other staff expressed anxiety about working with Joe. Finally, parents—terrified for the safety of their children—began demanding more effective safety measures from Principal Seaver. Several parents even contacted local community leaders and politicians, calling for strict disciplinary action against Joe and effective safety precautions to ensure the well-being of students at West High.

Questions for Discussion

1. Principal Seaver took immediate punitive action against Joe in this case. What about Joe's insistence that the webpage was "just a joke"? Should Joe have had an ability to defend himself prior to the suspension? Can alternative measures be taken—such as the involvement of a counselor—to help Joe learn to effectively deal with feelings of frustration and anger?
2. As Ms. Ambrose is forced to deal with Joe's anger, what clashes could emerge between her personal and professional ethical codes? Likewise, as Principal Seaver handles the situation, what clashes could emerge for him?
3. Whose voices are silenced in this dilemma? Why?
4. Why was Joe punished in school for an out-of-school activity? Does Joe's speech resemble "political speech" in any way? Should Joe's speech be protected? What rights does Joe have in this situation?

5. What level of turbulence is involved in this case? Suppose Joe contacts an attorney. What would be the likely result? What legal remedies are available to him? Conversely, suppose several parents contact the media regarding what they perceive as an unsafe learning environment at West High. How can Principal Seaver handle this situation to minimize the amount of turbulence? Compare and contrast the levels of turbulence felt by Joe, Ms. Ambrose, and Principal Seaver.

Sift or Shift: A Moral Dilemma to Censor a Student Newspaper or Change Discipline Implementation

"Oh, what a headline! 'Suffering Suffrage at Sutton High.' This just can't be published," thinks Mr. Jure, the high school principal, as he closes the latest edition of the student newspaper. In the top story, a senior has reported that girls in the school were rallying to revolt against the administration for unfair treatment. Supported with accurate statistics and candid personal interviews, the article outlines how girls have received demerits and suspensions from activities for disruptive behaviors, while boys have been only warned for the same behaviors. Having studied Susan B. Anthony in history class, these girls plan—as the articles forewarns—to wear arm bands to school and march for justice during an upcoming school board meeting hosted by the high school.

Immediately, Mr. Jure phones Ms. Clearview, the journalism teacher who had given Mr. Jure the prototype for his approval just the period before. "We have a problem, Joyce. We can't go to print with this issue. I would like you to come down during your planning period and bring Iysha Smyth with you."

That afternoon, Ms. Clearview and Iysha, the author of the article, report to the principal's office. They can imagine why they have been summoned to see Mr. Jure. Ms. Clearview had anticipated that the top story would cause distress with the powers that be. Iysha has prepared to debate the printing of the article but she fears that her graduation would be in jeopardy if she had fought the issue too far. Together, they sit in the leather wing-backed chairs facing the oak principal's desk, waiting.

Mr. Jure enters the small office and closes the door behind him. What follows is the conversation that took place.

Mr. Jure: "I am glad you are both here. We need to talk about the top story of the latest issue of Sutton's *Students Spotlight.* We just can't print the article. It would cause such a revolt that the learning environment at Sutton High would be destroyed."

Ms. Clearview: "Mr. Jure, we understand your point of view. The article may be seen as controversial. The topic is not the positive view of the school that you have stated you want to present to the community, but we feel that we have good reasons to print the article."

Iysha: "Respectfully, Mr. Jure, we have researched this article and the data show that the girls are correct. We are reprimanded more often than the boys in this school. We purposefully did not mention any students' names in the article so that we were not liable for printing slander. The reporting is accurate and truthful."

Ms. Clearview: "In all due respect, Mr. Jure, I have to agree with Iysha. This is an excellent example of journalism. If this were not a school, such reporting would make headlines and much media coverage. The facts are well researched and the interviews are well documented."

Mr. Jure: "Yes, I would like to know how you gathered your research. How did you get access to the discipline records for the students?"

Iysha: "We interviewed many girls and boys, and our other sources would prefer to remain anonymous. We have to respect their confidentiality, as good journalists. We have practiced all that we have learned in our class about freedom of speech and good journalism."

Mr. Jure: "Yes, but Ms. Clearview should have taught you that according to the *Hazelwood School District v. Kuhlmeier* (1988) case, students do not have the freedom of speech in schools. In the real world, investigative reporting may be honored in a democratic state; however, in a school such reporting may infringe upon the learning environment; therefore, according to *Hazelwood School District v. Kuhlmeier,* administrators may censor such student publications. Principals have the right to censor any student publication that they deem inappropriate or may possibly disrupt the educational system."

Iysha: "We agree with you, Mr. Jure; however, don't you agree that the disruption of the educational system is not due to this article? The chances of the girls' revolt will heighten if this article is not printed. The revolt, not this article, is and will be disruptive to the school day."

Mr. Jure: "I will deal with any student who demonstrates at the school board meeting with strong discipline, and that you can print! But this article, you will not print. We cannot put innocent children's lives and education in jeopardy because a few students feel as they are treated unfairly. Iysha, you are dismissed. Ms. Clearview, I will meet with you again tomorrow. And I want you to bring with you your curriculum for journalism and your lesson plans for this year."

Questions for Discussion

1. What would be the fairest decision Mr. Jure could make? Are there any laws to support his censorship? Do Ms. Clearview, Iysha, or the girls have any rights in this situation?
2. What actions could Mr. Jure take to show that he cares for the faculty, the *Spotlight* staff, the student body, and the community? What could Ms. Clearview do to show care to her staff, school, and principal?
3. Is using *Hazelwood School District v. Kuhlmeier*, in this case, supporting the student body or the administration? What critical questions would you ask each of the players in the dilemma?
4. Professionally, what actions should Mr. Jure take? How should Ms. Clearview proceed as the advisor of the newspaper? What actions support the best interests of learners in this dilemma?
5. What level of turbulence does this dilemma represent? How so? How might Mr. Jure lower the level of turbulence? What actions would raise the level of turbulence?

The Interrupted Party

As with any Monday morning, Dr. Lyle, the principal of Washington Middle School, entered his office and readied himself for the upcoming day. Part of his morning routine was to listen to his voicemail and respond to any immediate concerns. He was shocked when he heard the digitized voice say, "You have 14 unanswered messages." Considering that this was a Monday, Dr. Lyle's mind raced to come up with what would possibly warrant so many calls. Even before he listened to the first message, Dr. Lyle knew that something was wrong, and he prepared himself for the worst. As he listened to the messages, he heard angry parent after angry parent state how one of his teachers, Mr. Green, was seen visibly intoxicated at Patty's Pub and Restaurant.

Over the past two years, over fifty percent of Washington's teaching staff had retired, and most of them were replaced with teachers directly out of college. These new and younger teachers had really bonded and most of them associated with each other outside of school. This cohesiveness was something that Dr. Lyle and the school district supported and even promoted by having bowling parties, ice cream socials, and dinners at local restaurants. Besides these school-sponsored activities, the teachers regularly met at Patty's (a local bar and restaurant) each Friday to unwind after a long school week. Typically, Ms. Jones, Ms. Smith, Ms. Jennings, Mr. Carter, and Mr. Green could be found there every Friday. It was not unusual for each of these teachers to order an alcoholic drink upon arrival and some snacks to tide them over before dinner. Over the course of the next few hours, the teachers would continue to snack and drink. Later, they would typically take a cab to the Station Steak House and then off to Club Dimension to dance the night away.

On this particular Friday afternoon, the group (minus Mr. Green) arrived around 3:20 p.m., unusually early, but because Patty's was only two miles from the school, it was possible. As they entered, the group looked physically and mentally drained. "A rough week?" questioned Paul, the bartender. "You have no idea," uttered Ms. Jennings. The others seconded Ms. Jennings' comments with grunts and moans of their own. "Shall I start you off with the usual?" questioned Paul. "Sure thing, and keep them coming," stated Mr. Carter. As the drinks and food arrived, Mr. Green stormed through the door with a visible look of anger on his face. "That damn Lyle has forgotten what it's like to be in the classroom. He doesn't realize how difficult it is to control these kids!" exclaimed Mr. Green. Mr. Green was late because he was in a meeting with Dr. Lyle concerning an unsatisfactory evaluation that he had received that morning. The evaluation indicated that Mr. Green's class was unruly and the students were often off task. Although Mr. Green was having problems with his classroom management skills, Dr. Lyle considered him to be one of his best and brightest new teachers. The students really looked up to him, and the state test scores of his students were higher than those of the other new teachers. As Mr. Green pulled up a stool, Paul hurried over to him and suggested the usual, just as he had for the rest of the group. "No way, I need something much stronger. Make it a scotch on the rocks," stated Mr. Green in an exasperated voice.

After about two hours, the group was growing hungry and was contemplating moving the festivities to the Station Steak House for dinner. "Should we get going?" said Ms. Jones. "Yeah, I'm famished," uttered Ms. Smith. "Can we have just one more drink?" slurred Mr. Green, who by this time was visibly intoxicated.

Before anyone could respond, they were interrupted by the all-too-familiar shrieks and squeals of middle school girls. As they turned their heads to see what all the commotion was about, they recognized the smiling faces of Lisa, Mary, and Sara coming toward them. These girls were all in the seventh grade at Washington Middle School and they were the students of Mr. Green, Ms. Smith, and Mr. Carter. The restaurant at Patty's was a favorite place for the locals to eat and have birthday parties. On this day, Mary was celebrating her 13th birthday with her close friends and their parents. As the girls and their families were waiting to be seated, they noticed the teachers in the bar and were excited to see them outside of school.

With bright smiles on their faces, they—along with their parents—came to greet the teachers. "Like, oh my God, you guys actually have a life," said Lisa in a joking voice. "Yeah, we're allowed to have some fun," said Ms. Smith. "So, what is the occasion?" questioned Mr. Carter. "It's Mary's birthday, and we're here to celebrate with her," said Sara. "Well, happy birthday!" exclaimed the group. "Mr. Green, are you all right?" asked Bob, Mary's dad. "Sure, I'm fine. I think I just need some fresh air," slurred Mr. Green. As Mr. Green attempted to get up and head for the exit, he stumbled and fell to the floor. As he tried to pick himself up, he fell again, this time crashing into a couple sitting behind him, knocking their chicken nachos all over them. After this second fall, there could be heard rumblings from others in the bar, "Get that drunk out of here!" "Isn't he a teacher at Washington?" "What a mess!" Bob and the other parents had visible looks of anger on their faces. "Well, I think we'll be heading to our seats now. See you on Monday," said Mary with a look of sadness on her face. "Bye Mary, have a happy birthday," said the group in sullen unison.

As Dr. Lyle finished listening to the final phone call, he was at a loss for what to do. Most of the parents who had left messages were extremely angry and wanted Mr. Green fired. They were astonished that such an upstanding school as Washington would allow someone who they considered unstable and immoral—like Mr. Green—to teach their children. The parents were threatening to take this matter to the school board and even the press if something wasn't done immediately. Dr. Lyle felt that while Mr. Green may have used poor judgment, he really didn't think he should be fired.

As the rest of the staff began to arrive, Dr. Lyle called for the group to come to his office. When they entered, they could see that Dr. Lyle was visibly upset. He asked them to take a seat and he explained the situation to them: "Now, I know you all get along great and you enjoy each other's company, and that's great. It's something we encourage with all of the staff. However, a situation has come to my attention that I need to deal with. Several parents are calling for the firing of Mr. Green because of what happened at Patty's on Friday. I need some time to think about what I'm going to do, so please report back to my office at 3:15 this afternoon and I will give you my decision."

The day seemed to go on forever, and each second seemed like an eternity. Dr. Lyle knew that something had to be done to appease the parents—but what? He knew that he really didn't want to fire Mr. Green, and he also couldn't force the teachers to move their gathering outside of the district. As the 3:00 p.m. bell rang, signaling the end of the school day, Dr. Lyle was still at a loss for what to do. He reclined in his chair and pondered, "What should be done with Mr. Green?"

Questions for Discussion

1. What is the level of turbulence in this case? What could be done to decrease it? What could happen that might increase the level of turbulence? What level of turbulence might there be for Mary? Her father? Mr. Green?

2. Suppose Dr. Lyle decides to fire Mr. Green. Would his actions be justified? Why or why not? What legal agreement should Dr. Lyle consult in this case?

3. How might Dr. Lyle use the ethic of care in his decision making? Would it be possible to show care and concern for both Mr. Green and the parents? If so, how? What would the best decision be to show care for the students? Explain.

4. Do you believe Mr. Green acted in a professional manner? If not, how might he improve his actions in the future? In terms of professional responsibilities, what does Dr. Lyle need to do with Mr. Green? What decision might place the best interests of the students at the center?

5. Do you believe that teachers should be held to a higher standard than other people? Why or why not? Should teachers' personal lives impact how they are treated while at work? Why or why not?

Coaching in Intercollegiate Athletics:
The Pressure to Win versus Personal and Professional Moral Codes

Introduction

The shift in intercollegiate athletics over the past 15 years to a more revenue-driven market has put enormous pressure on coaches and administrators to win games. As more money is pumped into athletic programs, more coaches are being fired for not winning games. In 2000, then National Association of Basketball Coaches executive director, Jim Haney, said that there would likely be about 40 coaching changes in men's basketball programs after that season, most of which would be firings (Brown, 2000). Revenues and expenses of college athletics programs are increasing rapidly. In 2000, only 25% of Division I institutions received more money from outside sources (like ticket sales and television contracts) than they spent on their sports programs (Suggs, 2000). It used to be that coaches got into their field simply for the love of the game and the opportunity to share that and see its growth and benefits among student athletes. Today, fewer and fewer athletics administrators and coaches come from a background other than marketing, promoting, and generating funds in order to survive. It is no surprise that you cannot generate too much funding without fielding successful teams. The pressure to win is at all costs (Brown, 2000). The dilemma that many college coaches face, then, is how to work in this "win at all costs" pressure, with the personal and professional ethical codes that steered them toward the love of the game and coaching profession in the beginning.

The Dilemma

Elizabeth Buckley has been the athletic director at NCAA Division I "Character University" for five years. A former student athlete and Division I coach herself, Elizabeth knows the pressures, stress, and compromises associated with coaching at such a competitive level. Nevertheless, she is an administrator now and, from most accounts, is doing a very good job. The only major problem she faces at the present time is that alumni and donors are complaining about the lack of success the men's basketball program has had in the last few years.

Kevin Givens was hired by Elizabeth Buckley as the head men's basketball coach three years ago. Kevin played college basketball at Character University and was a two-time Academic All-American and member of the three-time conference champion team. He has over ten years of college coaching experience at highly competitive Division I schools. At the end of last season,

Elizabeth and Kevin met to discuss the team's so-so season. The team ended with a 15-18 record and a first-round win in the conference tournament. But the alumni and major donors are not happy, and revenues are suffering from three average seasons. Kevin has one more year on his initial contract at Character University. Elizabeth makes it clear that expectations are very high, and we need to win next year. She tells Kevin that he needs to do everything possible to make sure that happens. Keep kids eligible. Recruit the best. Win games and fill the arena. The message was clear: If these things did not happen next season, Kevin may have to consider "alternative solutions." He'd been around this business long enough to know the meaning of that statement. Win more games or find a new job. Elizabeth felt good about their meeting. She liked Kevin and felt he was a good coach. She admired his dedication and commitment to Character University, and knew he took pride in preparing his student athletes for life outside of sports. He had never had any NCAA violations of any sort, and had not caused her much stress other than his win-loss record.

The next season, the basketball team does better, making the finals of their conference tournament. In the final game, the score is tight; the referees have been making blatantly unfair calls on Kevin's players. He has been arguing with one referee constantly, feeling that he is making biased calls toward the favored team. Two of his players have fouled out, and it is only the beginning of the second half. On a particularly outrageous call, Kevin is irate, screaming at the officials once again. He argues nose to nose with the referee, pushing him backward into the scoring table as things get heated. Kevin is ejected from the game halfway through the second half and is forced to watch his team lose from the locker room. A media frenzy follows the game as fans, students, and university and athletic administrators question whether Kevin should be fired after another disappointing season has come to an end.

Kevin is devastated. He was under tremendous pressure to win this year, and his team did improve. His anger got the best of him in this game, but he does not feel that it should get him fired on the spot! Elizabeth is extremely disappointed. She questions Kevin's ethical decisions during the game. The university and athletic department are now under scrutiny, which is never a good place to be as the administrator. Now, she must make the decision of whether to fire Kevin or stand up for his actions. First, she has to deal with the media and how the university looks to the public after Kevin's despicable behavior.

Questions for Discussion

1. If Elizabeth fired Kevin after this game, would the turbulence level increase? Why? What could Elizabeth do to decrease the turbulence in this situation? What is the level of turbulence for Kevin? For the student athletes on his team? How might Elizabeth's decisions affect their turbulence levels?

2. What kind of example would Elizabeth set by firing Kevin? By not firing him? There are not rules stating she must fire him based on his actions. What should she try to teach the student athletes in this situation? Should Kevin be seen as a role model to the general public?

3. What is the fairest action for Elizabeth to take? If the referee's actions were indeed unjust, does that make Kevin's actions acceptable? Should Kevin be fired or reprimanded?

4. What is the most caring decision Elizabeth could make in this situation? For the student athletes? For Kevin? For the university? Could Elizabeth have done anything before this situation erupted to make Kevin feel less pressure?

5. What decision could Elizabeth take that would make the best interests of the players front and center? Are the best interests of the players exactly the same as the best interests of the general student body?

8

EQUALITY VERSUS EQUITY

*Cases contributed by Albert F. Catarro, Jr., Jamie R. Shuda,
W. Douglas Zander, and Yvonnette J. Marshall*

*E*QUALITY VERSUS EQUITY IS A PARADIGM that has been hard to delineate. However, for the purposes of this book, we are defining *equality* using Strike, Haller, and Soltis's (2005) definition of equal treatment. They wrote: "In any given circumstances, people who are the same in those respects relevant to how they are treated in those circumstances should receive the same treatment" (p. 55). While using a slightly different term, *equal consideration,* Gutmann (1999) describes this concept in a similar way (p. 203). Equality, in this instance, would view the individual and the circumstances surrounding him or her. It would not focus on group differences based on categories such as race, sex, social class, and ethnicity. This perspective, instead, is one of assimilation because it assumes that individuals, once socialized into society, have the right "to do anything they want, to choose their own lives and not be hampered by traditional expectations and stereotypes" (Young, 1990, p. 157).

Then, there is the term *equity,* which is not focused as much on the individual and more on a specific group. In this book, we are defining it as Shapiro and Stefkovich (2001, 2005) have done. It "deals with difference and takes into consideration the fact that this society has many groups in it who have not always been given equal treatment and/or have not had a level field on which to play. These groups have been frequently made to feel inferior to those in the mainstream and some have even been oppressed" (pp. 103–104). To attain equity for these groups, Young (1990) suggests, "Social policy should sometimes accord special treatment to groups" (p. 158). Equity, therefore, offers some justification for unequal treatment for those who have been disadvantaged. This concept makes it acceptable to have compensatory programs and benefits for those who have suffered ill treatment over time.

African-Americans, Native Americans, and other group movements have created legislation through pressure that has provided them with educational opportunities. For example, the women's movement fought for and eventually obtained the passage of Title IX of the Education Amendments of 1972. Title IX made it known that discrimination on the basis of sex was illegal in any educational program receiving federal funding (American Association of University Women, 1992, p. 8). The passage of Title IX opened the door for many gender equity programs and projects (American Association of University Women, 1995), enabling women and girls to be empowered and learn how to overcome the barriers that still exist today.

But it is not only in the area of racial, ethnic, and gender movements that the paradox of equality versus equity can be discovered. If one turns to the all-encompassing term of *diversity* and defines it broadly, then a range of differences can be explored that takes into account categories such as disability, sexual orientation, and exceptionalities (Banks, 2001; Cushner, McClelland, & Safford, 1992; Shapiro, Sewell, & DuCette, 2002).

In this chapter, dilemmas are presented that transition from school to college and university. In elementary and secondary schools, because education is compulsory, equity issues must be considered very seriously. Issues of educating special needs youngsters, for example, have to be explored. In the case of higher education, where there is no mandatory requirement of attendance, it is still reasonable to focus on those who have not been given the opportunity to study because of their differences. But post-secondary education need not be for all, at least from a legal perspective. However, using an ethical lens rather than a legal one, there is a moral imperative to provide access to disadvantaged students who need and desire post-secondary education, as well as offer them the necessary supports to achieve academically. In colleges and universities, then, an ethical stance could be used in regard to access to higher education for those who have been discriminated against in the past and even in the present.

The first ethical dilemma, Albert F. Catarro, Jr.'s "Rigor or Rhetoric?," focuses on special education in a secondary public school. In this case, a high-profile special education student defies the new rigor initiative and refuses to complete the final project for his class. A respected teacher of special education and English is challenged professionally and personally by the student and his family. She believes that she has been consistent with district policy in the decision she has made regarding the student's grade. Unfortunately, this case reaches higher levels, and the teacher faces charges of insubordination. The teacher's union president is involved as well, and there is the possibility of moving the problem beyond the school to the superintendent.

The underlying question of this case is: Do rules and policies apply equally to all public school students, or should one special education student be treated differently because of his disability?

In the next case, "Mission or Money Bound: A Dilemma of University-Based Community Service," written by Jamie R. Shuda, an urban university has gained a reputation for outstanding academics, research, and community service. Recently, the university has established a community outreach center to consolidate community-service efforts. The center director identifies education as the top priority of the new venture, and summer internships are suggested as a way to assist neighborhood high school students. At the second meeting of the board about the fellowships, one of the members shares that a neighbor is willing to donate $50,000. In return, the donor requests that students from his affluent district participate in the summer internships. The center director must now decide whether to accept the initial funding and service the "privileged" students or decline the generosity and support the mission of the center.

The following ethical dilemma is W. Douglas Zander's "Affirmative Action and the Urban, African-American Student Experience on Rural, Predominantly White Campuses: Is the Cure Worse than the Disease?" It focuses on a post-secondary institution's new plan to meet its diversity goals, requiring at least half of the students of color to be recruited to the university, without using the opportunity program designed for disadvantaged students. Unfortunately, the majority of students of color in the state attend urban schools that place them at an educational disadvantage. When the director of admissions tells his outreach counselors to enroll all high school students from the top 10% of their class through regular admission and not the opportunity program, they rebel. The counselors believe it is not fair to bring students from poor, segregated high schools in urban centers to middle-class, predominantly white rural campuses and expect them to succeed without special assistance. The university maintains it cannot afford additional supports.

The last case, "Bending of College Admission Standards," developed by Yvonnette J. Marshall, takes place in the West Indies. It deals with a mistake that occurs over the admission of high school students. The case extends well beyond the students, who were inadvertently admitted and arrive on campus, and is taken up by the students' families, the media, and even the government. This case illustrates the volatility of the issue of college admissions and standards, examining the reaction of the various stakeholders and how the issue might be resolved. It also deals with the problem of not having sufficient remedial or compensatory programs available on a campus.

Rigor or Rhetoric?

The anxiety and anticipation for the upcoming school year was different from the past ten summers, as this was Mr. Rogers first year as teachers' association president. He had to prepare an address for the first in-service day and he was excited about it. The school year was initiated in the auditorium of the high school and there were to be speeches. Each address turned out to be unique. The school board president complimented the support staff on a fine job of preparing the school buildings and wished the teachers well for a successful school year. The superintendent made a scholarly speech referencing educational leaders, spoke of the need for a school community, collaborative cultures, and stressed that although he was new to the district, his door was always open if he could help. The superintendent was hired during the last school year, and this was his first opportunity to address the entire faculty and staff. Since he was new, his ideas and ideals had yet to permeate the schools, and many of the district administrators did not share the vision of the new superintendent. Mr. Roger's address centered on how committed he was as the new association president and also discussed issues in a way that paralleled well with the superintendent's position.

Following the assembly, as was the custom, in-service training occurred in the individual buildings. The first afternoon event was a high school faculty meeting. The principal, Mrs. Stricton, began with her usual speech. The topics included the initiatives for the year, emphasizing strict enforcement of school rules, high standardized testing results, and her pet project, the need for academic rigor. The principal cited reasons for these foci, discussing the model of High Schools That Work and No Child Left Behind's (NCLB) state testing requirements. Also mentioned was a requirement for a complex writing assignment in every class as part of the new rigor initiative. Mrs. Stricton had a top-down managerial style of leadership. She firmly dictated from atop her chain of command.

Ms. Little, a special education teacher who was also certified in English, seized this opportunity to challenge her students with the rigor initiative. She proposed at a special education department meeting to adopt a district policy that allowed teachers to assign a final project instead of a final exam for her classes. This had always been an option but it had been efficient to issue an exam. Policy also stated that students who did not complete the final requirements did not pass the course. Ms. Little and the special education department modified the syllabus for each class to include the rigor initiative to replace the final exam with a final writing project. The project would consist of a five-page research paper on a topic assigned by the teacher. The rubric for the project included accommodations that would be made in the project to align with the IEP for the special education students.

Ms. Little was well respected in the district. She employed the ethic of care with her students and treated them as individuals with tremendous results. This year, however, she had Billy Winston in her freshman English class. Billy and his parents were well known in the district. They had an advocate and special education attorney on retainer to ensure that Billy received the type of education he needed. The district's special education supervisor, Mr. Abler, had regular interactions with the Winston family. In the past, the district avoided litigation threats by consistently accepting their demands. Billy's teachers had been forced to change grades, reduce discipline, and ignore infractions.

All of this came to a head in the first ten minutes of Ms. Little's class while she was reviewing the syllabus, which now included the rigor initiative and the research project. Billy boldly proclaimed there was no way that he would be doing a research project. He added that he would pass the class because his lawyer would take care of it. Ms. Little addressed the situation by requesting students not to call out in class, and explained school policy. She emphasized that completion of the final was required for every student to pass the course. However, she could see that Billy was not impressed.

Ms. Little prominently displayed a poster detailing the project in her classroom. On back-to-school night, parents were presented with a copy of the syllabus and the research project instructions. Ms. Little was deliberate in her presentation of the project, as she was well aware of the legal ramifications of special education and was secure that she was crystal clear in her expectations and followed school policy precisely. Although Ms. Little was not Billy's IEP teacher, she informed that teacher and Billy's parents about the expectations for the course, as well as his reluctance to complete the project.

The semester progressed and Ms. Little dedicated time to every student to personally assign a research topic related to ninth-grade English. The students were also allotted computer lab time for research and paper preparation. Ms. Little stressed the importance of the final project and reminded the students that the class time wasted would require that much more homework time on it.

Ms. Little considered the interests of the students in assigning the research topic. Billy was assigned an appropriate topic and spent most of his research time on the Internet viewing pictures of motorcycles and little time actually researching. He did, however, make token investigations and took some superficial notes. His notes in total would not fill five paragraphs, let alone five pages.

The due date of the project came, and Ms. Little collected the work. Billy was true to his word and did not submit a paper. Immediately, she called his parents at home to inform them. She was surprised at their response. The parents read the paragraph in Billy's IEP that stated they must be informed in writing if there was a possibility of Billy failing the class. Their position was that they were not properly notified, so he could not fail her class. Ms. Little replied that the failure was school policy concerning final projects, indicated as part of her syllabus, explained in a handout on back-to-school night, and clearly posted in her room. The parents stuck to their interpretation and advised Ms. Little that if Billy failed, then Mr. Abler, director of special education and secondary education, would hear from their attorney.

Ms. Little was steadfast in her conviction that she had covered herself with the amount of notification that she prepared about the failure consequences. She contacted Mr. Abler directly as a courtesy and explained the situation. She received yet another shock. Mr. Abler told her directly and emphatically that she should change William's grade and pass him. Taken aback by this response, she asked him numerous questions, including: Did he have any idea what he was doing? Did he understand how his decision would impact the school? Would all the special education students who did not complete the assignment question their teachers? Did he realize how the entire rigor initiative was being undermined?

Mr. Abler abruptly ended the conversation, stating the directive again. Ms. Little's reply was an emphatic, "No." Mr. Abler hung up the phone and immediately called Mrs. Stricton, the building principal. Mrs. Stricton summoned Ms. Little to a meeting and advised her to bring an association representative. Ms. Little called Mr. Rogers at once.

Mr. Rogers and Ms. Little had a discussion before the scheduled meeting with the principal. He gave her the usual advice for someone having this type of meeting. He cautioned, "Don't say anything. Just listen to what is said, and we will respond later."

The meeting was short and direct. Ms. Little was ordered to change the grade or be disciplined for insubordination and have an unsatisfactory incident letter placed in her file. Instead of remaining silent, Ms. Little blurted, "I refuse to change his grade." She proceeded to explain why, including the fact that this would undermine the principal's own initiative. However, Mrs. Stricton was following her orders and was not interested in hearing her comments. She informed Ms. Little that disciplinary proceedings would proceed. She also indicated that whether she did it or not, the grade would be changed.

Mr. Rogers felt he had to say something. He mentioned that he might speak to the superintendent and get him involved in this situation. This enraged

Mrs. Stricton, who said that if he broke the chain of command and went over Mr. Abler's and her head, he would face the same repercussions as Ms. Little. As he left the office with a visibly shaken Ms. Little, Mr. Rogers thought to himself that fortunately, this was a Friday, and he had time to consider this disturbing situation.

Questions for Discussion

1. What is the current level of turbulence following this meeting on Friday afternoon? It is the same for Ms. Little and Mr. Rogers as it is for Mrs. Stricton and Mr. Abler?
2. What could Mr. Rogers suggest that would lower the current level of turbulence, and what could he advise that would raise it?
3. Whose rules was Ms. Little following? The school's? The district's? What were the laws and regulations that Billy's family referenced?
4. Which were the right rules, laws, and regulations to follow in this case? Should special education students be treated very differently from other students?
5. About whom should Mr. Rogers and Ms. Little care? All the regular education children in the school, who had to complete a final assignment in each course? Some special education children, who might not be able to complete the assignment? Just Billy?
6. What about the ethic of the profession? How will Ms. Little's career be affected if she does not comply? What about Mr. Roger's position as president of the union? Is he jeopardizing his current post and his career? Above all, what is in the children's best interests? Which children, and why?

Mission or Money Bound:
A Dilemma of University-Based Community Service

Roosevelt University is a large urban institution that has gained a reputation for outstanding academics, cutting-edge research, and community service. The university prides itself in all of these characteristics but has recently received positive press about its community involvement. The community is impoverished, with many single-parent families and low-income households. Many people in the area have attained only a minimal education and hold poorly paying jobs. The K–12 schools are in severe need of resources and often struggle with low attendance and unsatisfactory graduation rates.

Roosevelt University strives to give the people within the community resources, such as professional training and medical support. The president of the university is proud of its gained reputation. To ensure that the university maintains its obligation to the community, all first-year students are required to do community service in local schools. There are several organizations involved in clothing and food drives during the school year, and the participation is high.

Because this outreach work is a priority of the university, the president and his administration decided to develop a specific center that prioritizes the community outreach, designs new initiatives, and fundraises for specific programs. It was named the Community Outreach Center and was in its first year of operation. The president appointed the dean of education, Dr. Scholar, to oversee the center. Dr. Scholar then hired the director for the center, Mrs. Givinings, a former educator who had many years of experience in social work and community development. Mrs. Givinings knew that she would need to recruit a supportive advisory committee to help determine the priorities of the Community Outreach Center. In her first few days as director, she approached local businesses, school principals, ministers, and professors at the university and asked Dr. Scholar to invite them to become members of the board. The first meeting would be a brainstorming session about the center's development.

The response was overwhelmingly positive, and Mrs. Givinings scheduled a roundtable discussion with the new committee. The group brainstormed about the components of the new center and the members agreed to make education and health the top priorities. Several local businesses agreed to advertise the center's programs at their stores and participate in job training sessions that the university would offer. The professors and the dean of education decided that the center would host summer internships and award stipends for high school students interested in attending college. These summer programs would provide extra writing and math workshops and mentoring from seniors at the university, as well as stipends so that the participants did not need to take on extra summer jobs. It was decided that recruitment for these initiatives would be within the urban community, and a set of criteria for participation would be discussed during the next board meeting. Before the next meeting, the board was asked to think about possible funding opportunities and the fundraising plan.

The advisory committee met three weeks later. One of the professors, Dr. Wilson, was very anxious to share good news with the board. He had persuaded a friend of his, a successful business owner in a local suburban community, to donate $50,000 to the center. Mrs. Givinings was delighted to hear that the program was already receiving the initial funding and immediately began to discuss on which initiative the money should be spent. One local businessman suggested running career-training workshops at the university. Another suggested launching the summer scholarship program for a few pilot students.

As the ideas were brought to the table, Dr. Wilson suddenly interjected a catch. Apparently, the donor asked that the monies for the summer internship program be spread to include high school students from the affluent suburban school district that his children currently attended. Immediately, Mrs. Givinings thought about the mission of the center and the university. This did not fit with the priorities recently adopted by the committee. Accepting the donation could distract the center from serving the population in the most need. The board expressed similar concerns. Dr. Scholar interrupted the several conversations that were going on, stating that soft-money fundraising was a high priority of the president's, and he would be very happy to hear that the center obtained some fiscal support relatively quickly. The meeting ended with no definite answer regarding whether the center should accept the funding, but rather concluded with mixed ideas about whether the accepting of the donation would be in the best interest of the center and the community in the long run.

Mrs. Givinings understood that this would be the first important decision she would have to make, and it would set the tone for her professional ideologies to the board and administration. She knew that by accepting the donation, it would appear to the president that her rapid success was due to her talent and ability to run the center. This was not untrue, given that she was able to create a hard-working and dedicated committee within the first month of her job. And yet, she struggled with compromising the core mission of the center by accepting the funding.

After the meeting, Mrs. Givinings struggled with one major question: How would the decision affect the urban students who might participate in the summer internship? On one hand, she believed it would allow one or two urban high school students to participate. On the other hand, fundraising elsewhere might provide more opportunities for the community's students and eventually get more recognition in the local media.

Then her thoughts turned to the advisory committee as she played out the overriding question: How would the board react to the decision to accept the monies with strings? It would appear that Dr. Scholar saw the benefits to accepting the funding but neglected to think about the potential outcomes of not directly servicing the urban community. Should she challenge his suggestions? More importantly, was she going to present to the board her decision to take the money or not?

Questions for Discussion

1. What is the level of turbulence in this case? Does the level vary for the different participants in the case? For Mrs. Givinings? For Dr. Scholar?
2. What might be done to lower the level of turbulence? What might be done to increase the level of turbulence, and what constructive purpose might that serve?
3. Are there any laws, rules, or policies involved in this case? Does the ethic of justice apply? If so, how?
4. Could there potentially be injustice in the resolving or solving of this ethical dilemma? If so, how and to whom?
5. Would the ethic of care be compromised if Mrs. Givinings accepted the money? Can the solution be a compromise? If so, what would it be? Does the compromise bring care for the urban high school students?
6. What of the ethic of the profession in this dilemma? If Ms. Givinings accepted the monies, do you think it could potentially conflict with her professional responsibility to the program's development? Would there be some way for her to make it up to the urban high school students? What is in their best interests?
7. What ethical perspective is Dr. Scholar exemplifying? If he were to make the decision, who would benefit the most?

Affirmative Action and the Urban, African-American Student Experience on Rural, Predominantly White Campuses: Is the Cure Worse Than the Disease?

William Pike was pleased with his new position as director of admissions at Milltown State University. Milltown had a great reputation in the region, and it was located in a bucolic, sleepy area that was far away from any major cities. This was very much in harmony with William's desires. Having spent many years working in a private university in a big city, he was thrilled at the opportunity to work at a public school in a quiet location.

One of his first surprises on the job came at a meeting of the enrollment management committee, where the topic was minority student recruitment. Several parties expressed their extreme dissatisfaction with the "high number of unqualified minority students who are admitted through the Step Up program." The Step Up program was an opportunity program designed to support students from educationally and economically disadvantaged backgrounds. It included a summer bridge program and provided tutorial and counseling support, but the enrollment was capped at 100 students. Although not a requirement, nearly all of the students in the program were minority students. What follows is some of the discussion at the meeting with Dr. Bellows, associate provost for student retention, Dr. Stevens, dean of student affairs, and Mr. Pike:

Dr. Bellows: Because we admit so many minority students through our Step Up program, it only serves to reinforce local prejudices about inferior academic abilities of people of color. So I hope we are clear, Mr. Pike. As the new director of admission, we want you to be sure our Step Up program no longer operates as a dumping ground for minority students who don't qualify for regular admission.

Dr. Stevens: I agree with Dr. Bellows. But keep in mind how important it is to enroll a diverse class of students. A large portion of our state appropriation is tied to our success with minority student enrollment. So even though we think it is important for you to bring in fewer underprepared minority students, we must see an overall increase in the number of minority students who enroll.

Dr. Bellows: And I suggest that you stop recruiting students from New City. Their high schools are notoriously poor. I don't understand why the admissions office doesn't spend more time recruiting well-prepared minority students from the suburbs.

Mr. Pike: Let me be sure I understand. You want me to increase the level of diversity on the campus with students who are well-prepared academically, and you want me to decrease the number of minority students who are enrolling through the opportunity program. Is that right?

Dr. Stevens: We know that is going to be a challenge, but that is what we expect of you, Mr. Pike. Please create a plan for minority recruitment with these objectives in mind.

Later that day, Mr. Pike went back to his office and began working on the minority recruitment plan. He created strategies to target students beyond the New City borders, and he set goals for modest numerical increases in the overall recruitment targets for Latino and African-American students.

He then added a goal that no more than 50% of all new Latino and African-American students would be admitted through the opportunity program.

When Mr. Pike shared his plan with the associate provost and the dean of student affairs, they received it enthusiastically. However, when he shared it with his minority student outreach counselors, they were far less enthusiastic. This can be heard in the discussion with Mr. Smith and Mr. Garcia, the two coordinators of minority student outreach, and Mr. Pike:

Mr. Smith: How do you expect us to increase minority student enrollment if you won't let us recruit in New City? That's where most of the African-American students live. I know you're new to the area, but take a look around. There aren't many people of color living in this area.

Mr. Garcia: The same is true for Latino students. Although there are many students of Mexican descent in this area, most of them are from migrant families, and many of them are illegals. They won't qualify for financial aid. Our best chance of recruiting Latinos who are United States citizens is to recruit in New City.

Mr. Pike: On a related note, how are we going to find students of color who don't need the support of the Step Up program? Surely, you don't believe that there aren't any students of color with good grades and strong SAT scores.

Mr. Smith: Sure there are, Mr. Pike. And all the private schools are offering them big scholarships to enroll. We're a state school, and we just don't have enough scholarship money to compete for large numbers of academically gifted students of color. And I think you probably also know that African-American and Latino students typically don't score well on SATs, even though their SAT scores don't correlate strongly with their likelihood of success in college. So the people complaining about students of color based on SAT scores really just don't get it.

Mr. Pike was skeptical about their comments until he did some research into the state's demographics. It seemed as if Mr. Smith and Mr. Garcia were correct. According to the census bureau, his state was among the most segregated in the nation. African-American and Latino families tended to live in intensely segregated communities, and their school districts tended to have high poverty levels. And in his region, more than 80% of the students of color lived in New City, about an hour and a half away. Nearly all of the high schools in there were failing to make adequate yearly progress according to the measures of the national No Child Left Behind legislation.

Mr. Pike decided to discuss the matter with his immediate boss, Dr. Singh, the university provost. Dr. Singh explained to Mr. Pike that the state university system had been under a court-ordered desegregation mandate for 25 years. In order to show compliance with the desegregation order, it was imperative that the university work hard to attract minority students, staff, and faculty. And in order to provide incentives to do so, the state system office tied funding to minority recruitment results on each of its campuses. Because most of its campuses were in rural locations and most of the state's minority populations resided in urban centers, recruiting minority students was a major challenge.

Dr. Singh advised Mr. Pike to be mindful of two imperatives. The first was to protect the overall academic profile of the university, which helped it perform well in the annual ratings of *U.S. News and World Report*. A strong reputation helped attract positive attention from prospective students and donations from alumnae and businesses. The second was to consider the need to bring in sufficient numbers of minority students in order to meet the goals of the state system to which significant funding was tied. He reminded Mr. Pike that the Supreme Court frowned on quotas and admissions systems that provided points on the basis of minority status. He added: "This issue has a way of solving itself," said the provost, "because the Step Up program can only take in 100 students. There's no money in the budget to increase the program size."

Mr. Pike then mentioned to him that the associate provost and the dean of student affairs told him not to bring in more than half of the minority students through the Step Up program. The provost's response was disturbing. He said, "That's a noble goal, but keep in mind that SAT scores don't count in our profile if students enter through the Step Up program. And they don't have to be considered at all if the student is in the top 10% of his or her high school class—even if the high school is in New City. The president of the United States endorses top 10% plans, so we are very safe in using them."

Mr. Pike continued to be distressed by these comments and asked: "So are you suggesting that I continue to bring students from New City, and admit the top 10% into the university without the Step Up program?"

The provost answered in an enigmatic way: "You're the one who wrote the recruitment plan, Mr. Pike, and you're the expert on admissions. We hired you to figure these things out for us. I have every confidence that you will do the right thing."

Once again, Mr. Pike went to his minority outreach recruiters with a new plan. He told them that they were correct—New City would have to be the main focus of recruitment. However, they should work hard to bring in students from the top 10% of their high schools through regular admission, and make sure that the numbers were balancing with those who were being offered admission through Step Up. Although Mr. Smith and Mr. Garcia began to raise objections, Mr. Pike cut them off and told them to move forward with the plan.

Over the next two months, as Mr. Pike watched enrollment figures he could see that almost every student of color was still being admitted through the Step Up program. He supposed that was because they just were not attracting enough students from the top 10% of their high schools in New City. Just to be sure, he started going through the files of Mr. Smith and Mr. Garcia. He was astonished to see that there were quite a few students who were in the top 10% of their high school class, but Mr. Smith and Mr. Garcia were still admitting them to the Step Up program. He immediately called a meeting with his outreach counselors once again.

Mr. Pike: I hope you two have a good explanation for what is going on here. I was very specific with you that we need to bring more students in through regular admission, and students in the top 10% of their high school class qualify for regular admission no matter what their SAT score is. Did you not understand me when we talked about this two months ago?

Mr. Smith: We didn't talk about this, Mr. Pike. You told us what you expected us to do, and you wouldn't even listen to our position. Do you have any idea what the schools in New City are like? Some of them don't even have books for the students. I graduated from a New City high school, Mr. Pike, and I was first in my class. When I came here to Milltown State, I was totally lost. They didn't put me in the Step Up program, and I almost didn't make it through my first year here. It wasn't just that the academics were hard (partly because they didn't teach any advanced math in my high school); it was mostly because I had no social group and felt lonely and isolated. There are 8000 students here, and only 200 of them are African-American. In my high school, there were 2000 students, and 1900 of them looked like me.

Mr. Pike: But don't you think it's a bad idea to label all the students of color as underprepared by putting so many in the Step Up program?

Mr. Smith: I think it's a worse idea to bring students from a poor, nearly all African-American high school in the middle of a big city to a nearly all-white college in the middle of nowhere and just expect them to succeed on their own. Until this campus provides some programs for students of color, like a multicultural center, I think students like me are better off coming into the Step Up program.

Mr. Pike: I'm not sure I agree with you. Did you read the article in the local paper about the experience of African-American students on our campus? They quoted one of our African-American students as being very angry that everyone assumes he's part of the Step Up program when he's really in the honors college. I don't think you can assume everyone shares your point of view.

Mr. Garcia: Look, Mr. Pike, the way I see it, you have a job to do. It's your job to bring in enough students of color so that the university can get its money from the state. But I see my job differently. I really believe that having a diverse campus is important for the different viewpoints and experiences students bring to the campus. I really believe that everyone can benefit when the campus experience is one that mirrors the world—and not just the isolated communities that most of us have been exposed to up to this point. But I worry that when you bring students from poor communities that are very different from this one, and then you just drop them on the campus and expect them to succeed, you are not being fair to them. The only outreach program this campus has that has a significant minority population is Step Up. For most students, it serves as an important social community; it helps them meet new people and get adjusted.

Mr. Smith: You do what you have to do, Mr. Pike. But don't expect me to turn my back on my own people to help you. I'll resign before I recommend regular admission for students who aren't going to make it without support.

Mr. Garcia: That goes for me, too.

Mr. Pike was thoroughly confused. He believed strongly in the benefits of diversity and in affirmative action. He had thought he was doing the right thing when he set up a program for minority recruitment. The goals had come from fellow administrators who knew the organization better than he did, and his boss had affirmed his tactics. How could he possibly turn around now and do the opposite of what he had agreed to and planned? And yet, Mr. Smith and Mr. Garcia made good points as well. He felt sure that if they quit their jobs in the midst of the recruitment season, he wasn't going to achieve his enrollment goals, period; forget about not having equal proportions of students of color in the Step Up program and admitted regularly. Not only would the university suffer from a lack of diversity in the incoming class, it would lose funding, and he might even lose his job.

Questions for Discussion

1. Suppose the Supreme Court decided that race could no longer be a factor in college admissions. Would you expect this change to increase or decrease the turbulence on Milltown State's campus from Mr. Pike's perspective? What about the perspective of Mr. Garcia and Mr. Smith? What about the perspective of future students of color on the campus?

2. The Supreme Court has said that quotas may not be used in college admissions. How can Milltown State ever achieve desegregation goals if it does not use quotas?

3. Mr. Smith knows that African-American students at Howard College have a much higher graduation rate than students who attend Milltown State. His performance is measured by the number of students from his territory (which includes New City) who enroll. According to the ethic of care, does he have an obligation to disclose graduation rates to prospective students of color who are choosing between Milltown and Howard, even if the prospects do not ask about graduation rates?

4. The Step Up program only has room for 100 students. Most of those seats will be used for students of color, although it means that white students from disadvantaged backgrounds will not get in. Justify this practice using the ethics of critique and care.

5. As an admissions professional, you are expected to be committed to the principle of the educational value of diversity. You are also expected to devise strategies that will achieve diversity goals for student enrollment. Keeping the best interests of students central to your plan, how will you achieve diversity goals on Milltown's campus?

Bending of College Admission's Standards

Concerns about the gradual decline in the performance of students on final examinations at New Forest College, located in the Caribbean, resulted in a program audit by the national accrediting body. Among the findings of the report was that students were accepted into the institution/program who did not meet the required matriculation standards. Based on the findings, the board of governors, newly appointed by the minister of education, instructed the management team of the college that under no circumstances were applicants who did not meet the required standards to be accepted as students.

This policy was in place at the beginning of a new academic year. The day all the troubles began was the calendar date on which residential students arrived on campus, received their room assignments, and settled in their rooms. The director of student affairs, Diane Smith, with responsibility for residential matters, faced a dilemma. A total of 20 potential students had arrived on campus whose names were not on her list of accepted students for that academic year. A check with the registrar's office, with responsibility for admissions, also confirmed that these individuals were not on the list of students accepted by the institution. The individuals, being informed that their names were not on the list, insisted they were sent acceptance letters by the college, and they were responding to the information in the letter, which advised them to report to New Forest orientation.

Ms. Smith immediately informed the president, Dr. Delroy Jones. Recognizing the possible crisis, Dr. Jones ordered an immediate investigation of the matter. The findings revealed that the office of the registrar had indeed sent out the letters to a total of 50 students, and these letters were actually signed by the vice president of academic affairs. This meant that in addition to the 20 students who had already arrived on campus, there were 30 others whose acceptance would be called into question.

Dr. Jones reacted at once and called an emergency meeting of his management team with the objective of seeking to control the damage. Mindful of the concerns raised by the recent report from the accreditation agency and the subsequent board policy, the team concluded that admitting the students would be in contravention of admission policy. The decision was therefore made to do the following: make every effort to contact individuals who had not yet arrived and did not meet the college's standards and inform them of the error; and meet with the students who did not reach the standards who were already on campus, apologize for the error, and refund travel expenses incurred, as well make arrangements to refund any fees that they had already paid.

Parents and students who heard the news were very upset with the new developments and appealed to the college to reconsider their decision in light of the facts that having received the acceptance letters they had made no alternative plans, and that it was now the beginning of the school year and would be too late for students to apply to other colleges.

The president consulted with the board of governors on the matter, and the board upheld the decision of the administration not to enroll the students and to send them home. On being informed of the board's decision, the parents and aggrieved students charged that this decision was very unfair to the students and further suggested that the decision constituted a breach of promise.

The issue did not rest with complaints to the college administration. Indeed, it was brought to the public forum as a result of students and parents airing their grievances on public radio talk shows. It was also reported in the national newspapers. There was a lot of public sympathy for the students, and there was a call for the minister of education to intervene and redress the situation, which was deemed to be an injustice to the students. Norman Hall, the minister of education, in the face of public outcry instructed the board and the college that the students should be admitted.

In a subsequent meeting of the board, although cognizant that the minister of education's orders had to be carried out, there was a general feeling that his decision had undermined the integrity of the college's admissions process. Moreover, the fact that these students were underprepared for the institution meant that there would be need for remediation, which was not in keeping with the mission of the college; and to top it off, there was not any funding for remediation programs available. Diane Smith questioned if the minister had made the right decision. While she knew legally that she should follow his edict, she could not help but think about resigning.

Questions for Discussion

1. What possible courses of action by the college would have resulted in a decrease in the level of turbulence in this case? An increase in the level of turbulence?
2. Are there any inherent inequities in this issue? If so, how might they be addressed?
3. Who determines admissions policies in colleges? Are the rules absolute? Should exceptions be made, and under what circumstances?
4. What do you see as the reasoning behind the admissions policy of colleges in general, and New Forest College, in particular?
5. What were the consequences of the decision taken by the management and board of New Forest College? What could be the possible consequences if the management of the college had acted against the policy of the board?
6. If you were Diane Smith, the director of admissions, what would you do?
7. What would be the fairest decision that Minister Hall could have made? Fairest for whom?
8. What would have been the most caring decision? What parties should Minister Hall consider in making a decision?

9

PERSONAL VISION VERSUS AUTHORITY

Cases contributed by Terry M. McDonald, Alison J. Staplin,
Maureen F. Linton, and Emily L. Gross

*P*ERSONAL VISION VERSUS AUTHORITY seems to be a paradox at the
heart of our existence. In an existential way, we wonder how we are
connected to any other living thing, what that connection means to us, and
how our connection might limit our freedom of action. The minute we enter
society, we face this paradox, making accounts of personal vision versus
authority easy to find in human culture. Adam and Eve pursued their personal vision and confronted authority at quite a cost. That is one lesson. But if
we merely obey authority, we are robbed of our humanity and the possibility
of living in a democratic community. The Nuremburg trials of the Nazi war
criminals showed not only that, they made it clear that claims of obedience
to authority were no defense for criminal acts.

Disobedience to authority has a long and noble history. Revolutions in
the United States and France were launched to secure individual freedom
from abusive governments through effective use of social movements (Tilly,
2004). Henry David Thoreau's (1964) famous essay laid the moral foundation for civil disobedience and inspired the thinking of heroic actors such as
Gandhi and Martin Luther King, Jr. Emma Goldman, an early leader in the
women's rights movement and an eloquently powerful defender of a humane
anarchism, stood her ground against the oppression of the powerless in early
20th-century America. Once deported and sent back to Russia, she stood
up to the leaders of the embryonic Soviet Union to demand they keep their
promise to govern a free nation. Lenin listened to her politely but did nothing
(Goldman, 1970). Goldman's story is instructive because in it we can see the
life of a brilliant woman who was made to wander the earth, never quitting
her pledge to defy authority, and thereby never finding a homeland willing
to accept her. Perhaps fearing such a fate, most of us seek a compromise.

One compromise is to embrace an inauthentic duality. Following this path, we seem to live two lives, one holding fast to the image of the heroic individual standing for identity and freedom and the other as the quiet participant in an organization that is itself part of a larger society. An interesting example of this paradox can be seen in the Kennedy administration. John F. Kennedy's book *Profiles in Courage* (1956) extolled the virtues of individuals willing to stand by their personal vision and, consequentially, stand up against the power of authority. Ironically, historians of that administration now blame the phenomena of "group think" for the poor planning that led to the ill-fated Bay of Pigs invasion of Cuba in 1961. How could a group of leaders so enamored with individualism fall victim to group authority? A similar incongruity became apparent when President Clinton, then leader of the world's most powerful organization representing the strongest political, economic, and military authority in the history of the world, revealed that *High Noon* was his favorite film. The supreme organization man, a United States president, most treasured the image of a lone Western marshal facing down a gang of outlaws.

This is a contradiction flowing from a paradox. We cheer whistle-blowers who reveal corporate or governmental misdeeds, yet we stand by and watch those same heroes lose their jobs and sometimes risk arrest while corruption quietly roots itself in new gardens. We study the works of Emerson (1993) and smile at the ideals of self-reliance while guiltily acknowledging the realities of conformity classically described in William H. Whyte's *Organization Man* (1956) and in David Riesman's *The Lonely Crowd: A Study of Changing American Culture* (1953). How can each of us face this paradox and find a response that honors our humanity and balances our uniqueness with our need to affiliate with others?

This chapter depicts four examples of the lived paradox of personal vision versus authority. In each case, the individual struggles over the right course of action. The concept of positionality in Turbulence Theory described in Chapter 3 of this book is especially important for these writers. Each of the four protagonists feels caught in a dilemma because of where they are in the organization. In one case, it is the individual's literal position, in the path of Hurricane Katrina, that may shape her perspectives and possible courses of action. In the other vignettes, it is their position inside the larger group. Each case demonstrates the crisis that individuals face when confronting their own conscience on the one hand and the demands of authority on the other.

Terry M. McDonald's dilemma, "Student's Wishes versus Faculty's Advice: Whose Vision will Prevail?," centers on the role a high school counselor will play in the case of a hard-working but stressed student who wishes to take an advanced course in mathematics. Will the counselor support the student or agree with the authority of three mathematics department faculty members who advise that the student take a lower-level course? Will the counselor defy the faculty members by taking the case to the principal? Whose vision will prevail?

In "Friend or Foe? One Student's Decision," Alison J. Staplin depicts the internal conflict facing a hard-working, somewhat overwhelmed student who is preparing for examinations at a highly competitive school. To her dismay, she discovers that her friends are planning to cheat on upcoming tests. The student must think through the dilemma by choosing among difficult alternatives that will define her own vision of right and wrong. Facing her vision are the double authorities of her friendship group and school officials.

Maureen F. Linton's case, "Revenue or Integrity: A Sacrifice for the Greater Good," also involves students cheating; however, now we will consider the dilemma through the eyes of a college faculty member. While an American student has been accused of cheating at this institution and faces serious consequences, a student from Asia—whose father is a major benefactor of the college—is similarly implicated. The professor must decide whether to follow his own vision of ethical behavior and risk confronting the authority of college administrators or quietly acquiesce.

In "Storm Warnings," Emily L. Gross describes the conflict of a college sophomore caught in the pathway of Hurricane Katrina. Should the young woman obey the authority of her parents and college officials and stay at a shelter, or should she follow her instincts and attempt to flee to the airport in an attempt to fly out of the area before the storm reaches her?

Student's Wishes versus Faculty's Advice: Whose Vision Will Prevail?

As school counselor Alden left the office mid-morning on May 24, 2005, to meet with a student that period, three math teachers arrived at the door. They wanted to discuss a situation regarding JM, a high school junior. The three teachers were JM's current Algebra II-Academic teacher, the teacher who is tutoring JM in Algebra II-Academic, and JM's sophomore Geometry-Academic teacher. The problem is that all three believed that JM would be better served by a lower placement in math, called Math Analysis-Academic. There is a prerequisite for student placement in this course, such as a "C" average coming from Algebra II-Academic.

Prior to this discussion, counselor Alden had a college planning session with JM. JM conveyed that these teachers had recommended Math Analysis in the senior year program. Alden suggested that based on JM's college planning list, Precalculus would be the best option for college selectivity.

The student disclosed that her parents did not want to continue to pay for tutoring next year. JM had entered high school in an honors curriculum in history, English, and world language. Alden offered that before making a decision, they would call several colleges that were on the student's college planning list, and JM was agreeable to this idea. In every effort to support the student, the counselor said that as an additional option, JM could go into Precalculus for a few weeks, make an assessment, and decide what would be the right decision.

Alden did not anticipate that these three math teachers would be stopping by the counseling department. All three strongly opposed the student going into Precalculus, although JM had a "B" average for this class and had maintained a "B" average in math since her freshman year. Professionally, Alden shared with the teachers that the student at times superimposed anxiety, trepidation, and negative comments of failure. JM seeks challenges but often ends up avoiding them due to these emotions. Alden and JM have been working on self-efficacy skills for three years and have cultivated an authentic relationship. The math teachers were concerned that JM would have an emotional setback by struggling in Precalculus. Alden explained that the list for math recommendations was given to the school counselors by the math department chairperson, and her Algebra II-Academic teacher had not listed JM's name to be placed in Math Analysis.

After this information was presented to the three teachers, they commented that "We are math teachers and we know what is best for this student." Alden validated their feelings and added, "With this student, I have had an ongoing counseling relationship built upon trust." Alden reiterated that these behaviors are often seen in students of high anxiety. They take themselves out of academic challenges. This particular student enjoys being with other students in the honors curriculum. The teachers continued to defend their assessment that JM should not go on to Precalculus. They said that JM did not want to take a math next year, and that this would impact his GPA. Alden stated that that was not true: "GPA is based on six semesters, ending the junior year." The teacher tutoring JM asked, "Will colleges prefer an 'A' in Math-Analysis versus a 'B' in Precalculus?" Alden responded that "In a higher-level math course, a 'B' is fine." Alden disclosed that JM strives for perfection, works extremely hard, and works well under pressure. The teachers wanted the school counselor to support their decision but Alden did not and replied that the schedule change policy states that the parents needed to give written permission for JM to make a math level change before any change would be implemented. Before leaving, Alden once again acknowledged the three teachers' professionalism with positive reinforcement of their caring qualities as teachers.

After the teachers had left the office, Alden had some time to reflect on their comments. Alden was perplexed. The counselor questioned whether JM's parents should be called. More importantly, Alden was aware that JM's tutor is a fine teacher but had never taught any higher-level math courses. Alden also contemplated whether it was appropriate to bring the dilemma to the math department chairperson. It did cross Alden's mind that this ethical dilemma might end up before the school principal.

Questions for Discussion

1. How do the two sides, the math teachers and counselor Alden, demonstrate conflicting concepts of care?
2. Who most thoroughly and convincingly speaks for JM's best interests—the math teachers or Alden? Explain.
3. Where in this dilemma is JM's voice? How might she be brought into the decision-making process?
4. The three math teachers were aware that the list for math recommendations was given to all the school counselors by the math department chairperson. Were they putting JM's college admission in jeopardy? Why was the schedule change policy stated to the three teachers?
5. Where on the turbulence gauge would you place this dilemma? How turbulent is this situation for JM? The math department chair? Counselor Alden? How might positionality help explain the differences in perceived turbulence?

Friend or Foe? One Student's Decision

Emily finished her second violin lesson for the day and began packing all of her belongings to go home. She felt sick to her stomach but she knew she was not ill. She was nervous. It was Friday, and Emily had a long weekend ahead of her. She had four hours of violin lessons on Saturday and a major competition on Sunday. The competition was extremely important because it determined whether or not she would be accepted and receive a scholarship to the prestigious conservatory she wanted to attend. She was excited about graduating from high school in two months but nervous for her future and the competitive atmosphere at the conservatory. She was exhausted and she wanted to relax, but she knew she needed to get home quickly to work on her projects and study for her school classes. The projects were worth major semester grades and she had several tests coming up, too. Emily wasn't sure how she was going to manage to complete everything over the weekend with her hectic schedule.

Everyone at Harrison High pursues a career in a competitive arena. The private school's population consists of musicians, ice-skaters, competitive horseback riders, and dancers. Harrison's coursework and schedule is flexible to cater to the schedules of these talented students. Students' coursework/testing is online and there is additional coursework offline to foster socialization. Emily is particularly close with her graduating class of 30 students. They began freshman year together and have supported each other through the ups and downs of high school and training in competitive arenas.

During the car ride home from her violin lessons, Emily thought about the conversation she had with her friend and classmate, Reina, that day at school. Thinking about the conversation made her feel sicker. Reina and Emily were talking about the upcoming projects and tests that had to be completed and their hectic schedules. Reina was a competitive horseback rider and she had a major show this weekend, but she told Emily she was not worried about completing everything and getting good grades while balancing her busy schedule.

Emily knew why she was not worried, and it really upset her. Two weeks previously, Emily had walked into what she thought was just a study session with some of her classmates. It turned out to be a group of five or six classmates sharing answers to their online coursework. In addition, one of the students had gained access to the secured area on the school's computer network where the teachers upload the tests that the students take online. Emily's classmates were utilizing these tests to cheat. She was shocked and walked out of the room feeling disappointed in her classmates. Emily considered them all to be good friends and good people. She knew they worked extremely hard, especially in their competitive arenas.

Emily spent a lot of time over the previous two weeks thinking about what she saw and debating about how to handle it. She was upset, disappointed in her friends, and angry that none of them had to spend the time she did on her schoolwork. She also knew personally how difficult it was to balance the advanced schoolwork and a busy music schedule. Emily was considered an accomplished young musician with a bright future; however, at her level she was practicing about four hours every day and competing for limited spaces and scholarships. The pressure was high, and she knew that all of her classmates felt the same way. In a way, although she disapproved if it, Emily understood why they made the decision to cheat.

It was hard for Emily to talk to the people involved, and she knew they sensed she was upset with them. Emily thought they would eventually get caught, but it had been over two weeks and none of the teachers or administrators seemed to be catching on. It was not until Emily spoke with Reina that day that she felt truly torn about the situation. In their conversation, Emily told Reina how nervous she was about her competition and balancing her schoolwork and music schedule. Reina said she understood, and that her life was the same way until she found "a little help." Reina told Emily that she was welcome to join their study session that night around 8:00 p.m. at her house to get some help.

When Emily got home that night after her lessons, she went straight to her room and started unpacking her backpack. All of a sudden, she started to cry. She was exhausted and the work of the weekend seemed to loom in front of her. Her parents were still at work and probably would be for another hour. Emily knew they worked twice as hard to provide her with special schooling and all of the lessons she needed; that made her cry even harder. Emily thought about Reina and her other friends. They were all good people and seemed to justify what they were doing very easily. Reina wondered what would happen to them if the administrators found out. She knew Harrison had a very strict plagiarism and cheating policy. Emily was afraid that if they found out about the cheating, her friends would not be able to graduate.

Emily knew she had three options: to turn them in, not to say anything, or to join in. Emily did not want to turn her friends in. She was close with them, and they had always supported her through high school. She was afraid for them, and did not want them to be unable to graduate—or worse, be expelled, which would affect their college acceptances. However, Emily also thought about how hard she worked for her grades and to balance her schedule. She was proud of her time management skills, and she knew that this character trait would help her later in life. She felt it was unfair that these students had an advantage over everyone else in her class. On the other hand, feeling all of the same pressures, Emily understood why they made the decision to cheat. In a way, Emily felt like they justified what they were doing, and that they were continuing to support each other through some tough times. Sitting alone in her room, she felt like she could use some support, too.

Emily's mom came home from work and came to her room to see how her day was, and to ask her what she wanted for dinner. Emily was in a heap in the middle of her bedroom floor with a box of tissues. Emily's mom immediately sat down on the floor and hugged her for a while. Then she asked Emily what was wrong. Emily told the whole story to her mom. Her mom recognized that Emily had been acting strange the past few weeks but she thought she was just nervous about the upcoming audition for the conservatory. Her mom suggested that they make a pro and con list of all of Emily's options, so that they could look at all of the outcomes in each situation. Once the list was created, Emily knew she was not going to Reina's house that night to "study." She did not want to risk everything she had worked so hard for in high school. But Emily still could not decide whether to tell on her friends or to not say anything at all. Emily did not want to make any enemies, but she also wanted everyone to be on the same playing field in terms of their schoolwork.

Emily's mom suggested she talk to Ms. Spelling, one of the school's administrators, who used to be the school counselor. Emily really respected Ms. Spelling because she was a great mentor, and she used to be a concert pianist, too, so she understood the pressures the students faced every day. Emily's mom told her that she could just ask Ms. Spelling about the situation hypothetically, so that she did not have to tell on her friends, but she could get some good advice. Emily spoke with Ms. Spelling on Monday. Ms. Spelling told Emily that she did not need to disclose names because the school was already aware of what was going on. One of the computer administrators realized someone was logging into the teacher's network outside of the school and they were able to pinpoint the people that week by looking at the assignments and tests.

The students were disciplined and were not allowed to participate in any of the senior activities. Emily felt relieved that she decided not to participate and that she was able to keep her friends, too. The following year, Emily attended the music conservatory on full scholarship and she became even more appreciative of her time management skills.

Questions for Discussion

1. What is the level of turbulence for Emily in her situation? What is the level of turbulence for the school? How might these levels be changed given Emily's decision?
2. Were the consequences of violating the plagiarism and cheating policy clear for the students at Harrison? Why or why not?

3. Why do you think these students seem to justify cheating and don't seem to think it is wrong?
4. How did Emily's thought process show care for her friends? For her school? For herself?
5. To what extent did Emily's mother and Ms. Spelling place Emily's best interests at the heart of their thinking?

Revenue or Integrity: A Sacrifice for the Greater Good

Medgar University is highly ranked nationally in science and technology. For many years, Medgar consistently graduated brilliant, top-performing scientists, researchers, and winners of prestigious science awards from NASA and other nationally acclaimed research foundations. Medgar boasts of its tolerance for diversity, and the large international enrollment in the College of Science and Technology certainly supported this claim. However, since September 11, 2001 and the new laws regulating the recruitment of foreign students, international admissions plunged dramatically, resulting in the closure of many science concentrations and the layoff of faculty members.

Tom Evers, associate director of international admissions, and Jeremiah Crusoe, head of science and technology, met frequently to plan recruiting strategies. In the fall of 2000, after a very successful meeting with a group of local entrepreneurs, the existing situation took an exciting turn toward a solution. Ralf Amagucci, a well-known and powerful Asian businessman, made good on his promise and influenced a large contingency of wealthy Asian science majors—including his son, Aladdin Amagucci—to transfer to Medgar University. For many years, Ralf worked to raise money for Medgar University. Both administration and faculty respected him as a reliable, cooperative, and dependable person. All students in the group he identified transferred from local community colleges. All agreed to prepay tuition fees, as well as room and board, for an entire year. This brilliant move brought much excitement as it rejuvenated the science program and brought increased revenues to the university. Many of the incoming Asian students took advantage of transfer articulation agreements between local community colleges and Medgar University, and were prepared to transfer directly into Medgar's science and technology program.

Enos Morgan, a long-standing faculty member in the physics department, complained frequently about the poor writing skills of science students generally. Enos was well known for his deep commitment to uphold the integrity of Medgar. He implicitly believed that the university's untarnished reputation was the key to gaining respect and staying strong. Recently, Ray Pitter, an American physics major, was caught plagiarizing by Professor Morgan and was reported to the disciplinary committee. His chance of receiving academic dismissal was very real. While Ray remained fairly quiet, his twin brother, Roy, frequently complained bitterly about the administration's unfair treatment of students. Roy considered himself an activist and felt it was his right to rally students to demonstrate against oppressive college policies. Roy and other local students were wary of the influx of foreign students and resented the attention given to them by the entire university's hierarchy. Morgan was aware that these Asian students were a great asset, although many struggled with writing-intensive programs, a condition that was never properly remedied in the two-year college setting. When Aladdin turned in his capstone paper at the end of the semester, Morgan was stunned. Blatant plagiarizing was evident and numerous quotes were included in the final paper without the attribution of sources. He wrote appropriate notes in certain sections of the paper, which he tucked away at the bottom of his daily pile of urgent work on his desk.

Morgan immediately thought of his role in the disciplining of Ray Pitter, the precedent set, and the seething anger of his twin brother, Roy. He had no regrets for his actions, as he was guided by his professional code of ethics and was always ready to fight to uphold the integrity of the institution he dearly loved. As a founding member of Medgar University, he cared for all students profoundly, but he knew that above all, he was committed to the greater good, the protection of the reputation of the institution.

Morgan sat pensively at his desk in the staff lounge. He opened his e-mail and scrolled to a caption marked "urgent." His heart froze as he read the president's upbeat announcement that yet another group of wealthy Asians had been identified to enter Medgar's science program. He could not shut out the sounds of celebration in the lounge as his colleagues cheered the brilliant move of the business community.

Morgan walked out of his office, deep in thoughts. Suddenly, his thoughts were interrupted by fast-approaching footsteps. Looking around, he squarely faced a very angry Roy Pitter. "I believe you left this file on your desk," he said, holding up Aladdin's paper with his own handwritten notes written all over. As he confronted the seething anger of the student, Morgan could only envision a real threat to his beloved institution. His mind was finally made up; he decided to report Aladdin Amagucci to the university's disciplinary committee at once.

ᔐ

Questions for Discussion

1. In applying the ethic of care, what strategies could Professor Morgan use to diffuse the anger Roy Pitter displays toward him?
2. Based on the contributions of Ralf Amagucci to Medgar University, would justice be served if the disciplinary committee handles his son's misconduct in the same way it handles Ray Pitter's misconduct?
3. After the professor discovered Aladdin's plagiarized paper, he did not react immediately until he was confronted by Roy Pitter. Based on the ethics of critique, what questions could he possibly ask himself within this timeframe?
4. When Morgan made his final decision, he seemed less worried about the consequences of his actions, as his professional code of ethics guided him to carry out his mission, and let the process take its course. Reflect on your own experiences when you had to resolve tough decisions based on your professional code of ethics. What was the outcome? Discuss.
5. In your opinion, what is the current turbulence level of this case, and what should be done to lower the level?
6. Describe potential effects on the turbulence level if the disciplinary actions for Aladdin's plagiarism coincide with the incoming class of Asian students.

Storm Warnings

Robin Lanza could not wait for the summer to end. There were a number of reasons for her impatience: the weather was uncooperative, raining much of the time; her friends were busy in other parts of the country; she attended an advanced course in chemistry that she really did not want to take; but most of all, she was about to transfer to Roland University in New Orleans. The prospect of leaving her rural New England town for the electric sparkle of America's liveliest city was part of the reason for Robin's excitement. But there were deeper reasons. Roland was known for its academic quality, relatively small and highly motivated student body, and excellent programs in her chosen field of pre-med. Besides, two of her closest girlfriends, Lucy and Ellen, were about to be entering Roland as first-year students.

The attraction of her new life at Roland, mixed with her desire for this particular summer to end, only made the early days of August seem to drag. Then there was the issue of her parents. Roland was a great deal more expensive than the state university she was leaving. That was an issue but not a crucial one, if they were being honest with her. Yet her parents were anything but enthusiastic about this transfer. "You're doing so well where you are, Robin. Why risk that just to go to New Orleans? We are worried about this decision," her mother told her. Her father seemed a bit more supportive, but Robin knew that he was only following his instinct, that it was her education and she needed to have the final say. Shopping for clothing and supplies together, Robin easily saw through her parents' facade of cheeriness. She knew that transferring to Roland was a bit of a gamble and that she would be somewhat on her own. Still, it was her dream and she was determined to make it work.

The dog days of August passed, and it was soon time to drive to the airport and fly south. With two large suitcases and two huge carry-on bags, Robin made her way onto the plane. Saying goodbye to her parents was less difficult than she imagined, and she was glad that they smiled as she turned to wave after she passed through the security checkpoint. At least they were trying to be happy for her. The flights were smooth and late that Thursday afternoon, Robin landed at the Louis Armstrong International Airport and then went on to her hotel, as her room at Roland's sophomore dorm would not be ready until the next morning. Friday was almost dream-like and something of a blur as Robin moved into her dorm, met her new roommate, shopped for supplies at the school store, and strolled through the campus, imagining her future. She listened to the radio a bit but the news of a Category One hurricane named Katrina that was passing over Florida made no impression her. What would be her only day at Roland ended calmly as she left the welcome party for new students and climbed the four flights to her well-organized, air-conditioned room.

The contrast between Friday and Saturday could not have been greater. Whereas university faculty and staff were filled with good cheer and welcoming wishes for Robin and the other new students just 24 hours earlier, a tone of serious order permeated Saturday's emergency meeting. Hurricane Katrina had taken an unexpected turn toward New Orleans and was ominously growing in size with each hour. Students were told that as a precaution, they were going to be bussed north to Mississippi and the campus of Tether State University until the hurricane passed the city. Robin and her two girlfriends were only a little worried as they boarded the chartered buses, but the well-organized response of the university staff and the obvious planning for emergencies like this gave her a sense of security. She smiled a bit as she turned to her friend, Lucy. "Look, where I came from, it was winter storms and blizzards. Here, a hurricane or two is just part of the deal. We'll be back soon." Lucy seemed convinced and though it could hardly be called a party atmosphere, the bus ride to Tether State was almost pleasant.

Conditions at Tether were not quite what Robin expected. Roland students were gathered in the school's gymnasium and asked to stay there. Tether students were not particularly friendly and seemed to mind the imposition of so many strangers in their midst. Roland and Tether officials did their best to keep everyone occupied and well fed, but as night fell over the campus, two things became clear to everyone in the gym: there were not enough cots to go around and, more importantly, the hurricane headed for New Orleans was no ordinary storm. Trying to sleep on the hard gymnasium floor without a pillow, Robin started to see her dream fray at its edges as she, Lucy, and Ellen quietly shared their anxious feelings until they drifted off to a fitful sleep.

Then there was Sunday. Roland officials were clearly doing their best but the situation was not encouraging. Hundreds of students needed to be informed, fed, entertained somehow, and kept safe at someone else's campus. Cooperation between the institutions was excellent but this extraordinary situation at the start of both of their semesters was a challenge. On top of that, it now appeared that the hurricane was not only headed for New Orleans, its path also now included Tether State. Despite all of these problems, the situation was well under control—for now. But nothing could keep the students from worrying about the massively destructive storm. Some students started to make their own plans. Lucy began to make a series of calls on her cell phone and then turned to say: "Look, Robin, staying here is just crazy. The storm is coming this way, and we will be in danger. I don't want to spend another stupid night trying to sleep on the floor, and who knows when we will be able to go back to New Orleans? I'm getting out of here. All we need is a ride to the airport and we can be home by tonight, tomorrow at the latest. What do you say?"

Robin thought about it and called her parents. Her father said: "Listen to me, Robin. Things seem very serious down there. Now, you are being fed and taken care of by the Roland people and they are responsible for your safety. If you leave, anything could happen. You might get stuck at the airport or caught in the storm. Mom and I really want you to stay put until things are safer. Please forget about trying to fly home in this mess."

Her dad seemed to be almost angry, thought Robin, but he's not the one trapped in this situation. How can my parents know how I feel, and how can they be so insensitive in this emergency? Robin asked Roland officials about getting to the airport. An official from the Dean of Student's office told her: "We can get you to the airport, if you leave right now. But you have to know that once we drop you off, you are on your own."

So there it was. Hurricane Katrina, a Category Five storm, was now headed right for them. On one side, her parents and Roland officials told her to stay. On the other side, her friends were leaving for the airport in ten minutes. Should she agree to stay and be without friends at the gym for who knows how long, or should she follow her instincts by defying her parents and Roland authorities and try to make it out of the region? Time was running out, and Robin had to make up her mind.

Questions for Discussion

1. What do you think of Roland's policy? Would you suggest alterations to the policy of allowing students over the age of 18 to decide for themselves whether or not to leave the area?
2. How might Robin employ the ethic of care to herself in this situation? How might she apply it to others, including her friends and family, regardless of her decision?
3. Is Robin being unduly pressured by contradictory voices?
4. Consider the dilemma from both sides—the advice of Robin's friends and Roland officials as well as the demands of her parents. How does each try to frame her best interests differently? Which seems more compelling to you and why?
5. What level of turbulence was Robin experiencing at the shelter? How might a decision to leave for the airport change that level for her in the short run? In the long run? How does Robin's position *vis-à-vis* the storm color seem to color her reaction?

10

RULES, REGULATIONS, AND POLICIES VERSUS INDIVIDUAL NEEDS AND CONCERNS IN STUDENT TEACHING

Cases contributed by David X. Fitt,
Joseph P. DuCette, and Sara M. Becker

*T*HIS CHAPTER IS DERIVED FROM DAY-TO-DAY EXPERIENCES over a ten-year period in the teacher preparation process in general, and on experiences overseeing the placement of student teachers in the field specifically. The chapter relies on a series of case studies to bring to life some of the ethical dilemmas that evolve from the complex interaction of federal and state rules, regulations, and policies governing K–12 education. These regulations affect all aspects of the teacher training process: the schools, the school districts, principals, pre-service teachers, cooperating teachers, university supervisors, and the university itself. While these regulations are completely understandable as one mechanism of accountability, the way they are applied sometimes creates situations where the vested interests of the stakeholders in the teacher preparation process come into direct conflict. The purpose of this chapter is to present some of these conflicts as demonstrations of ethical dilemmas.

The Teacher-in-Training: Expert or Novice

Student teaching is the culminating activity of almost all teacher preparation programs. Because it plays such a critical role in the preparation of new teachers, this part of the program has been infused with a complex set of rules, procedures, and regulations designed to ensure that the prospective teacher is qualified to obtain a certificate to teach. At no other time in the pre-service teacher's program of study are the stakes so high and the stakeholders so numerous. For the teaching profession itself, it is mandatory that all candidates for licensure be qualified in the multiple dimensions of content, pedagogy, and character. Teachers need to come into the workforce with the knowledge and skills that will help them understand their students and their learning capabilities. They also need a solid understanding of content and pedagogy. Moreover, they need the ability to design and implement effective assessment tools and the ability and desire to work collaboratively with other teachers, families, and communities (Darling-Hammond, 2000; Holm & Horn, 2003; Kruse & Louis, 1997). For the university, it is critical that the student teachers—who are the university's external representatives to school districts—act professionally and responsibly. For the teacher preparation program, it is essential that the student teachers demonstrate those qualities that characterize the philosophical basis underlying its programs. All of these entities have a vested interest in ensuring that the student teachers are competent, ethical, and professional at all times.

The conflict, of course, occurs because the stakes are even higher for the student teachers under precisely those conditions where failure is such a likely possibility. In Mezirow's (1991) terms, student teaching should be a transformative experience where the student teacher evolves into the role of a teacher from the previous role of a student. This type of transformation is always gradual and always involves a lengthy trial-and-error process. Unfortunately, the typical student-teaching situation mandates almost exactly the opposite reality. By definition, a student teacher is an amateur judged against professional standards.

Perhaps the dilemma in this situation can be better understood by comparing the actual student-teaching situation to the ideal on which it is based. Teacher preparation is based, essentially, on an apprentice model. In the guild system that developed and refined the apprentice model, a candidate for a profession was apprenticed to a master craftsman to learn a trade. Through a series of increasingly complex and increasingly responsible situations, the apprentice learned the trade through one-on-one contact with the master. Under this system, failure was expected but was limited by the extent of responsibility given to the apprentice. Only when the master craftsman determined that the apprentice was ready was the person allowed to begin life as a member of the guild. In this system, individuals were allowed to learn and grow at their own rate. The rules and regulations of the trade were not applied to the apprentice, since ultimately it was the master craftsman who assumed responsibility for the final product.

Compare this model to student teaching. Since the student teacher is learning the trade, failure should be expected and individual learning rates should be honored, a point made strongly by Koetsier and Wubbels (1995). Student teachers should not be expected to demonstrate professional-level behaviors because they are not as yet professionals, nor do they have the skills of a professional (Darling-Hammond, Chung, & Frelow, 2002). Student teaching, however, is typically only a one-semester experience, and an experience that is usually graded in a manner similar to all other experiences in the student's program. Moreover, the student teacher is governed by essentially the same rules and regulations that govern fully licensed members of the profession. Under this condition, it is inevitable that those who supervise the student teachers will be continuously faced with the dilemma of judging the student teachers as professionals and yet allowing them to be amateurs. The stories presented in this chapter demonstrate some of the issues when this type of dilemma is encountered.

The Ascendance of Field Experiences in the Preparation of New Teachers

The preparation of new teachers is increasingly relying on field experiences as a core element of formal professional preparation. Field experiences are typically embedded in courses, and they are designed by the university with the understanding that each new pre-service teacher eventually will affect the lives of thousands of students. Increasingly, university classroom-based instruction is being replaced with or augmented by some form of field experience (Keller, 2003; Shen, 2002) where the student teacher can be given "guided induction into the tricks of the trade" (Tigchelaar & Korthagen, 2004, p. 670). These field-based experiences create high visibility and provide a rich environment where the university can interact with and provide service to its surrounding community. On the other hand, the intensity of these experiences also provides numerous opportunities for friction to occur.

In-service or cooperating teachers volunteer for, or are assigned, the responsibility of mentoring a student during the student-teaching experience. This assignment is based on the assumption that the teacher, at least in theory, has successfully taught for several years and that he or she has a sufficient degree and type of mentoring skills to competently perform the role. Now that more teacher training programs are investing heavily in early and ongoing field placements, the role of the in-service teacher is becoming increasingly important and influential to the professional lives of new teachers. One of the more interesting and unintended outcomes of this increased emphasis on field-based training is that the university is getting a much closer look at what is really happening in the schools, and the schools are obtaining a deeper understanding of how teachers are trained. As before, this has the positive potential of creating opportunities for meaningful interaction but also has the negative possibility of allowing both entities to observe the other under circumstances that are not always flattering.

From the perspective of the university, the many layers of external regulation and assessment are tremendously expensive and they are viewed as being foisted upon teacher preparation programs by government as unfunded mandates. This complex mix of regulatory bodies, schools, university supervisors, and cooperating teachers provides fertile ground for the development of systematic turbulence and prolific ethical dilemmas.

The five vignettes presented below contain a number of real-life dilemmas that involve some aspect of the student-teaching process. Each one is based on actual experiences encountered in administering a large student-teaching process in an urban setting. The dilemmas, however, can occur in any setting of this type—large or small, urban or suburban. They are intended as case studies of what can happen when the reality of student teaching clashes with the theory on which it is based.

The story entitled "When Enthusiasm Is Not Enough" presents a dilemma often encountered in student teaching. The student teacher in question clearly wants to be a teacher and brings youth, motivation, and enthusiasm to her placement. When faced with the reality of teaching material with which she is not completely comfortable, however, her deficiencies become evident and her motivation wanes. This case demonstrates the dilemma of forcing pre-service teachers through a process that is too removed from the apprenticeship model on which this experience is theoretically based.

"Whose Values Should We Accept?" presents the dilemma encountered when contradictory value systems clash. The retired principal in the story brings to her role in student teaching a long history of working with students and teachers who have looked and acted in ways that she believes are correct. When confronted with student teachers who are very different from those with whom she has interacted in the past, she concludes that these diverse pre-service teachers will not succeed. In indicating her disapproval of these teachers, she is acting upon an established sense of what is correct in a setting that she understands. The dilemma that is posed in the story is how these established values should be balanced against a competing ethic.

In "When Principles Meet Reality," a supervisor of student teachers stumbles upon a situation where she believes unethical and abusive behavior is occurring. Although she has no legal standing to intervene, she informs the proper authority—the principal of the school—about her concern. The story touches on a set of real-life issues in many urban school districts, where choices must be made not between good and bad but between one type of bad outcome versus another.

The story "When Is the Tried and True No Longer True?" presents a case of where established practices encounter innovation and change. Similar to the second story in this chapter, the cooperating teacher here has a long history of teaching, during which she has created for herself a set of principles that she believes are correct. When confronted with a student teacher who practices a very different kind of pedagogy, the established teacher concludes that the student teacher is inadequate. The story addresses the question of how these opposing philosophies can be balanced.

In the fifth and final story, "When Is Telling the Truth Not Good Enough?," the assistant professor who has been asked to provide an honest evaluation of the student-teaching program confronts the reality that truth is not always a desired commodity. The dilemma for her, and for the dean to whom she is reporting, is to balance a straightforward evaluation with the need to protect the reputation of the college and the student-teaching program.

When Enthusiasm is Not Enough

Susan Jenkins is a 20-year-old senior at City University majoring in elementary education. She transferred to City after obtaining an associates degree from the community college near her home. She has performed adequately in her teacher preparation program, obtaining a GPA of 3.1 out of 4.0. She passed the pre-professional tests of the PRAXIS series, although she did have to re-take the math test in order to meet the state's minimum passing score. Overall, Susan would be considered a good but not outstanding student. She decided to become a teacher because she has a special fondness for young children in kindergarten and the early elementary grades and because her mother is a teacher. In fact, her mother, who has taught for many years in the city schools, has now achieved the rank of lead teacher in the Green Lane Elementary School, one of the better elementary schools in the district. Because of her seniority and connections in the district, Susan's mother has been promised that her daughter will be given a job in the district when she graduates and obtains teacher certification.

Susan was placed in the one of the university's professional development schools for her student teaching. Although her preference was to student teach in a kindergarten or first grade, there were no available classes at that level. Consequently, she was assigned to student teach in Mrs. Crane's sixth-grade class. While the grade level was not what she wanted, Dr. Olson, the director of student teaching, thought that this placement would be beneficial since Mrs. Crane had taught for more than ten years and was considered a superior teacher and mentor. Her university supervisor was Dr. Blake, a former principal, who had successfully supervised student teachers for several years after his retirement.

Susan began her student teaching experience by observing Mrs. Crane for one week. She was then asked to take over the class for a reading lesson. This was followed by an assignment to teach math, after which she was asked to teach science. While Susan clearly enjoyed interacting with the students, it became evident rather quickly that she had significant deficits as a teacher. Although she carefully prepared her lesson plans, she did not seem able to respond to the students' questions or to modify her lessons to handle the ebb and flow of the classroom. This almost always led to classroom management problems as the students became aware that she was uncomfortable and anxious. Inevitably, Mrs. Crane had to intervene and take over the lesson from Susan. Mrs. Crane and Dr. Blake began to realize that the core issue was that Susan did not have enough content knowledge to teach at this grade level.

Although both Mrs. Crane and Dr. Blake tried to help Susan throughout her student-teaching experience, no significant improvement was noted. In fact, her repeated failures led Susan to become even less successful in her teaching, so that the point was eventually reached where Mrs. Crane no longer asked her to assume control of the classroom. At the end of the semester, both she and Dr. Blake agreed that they could not give Susan a passing grade. When informed of this, Susan argued that she did not intend to teach at the upper elementary grade level, and that she was sure she would do well as a kindergarten or first-grade teacher. While this might be true, it was noted that the certificate that she would obtain from the state entitled her to teach all the way up to the eighth grade. Given this reality, a grade of "C" was recommended to Dr. Olson. Since a minimal grade of "B–" is required for certification, Susan could not be recommended for a teaching certificate with this grade on her transcript.

When Susan informed her mother that she was going to obtain an unsatisfactory grade in student teaching, her mother immediately called Dr. Olson. She informed him that allowing Susan to obtain the unsatisfactory grade would mean that Susan could not assume the job that she had been promised. She implied, but did not explicitly state, that she would no longer look favorably on placing student teachers from City University in her school, or perhaps in any of the schools in the district. She also informed Dr. Olson that the long relationship between the district and the university meant to her that some leeway should be allowed in specific cases. In her mind, one implication of this was that Susan should be given at least a "B–" in student teaching, and should be recommended for a teaching certificate.

Questions for Discussion

1. What do you think about the original decision to place Susan at a grade level for which she was not preparing to teach? Was it appropriate to place her with older children? Discuss.
2. Why give out a teaching certificate that extends to grade eight? Does this rule for certification make sense for teachers who want to work with only young children?
3. What do you think Dr. Olson, the director of student teaching, should do? How do you think he should balance the ethic of justice, the ethic of care, and the ethic of the profession in this case?
4. How can the thinly veiled threat to not accept future student teacher candidates relate to the ethic of care and the ethic of profession, particularly in light of the fact that all stakeholders are equally obliged to prepare new teachers?
5. Where do you see turbulence in this dilemma? How might it spike? How might Dr. Olson act to modify the level of turbulence?

Whose Values Should We Accept?

Dr. Ruth Jamison is a 65-year-old widow who has recently retired from the Metropolitan School District. She had spent more than 40 years in the district, starting as a kindergarten teacher, moving into the position of lead teacher in her school, and eventually becoming a full-time administrator. She spent her final 15 years as the principal of the Washington Elementary School, a position that provided her with great job satisfaction and enormous respect by the teachers and parents with whom she interacted. Now that she has retired, she wants to give back some of what education has given her. Since she had worked for many years with student teachers from City University, she decided that the best way she could provide service to her profession was to assume a position as a supervisor of student teachers. Since her experience and credentials were exactly what the state required for this position, she was readily hired by the university's director of student teaching, who assigned her four student teachers to supervise. To make her comfortable with this assignment, Dr. Jamison was assigned to supervise all four student teachers at Washington Elementary.

At the first meeting with her group of student teachers, Dr. Jamison found four distinctly different individuals. Mary Kline seemed like the typical elementary teacher that Dr. Jamison had interacted with during her 40 years in education: she was a petite woman who had always wanted to be a teacher. She dressed conservatively and was clearly respectful of Dr. Jamison's expertise. John Roberts, on the other hand, was a 23-year-old African-American male who believed that he could make an impact on the African-American boys in his class. He was an avid fan of rap music and had developed innovative ways of using this music to reach these boys. Theresa Hopkins was a 45-year-old woman whose children were now in school and who had decided to complete her own education. In order to fit in, she had chosen clothes that her own teenage daughter would wear. Finally, Katie Halpern, a 24-year-old Caucasian woman, arrived in a wheelchair, having been partially paralyzed in a car accident.

Dr. Jamison was quite upset by what she saw. In her experience, the only one of her student teachers who had a reasonable chance of becoming a good teacher was Mary Kline. She simply could not see how the other three could make it through student teaching or, if they were able to get past this experience, how they could survive as teachers. Since she believed it was her responsibility both to the students and to the field of education to be honest, she stated publicly that John, Theresa, and Katie would probably have a very difficult time with student teaching. She also publicly asked each of them if they really wanted to be a teacher, and indicated that other careers seemed a better choice.

Immediately after this initial meeting, the three students went to the director of student teaching and requested that they be given another supervisor. Moreover, they indicated that they felt that Dr. Jamison was inappropriate as a student teaching supervisor, and that she be dismissed from this role. The director of student teaching was left with some difficult choices.

Questions for Discussion

1. Was there a rule, procedure, or policy that Dr. Jamison followed when she indicated publicly that three of the four student teachers would not make it through the probation period? If so, what was the rule, procedure, or policy? If not, should there be a rule, procedure, or policy to address Dr. Jamison's behavior?

2. What of the ethic of care? Did Dr. Jamison really think that she was caring for three students who she deemed to be inappropriate for teaching? How do you think each of the students felt about her behavior?

3. What direction should be given to Dr. Jamison so that she can act in the best interests of all students?
4. What is the current turbulence level in this dilemma? What could Dr. Jamison do to bring down the level of turbulence? What could the director of student teaching do to make the turbulence level even worse? What about the students? How could their decisions create more turbulence or lower it?

When Principles Meet Reality

Mary Ellen McGrory is the supervisor of a student teacher who has been assigned to the Benjamin Franklin Elementary School. Benjamin Franklin is located in one of the poorer sections of a large city. The building was constructed in the 1920s and has not had significant improvements for more than 20 years. The student teacher who Ms. McGory is supervising has been doing a superb job, and Mary Ellen has had only praise for her work.

During one of her site visits, however, Mary Ellen observed an incident that occurred in an adjacent classroom. Since there are no walls between the two classrooms (just bookshelf dividers), she was able to clearly hear what transpired. The teacher in the adjacent class, Mrs. Adams, spent 25 minutes berating a student regarding her behavior in the halls. The rest of the students in the class were sitting quietly in their seats listening to this harangue. The teacher's voice was not only heard by Mary Ellen but also by the students sitting in the back of the classroom in which she was observing her student teacher. Next, Mrs. Adams used her cell phone to call the student's mother regarding the student's behavior. Again, the entire class was privy to the conversation. This telephone call lasted about 45 minutes. After 15 minutes of the telephone conversation, the student being chastised began sobbing and continued sobbing until the telephone call ended. When the phone call ended, Mrs. Adams turned her attention to a special education student who had refused to eat the pizza that was part of the lunch meal for the day. The student had put the pizza into the wastebasket in the front of the room. Mrs. Adams took the pizza out of the wastebasket and insisted that the student consume some portion of it in front of the entire class.

Mary Ellen was visibly upset by what she was observing. It was clear to her that what was happening in the adjacent classroom was, at the very least, inappropriate and pedagogically unsound. In fact, a reasonable case could be made that the behavior was abusive. Although she had no legal standing regarding Mrs. Adams, she felt that something had to be done. Consequently, when she had completed the observation of her student teacher, she asked to see Mr. Hopkins, the principal of the school. She reported what had occurred to him. He replied that he was not surprised by what he was hearing. Mrs. Adams had been reported on several occasions for exactly this type of behavior. However, on each occasion, because Mrs. Adams was a tenured teacher, she appealed to the teachers' union and charged Principal Hopkins with harassment. In each case, the teachers' union had intervened and the case was dropped. In fact, Mr. Hopkins had been warned by the district's personnel office that he should make sure that this type of situation did not get as far as a union hearing because these cases made the district look bad. To make the matter worse, the principal was already short two teachers in his school. Even if he could get Mrs. Adams removed, it was very unlikely that he could get a replacement. Finally, he said that while some of what Mrs. Adams did was questionable, most of the parents of her students did not object to the way she handled their children. In fact, many of them felt that her behavior was appropriate to keep their kids from misbehaving. He told Mary Ellen that he empathized with her concerns but that the situation could not be changed. The supervisor left the office angered and determined to act but not knowing how.

Questions for Discussion

1. What does the law say about the treatment of children by a teacher in your state? Would the actions of Mrs. Adams be tolerated? Discuss.
2. If there is no law or policy in your state regarding Mrs. Adams' behavior, should there be? Explain.
3. In what way is the teachers' union upholding the ethic of the profession? Or is it?
4. If the system tolerates this type of treatment of poor students, how can Mary Ellen use the ethic of critique to build a case for serious change?
5. Is the ethic of care being used at all by parents who agree with Mrs. Adams?
6. How might Mary Ellen use the current turbulence in this situation to help create change?

When is the Tried and True No Longer True?

James Morgan is the principal of the Harrison Elementary School. He has been at Harrison for several years and is considered an exemplary administrator. During his years as principal, he has encouraged his faculty to become cooperating teachers to work with students from the local university. In general, this arrangement has worked well, because in encouraging faculty to mentor students, he found that the in-service teachers themselves seemed to improve in their own teaching. This success has led the university to place a larger cohort of student teachers at Harrison because the experience has proven to be so rewarding.

One of the unintended outcomes of this situation, however, is that student teachers have had to be placed with teachers who have not traditionally served as cooperating teachers. One of these teachers who was new to the role of cooperating teacher was Ms. Helen Creighton. Ms. Creighton has taught fifth grade students at Harrison for more than 30 years. Respected more than loved, Ms. Creighton was considered one of the "old guard" at Harrison; she believed in strict discipline in her classroom and in the traditional roles of teacher and student. She was asked to mentor Susan Kaiser, a 22-year-old senior at the university.

Near the end of the semester, Ms. Creighton requested a meeting with Principal Morgan. She informed Mr. Morgan that she has been extremely dissatisfied with the performance of Susan from the start: she has poor classroom management skills, unrealistic expectations for students, is too friendly with the students and interacts with them in an unprofessional manner, creates inappropriate lesson plans, and is generally not suited for the profession of teaching. She indicated that she intended to recommend that Susan be given a grade of "C" for student teaching. She also mentioned that from now on, she wanted to be given a student teacher each semester because it was clear to her that the university was not preparing the next generation of teachers very well, and she wanted to be in a situation where she could act as a gatekeeper for the profession that she holds in such high regard.

In response to this complaint, Principal Morgan called Susan into his office and asked how her student-teaching experience had been going. Susan replied that her situation had been intolerable throughout the entire student-teaching experience. She explained that Ms. Creighton had used only one type of instruction for all students, although it was quite clear that the students demonstrated a variety of learning styles. Any attempt to implement new concepts for good teaching that she had learned in her methods classes was rejected. She said that Ms. Creighton was always negative, she disliked and distrusted students, and she rejected any suggestions about changing the way instruction was handled in the classroom. She felt that Ms. Creighton disapproved of everything she did or wanted to do. Susan was convinced that her cooperating teacher would recommend that she receive a "C" in student teaching, an outcome that would require her to retake the course or to graduate without certification.

After both meetings, Principal Morgan was left to ponder the problem. Should he intervene, and if so, what actions might be justified?

Questions for Discussion

1. Who should be responsible, by university rules, for giving the final grade in student teaching?
2. To what extent is this situation a generational conflict? A philosophical conflict? A class conflict?
3. What is in the Harrison Elementary School students' best interests? What is in Susan's best interests? Is there a difference?
4. Is it possible for Principal Morgan to counsel Mrs. Creighton not to have student teachers in a way that will preserve her dignity and demonstrate respect for her?
5. Is the turbulence level greatest for Mrs. Creighton, Susan, or Principal Morgan? Explain.

When is Telling the Truth Not Good Enough?

Samantha Shen was an assistant professor at City University. She had taught third grade while completing her PhD degree in elementary education and was hired to teach in the College of Education at City and to coordinate the student teaching placements. During her first year as an assistant professor, the college's teacher preparation programs were scheduled to be reviewed by the state's Department of Education. The dean of the college, Richard Frampton, had also been hired at the same time as Dr. Shen. In his interview for the job, he had made it clear that he perceived serious problems in the college and that his immediate job was to make significant changes. He believed that the state review would serve as one of the ways to find out where the changes most needed to be implemented. He asked Dr. Shen to complete that section of the review relevant to student teaching. He informed her that the state's program officer had told him that he wanted to pay special attention in the review to all of the college's field experiences, with a special focus on student teaching. The dean indicated to Dr. Shen that while he recognized that the review was summative from the state's perspective, he wanted the review to also serve a formative purpose because he was especially interested in improving the student-teaching program.

As she was new to the job, Dr. Shen asked a group of principals and cooperating teachers who had worked with the college for several years to meet with her in a focus group to give her their feedback about the student-teaching program, as well as discuss the quality of the students who were being placed in the schools. While the principals and teachers had some positive things to say about the students' enthusiasm and willingness to learn, their general consensus was that the students were not prepared well for their jobs. Moreover, almost all of the members of the focus group agreed with the following: the student-teaching program was badly managed; the students received inappropriate placements; no training was given to the cooperating teachers (although the state mandated such training); and City University clearly had the worst student-teaching program of any of the universities with which they had worked.

Dr. Shen completed her report for the state review by including as many of the positive aspects of the program as she could find. However, consistent with her charge from the dean she listed all of those aspects of the program that needed revision and put forward a lengthy series of modifications that she believed would remediate the problems mentioned by the focus group. When she submitted her report to Dean Frampton, he informed her that she would have to remove all suggestions that there were problems in the student teaching program. He told her that he did not want the college "to look bad" when it was reviewed by the state. He also said that he had recently met with City University's president, who had said that he did not have a good impression of the college nor with the job that Dean Frampton was doing. Although it was not said explicitly, the impression that the dean had taken from the meeting was that he believed the president might close the college if the state review did not go well. With all of this at stake, the dean believed that only the most positive things should be said in the review. When Dr. Shen mentioned that she had asked several of the principals and cooperating teachers who had been in the focus group to meet with the visiting team from the state, the dean said that she must make sure that none of these individuals were invited to the meetings, nor that any member of team be allowed to visit any of the schools in which these individuals worked.

Dr. Shen could not believe what she was hearing. Had she come to work in higher education only to be faced with such an ethically compromising set of demands? As she prepared to meet with a friendly senior colleague who acted as her mentor, Dr. Shen wondered what she might do.

Questions for Discussion

1. Are there any legal requirements regarding how a program should be reviewed? Discuss.
2. What advice would you give to Dean Frampton for dealing with the university president's allegations regarding the College of Education?
3. What advice might Dr. Shen's mentor give her that would demonstrate concern for her as a professional and for her as a person?
4. What feedback should program leaders use if they want to make improvements for the best interests of all students? And how and where should this feedback be presented?
5. What could the university president do to lower the level of turbulence and help to create a climate for an effective program review? What could the dean do to lower the turbulence level? How could the turbulence level be raised? Discuss.

Part Three

INTRODUCING THE NEW DEEL

*I*N THIS LAST SECTION OF THE BOOK, the New DEEL (Democratic Ethical Educational Leadership) is introduced as a movement. This innovative approach, with its core values based essentially in democracy and in ethics, has been accepted by a number of universities and colleges in the United States, Australia, Canada, and the United Kingdom. It is also growing in numbers through the active engagement of diverse practitioners in Canada, Australia, Taiwan, and Sweden. In addition, the University Council of Educational Administration (UCEA) has recognized and even highlighted this concept at its annual conventions.

The New DEEL is a concept that dovetails well with the Multiple Ethical Paradigms and Turbulence Theory. A major thrust of this movement is to reintroduce ideals that made meaning to many of us when we entered education. The effects of returning to our roots will hopefully enable us to move away from the current emphasis on external standards, high-stakes testing, and accountability and bring us back to a high regard for civic responsibility and to the values inherent in the ethics of critique and care. This movement offers guidance enabling us to think deeply upon the content of courses and programs for educational leaders. And reflecting more broadly, the New DEEL requires that we return to instilling a joy of learning in young people, provide them with the critical thinking skills necessary to challenge and modify the status quo, and offer them the hope needed to build a better society for their progeny.

11

CONTROL VERSUS DEMOCRACY

*I*N HIS INSPIRING BOOK *The Moral and Spiritual Crisis of Education*, Purpel (1989) provided some excellent examples of paradoxes. Probably the most relevant one, for this book, is the paradox that exists between control and democracy.

Turning to control, Purpel wrote that most of us wish to control our destinies. He went on to say that this is difficult to do in a world riddled with nuclear bombs and internal violence; where there are economic depressions, tidal waves, famines, pollution, volcanoes, and hurricanes. (If this book had been written later, terrorism would no doubt have been on his list.) Purpel added that because of this desire for control in our bureaucratized, computerized culture, we value "work, productivity, efficiency and uniformity over play, flexibility, diversity and freedom" (p. 48).

Focusing on democracy, Purpel spoke of how bureaucracy "sharply conflicts with our dedication to democratic principles which stress self-determination and a process for both sustaining autonomy and adjusting conflicts" (p. 49). He went on to speak of John Dewey's conceptualization of the school as a "'laboratory' of democracy where students and teachers could wrestle with the challenges of the democratic experience" (p. 49).

Currently, in American public schools strict discipline and school policies are major concerns. Meeting standards through the raising of test scores is a central focus. Accountability is in vogue. While in the same era for the most part, student government is lying low. The debating society is not emphasized. Controversy and critique are not desired, nor is there really any time for it in a curriculum that is driven by high-stakes testing. Civics education seems to receive little attention in many schools that are focusing on testing and a very basic education (Shapiro, 2005).

While schools can and should be the way to encourage democracy by teaching young people to be good citizens and by helping them become aware and engaged in at the very least their local society, this is clearly not the case in most public schools at the present time. However, despite this trend there does exist a counter trend. For example, there is an increasing cry for more service education (Keith, 1999, 2005). Service learning does ask students to go beyond the school and help appropriate organizations within society. In addition, there are a number of scholars (Aiken, 2002; Boyd, 2000; Crow, 2006; Driscoll, 2001; Furman-Brown, 2002; Gutmann, 1999; Gutmann & Thompson, 2004; Mitra, 2004; O'Hair, McLaughlin, & Reitzug, 2000; Reitzug & O'Hair, 2002; Shapiro & Purpel, 2004) who believe that students should have a solid, engaged civics education to be prepared to play strong roles in the democratic process.

Democracy and Public Schooling

> The barrage of accountability measures aimed at schools has caused edu-
> cators to focus on varied and questionable purposes, such as teaching to
> the tests and "dumbing down" the curriculum (McNeil, 2000) rather than
> preparing students to become useful and productive citizens (Kochan &
> Reed, 2005).

In the above quote, Kochan and Reed speak to the control-versus-democracy paradox currently being played out in schools and warn educators that accountability, at its extreme, can hurt students by not preparing them to be useful and productive citizens. Unfortunately, as the authors warn, the continuing focus on accountability, with its focus on high-stakes testing, places social studies and civics education off to the side. A major reason for this is that currently reading, writing, and arithmetic (the 3 Rs) figure prominently on the tests while social studies and many other subjects are too often treated as peripheral disciplines within the curriculum. Even if social studies is included on the tests, the citizenship piece is something that requires much more than answering questions on a high-stakes exam. It requires dialogue, debate, and decision making.

Although it is clear that democracy is extremely powerful and important and needs to be taught in schools, Gutmann (1999), in *Democratic Education*, raised what she considers to be the central question of the political theory of education: "How should citizens be educated and by whom?" (p. xi). She frames her discussion around two paradoxes: the tension between multiculturalism versus patriotism as well as the inconsistencies surrounding parental control versus public control. In her discussion, she speaks of civic minimalism that some parents think appropriate for public schooling. It is these parents' belief that they should "have the right to exempt their children from any part of the school curriculum as long as the education that they wish to substitute satisfies the civic minimum" (p. xii). Gutmann also speaks of the democratic educationalists who offer "a principled defense of

schooling whose aim is to teach the skills and virtues of democratic deliberation within a social context where educational authority is shared among
parents, citizens, and professional educators" (p. xiv). Gutmann makes a
sound case for what she calls "deliberate democracy."

Deliberate democracy asks all parties to come together to discuss in depth
controversial issues and attempt to deal with them in such a way that the
problems can be resolved. She asks for a more principled educational debate
on the difficult problems related to education. Gutmann asks for education
that teaches students to handle complex problems. She wants them to learn
about the civic values that make up their own country and the moral purpose
of other nations. Gutmann's approach requires a great deal from our teachers
and from our educational administrators. She emphasizes tolerance as well
as critical discussions of the concept itself. To teach this type of democracy,
there is really no place for the back-to-basics movement. Gutmann's curriculum is comprehensive and broad-based. She advocates a type of democracy
where the process itself—the deliberation—is significant and must be taught
and practiced.

The New DEEL

The paradox of control versus democracy is at the heart of Democratic Ethical
Educational Leadership ("The New DEEL"). This movement came about in
response to the challenges facing the field of educational leadership. The New
DEEL attempts to respond to some critics of the field who have claimed that
it has tended to reinforce social inequalities and hierarchies (Rapp, 2002).
It follows a trend in educational administration flowing in the opposite
direction. One of the strengths of the New DEEL is the rich historic tradition
of democracy and ethical leadership upon whose shoulders it stands.

For example, early in the 20th century, Ella Flagg Young, the first woman
to run a major city school system and a close associate of John Dewey,
pioneered the use of teacher councils, which were an early form of shared
governance. While some credited Dewey with this invention, he eagerly
pointed out that he learned the workings of this practice from Young (Webb
& McCarthy, 1998). Dewey is certainly the clearest early proponent of the
requirement for democracy in schools (1903) but the tradition does not end
with him. In the depths of the Great Depression, George S. Counts criticized
the progressive education movement's limited impact on social justice and
raised the possibility that education could lead the United States into an era
of greater equality and democracy in his book, *Dare the Schools Build a New
Social Order?* (1932). Later in that decade, facing the threat of Nazi Germany

and her axis allies in Italy and Japan, the field of educational administration again took the lead. The democratic school administration movement spearheaded by Teachers College faculty including Alice Miel (Koopman, Miel, & Misner 1943) and Harold Rugg led to new texts and a refreshed emphasis on civic equality and shared power in the school (Kliebard, 1987). By the early 1960s, as the United States began to awaken from McCarthyism and the panic spread to schools by the success of the Soviet Union's *Sputnik*, a new breed of social critics arose who emphasized democracy and a moral imperative for schools. Writers like Herbert Kohl, John Holt, and Jonathan Kozol found democracy sorely lacking in the schools of America and pressed leaders at every level to raise moral questions aimed at the heart of their practice.

Beginning in 2004, faculty and practitioners, as well as the University Council of Educational Administration (UCEA), launched a new movement in the field of educational leadership. Currently, well over 20 universities and practitioners from the United States, Canada, the United Kingdom, Taiwan, Sweden, Jamaica, and Australia are involved in the New DEEL. This ever-increasing group promotes democratic action using a moral framework focusing on leadership in schools, in higher education, and in the wider community. It aims to change the direction of educational leadership away from an overly corporate and controlling model towards the values of democratic and ethical behavior (Gross & Shapiro, 2005).

Those who are part of this movement believe that the first job of the school is to help young people become effective and ethical citizens in a democracy. Democratic citizenship in any era is a complex task, but it seems especially difficult at this time when international conflicts and growing economic and social inequality are the rule and not the exception. The spirit of the New DEEL is toward a liberating education, enabling students to make intelligent and moral decisions as future citizens.

The mission of the New DEEL is to create an action-oriented partnership dedicated to inquiry into the nature and practice of democratic and ethical educational leadership through sustained processes of open dialogue, a right to voice, community inclusion, and responsible participation toward the common good. The group strives to create an environment to facilitate democratic ethical decision making in educational theory and practice that acts in the best interests of all students.

Moving Educational Leadership Forward

Changing the course of an academic field is a daunting prospect, yet one that New DEEL members are dedicated to attempt. In order to bring about such a sea change in educational leadership, six inter-related projects are currently underway. These include work on a code of ethics, curriculum design, research into critical areas such as student engagement, publication of new scholarly articles and texts, technology infrastructure, and the pursuit of funding opportunities.

As the New DEEL moves forward, those involved keep in their minds the profile of a very different type of educational leader. To be a school leader in the 21st century, additional skills are needed and a broader definition of leadership itself is required. To facilitate the emerging profile of this type of leader is to attempt to contrast the characteristics that the current movement, emphasizing control, promotes from those that sit more reasonably with the concepts of democracy and ethics. This distinction is illustrated in Table 11.1. Some clear distinctions are noticeable in this table between the traditional model of an educational leader and the one that is envisioned for the future. Included in the New DEEL perspective are the skills of community building, deep ethical understanding, and a theoretical and practical knowledge of turbulence driven by the internal desire to lead from an ever-expanding sense of mission and responsibility. While the traditional leader seeks to climb the existing power structure largely for the sake of greater power and prestige, the New DEEL leader may be at the top of a given system but is never satisfied with that. Rather, the goal is one of a transformed community through education that will likely include working through turbulent conditions and knotty ethical dilemmas. Whereas the traditional school leader shies away from such responsibilities, the New DEEL leader understands that these challenges are part of the work of leadership in our era and has a clear educational foundation for this reality. In sum, the traditional leader is a functionary of a system that is becoming ever more centralized, corporate, and removed from the influence of students, families, and communities. The New DEEL vision promotes democratic life and ethical reasoning growing from the heart of the community toward the wide world.

Ethical Leadership from the Heart

Moral leadership, therefore, is broader than traditional school management. It demands a deep investment of the genuine or authentic self of the educational leader. Moral leaders have the courage to locate their work in a broader as well as deeper space as they work to bring about societal transformation. (Dantley, 2005, p. 45)

Table 11.1 Comparison of the New DEEL Vision for Leaders with the Traditional Behaviors of School Leaders

New DEEL Vision for Leaders	Behavior of Traditional School Leaders
Transformational	**Transactional**
Guided by an inner sense of responsibility to students, families, the community and social development on a world scale	Driven by an exterior pressure of accountability to those above in the organizational/political hierarchy
Leads from an expansive community-building perspective	Bound by the system and the physical building
A democratic actor who understands when and how to shield the school from turbulence and when and how to use turbulence to facilitate change	A small part of a monolithic, more corporate structure
Integrates the concepts of democracy, social justice, and school reform through scholarship, dialogue, and action	Separates democracy and social justice from guiding vision and accepts school improvement (a subset of school reform) as the dominant perspective
Operates from a deep understanding of ethical decision making in the context of a dynamic, inclusive, democratic vision	Operates largely from perspective of the ethic of justice, wherein obedience to authority and current regulations are largely unquestioned despite one's own misgivings
Sees one's career as a calling and has a well-developed sense of mission toward democratic social improvement that cuts across political, national, class, gender, racial, ethnic, and religious boundaries	Sees one's career in terms of specific job titles with an aim to move to ever greater positions of perceived power within the current system's structure

Gross, 2005a.

What the New DEEL hopes to inspire is a focus on educational leadership and not educational management. One difference in creating these types of leaders is that they have been prepared, through the study of ethics, to appreciate a difficult paradox or inconsistency when they meet it, and then know how to deal with it in ways that are not purely managerial in nature, but instead are morally sound.

In this complex and chaotic era, to educate leaders and not just managers it is important that morality and ethics are at the center of educating leaders. The New DEEL treats ethical decision making seriously. Educational leaders need to know when they meet paradoxes, such as control versus democracy, and then must learn ways to solve or at least resolve them. Modeling rational and intuitive decision-making abilities is powerful as it is bound to have an effect on staff and students. Hopefully, at its best this type of decision making can lead over time to the societal transformation that Dantley mentions in the above quotation.

It is important to realize that ethical leadership is not always rational in a narrow, linear sense. There is a need for the type of leadership Sergiovani (1992) speaks of that is not just with the head and the hand but also with the heart. Emotions enter the picture where good leadership, not management, is concerned. It is important for leaders to be aware of their own emotions as well as other people's reactions, and know how to channel them appropriately.

This type of leadership takes into account issues of motivation and self-knowledge that are so much a part of Begley's (1999, 2004) "onion model" of educational leaders that places "self" at the center. This type of leadership should take into consideration Gross' (1998, 2004, 2006) Turbulence Theory, that asks leaders to gauge the level of turbulence when making an ethical decision, and to determine in advance if the decision that will be made will increase the level of turbulence or decrease it.

Ethical Leadership from the Head and the Hands

Not only does ethical leadership take into account emotions but it especially turns to the moral groundwork laid by Starratt (1991, 1994a) in his writings about ethical schools, and the thoughtful work of Noddings (1984, 1992) and Sernak (1998) on the ethic of care. It also takes into consideration the writings—for example, of Davis (2000, 2001), Shapiro and Purpel (2004), and Young, Petersen, & Short (2002)—who turn to the ethic of critique to highlight issues of social justice. In addition, this type of leadership relates well to the model of ethics that focuses on the ethics of justice, critique, care, and the profession (Shapiro & Stefkovich, 1997, 1998, 2001, 2005; Stefkovich & Shapiro 1994, 2003).

This type of leadership asks us to prepare individuals who can deal with the hard questions such as: What is the law? Is it appropriate in this particular ethical dilemma? Could the law be wrong? Who will I hurt by my decision? Who will I help? Above all, what is in the student's best interests? And finally, what happens if my decision is in the best interests of some students but not all?

Because this is leadership preparation, the ethic of the profession requires particular attention. In this ethic, students are placed at the center instead of focusing on budgets, efficiency, accountability, and control. It means that educational leaders will think of what is good for their students throughout the decision-making process.

Empirical Studies of Ethical or Moral Leadership

One major goal of the New DEEL is to carry out studies related to its theoretical underpinnings. With regard to ethical or moral leadership, the intent is to build on some of the current empirical investigations already in the literature (e.g., Friedman, 2003; Greenfield, 1991, 1995, 2004; Gronn, 1999; Marshall, 1992; Marshall et al., 1996; Reitzug, 1994) as well as carry out studies that focus on the use of the Multiple Ethical Paradigms and Turbulence Theory. In addition, a few of the New DEEL members have written about some current exemplars in the field (e.g., Aiken, 2005; Cate, 2005; Gross, 2005b; Sernak, 2005; Zaretsky, 2005). These stories of authentic and outstanding leaders should be helpful in providing ethical guidance for students in the field of educational administration.

However, a caveat to consider is that studying ethical leadership is far from easy at the best of times, and it is more difficult to do so during a paradoxical time; in this instance, we are part of an uncertain era that is trying to establish control over its schools. Nonetheless, it is clear from the studies that have been conducted thus far that positive values are an essential ingredient for the development of good educational leaders. Those engaged in the New DEEL hope to continue the investigative work in this area to gain better understandings and insights into the ethical responsibility of educational leaders.

The New DEEL: Control versus Democracy

The paradox of control versus democracy has become a bit more complex in public education in the United States at the beginning of the 21st century, but it is still very much with us. Kochan and Reed (2005) wrote:

> Recent trends in education suggest two possibilities: Either greater control will be exerted over public schools and schooling, or conversely, educational autonomy will be expanded in the form of charter and independent schools, which would be unfettered by external controls and perceived as an alternative to public education (Goldring & Greenfield, 2002). No matter what the requirements or configurations of schools, educational leaders in the public sector will likely face greater stresses and increased demands for the successful performance of all students and for outcomes established by governmental and community groups. (pp. 71–72)

Kochan and Reed (2005), in the above quote, point out that charter and independent schools may allow for some relaxation and freedom from external controls for public education. However, they also speak of the problems that educational leaders will still face because of increasing accountability.

The New DEEL (Gross & Shapiro, 2005) does not focus on restructuring some public schools by turning them into charters or independent institutions. Instead, this concept asks educational leaders to return to the historical mandate of the public schools to prepare citizens for participation in a democratic society. It also goes beyond that mandate by asking educational leaders to create schools that prepare all students to be thoughtful, caring, and even critical citizens who are able to make wise, ethical decisions.

The New DEEL, while innovative and broad in scope, still aligns well with Standard 5 in the Interstate Licensure Standards (ISLLC) that states: "A school administrator is an educational leader who promotes the success of all students by acting with integrity, fairness, and in an ethical manner" (ISLLC, 1996, p. 18). To meet this standard, an administrator—among other things—must: (a) possess a knowledge and understanding of various ethical frameworks and perspectives on ethics; (b) have a knowledge and understanding of professional codes of ethics; (c) believe in, value, and be committed to bringing ethical principles to the decision-making process; and (d) believe in, value, and be committed to developing a caring school community. While this standard is well written, it could go further by asking for more than a caring school community—which would be a fine start—but also for a democratic school community.

Conclusion

In this final chapter, the paradox of control versus democracy is illuminated. This profound contradiction highlights the ethical underpinnings of the New DEEL. It focuses on both the hierarchical management style and attribution of blame that are noticeable in this era of increasingly diverse forms of accountability in public education. It also speaks to the importance of creating more empowering and engaging experiences for young people through the use of deliberative democracy, as well as avoiding the back-to-basics curriculum that occurs because of high-stakes testing. In addition, this chapter considers the importance of leadership that emphasizes not just the head but also the hands and the heart. Knowing how to make sound ethical decisions, taking into account both the rational and emotional contexts, is essential for educational leaders, especially in this challenging time.

Scholarship, activism, and a powerful, positive vision for the future seem required ingredients if the ideals of the New DEEL are to take root and move educational leadership and education itself away from today's alienating values of control from above toward democratic-ethical community building around our world. It may be a daunting challenge but one that we believe educators can attain.

With the inconsistencies, complexities, and turbulence in this early part of the 21st century, it is imperative that those of us who prepare educational leaders keep a dialogue going to widen the discussion of democratic, ethical leadership so that we begin to have common understandings. This agreement should hopefully lead to implementation of the inherent ideas—that is, to develop educational leaders who are knowledgeable of diverse students and different communities, who are compassionate and supportive of their intellectual and emotional needs and their dreams, and who prepare them to be democratic and moral citizens.

REFERENCES

Aiken, J. (2002) "The socialization of new principals: Another perspective on principal retention." *Educational Leadership Review*, 3(1); 32–40.

Aiken, J. and Gerstl-Pepin, C. (2005) "The New DEEL: Democratic responsive practice for school leaders." Paper presented at the annual convention of the University Council of Educational Administration, Nashville, TN, November.

Alcoff, L. (1991) "The problem of speaking for others." *Cultural Critique*, 20; 5–32.

America 2000: An Education Strategy. (1991) Washington, DC: U.S. Government Printing Office.

American Association of School Administrators. (1981) "Statement of ethics for school administrators." Arlington, VA: American Association of School Administrators.

American Association of University Women. (1992) "How schools shortchange girls: A study of major findings on girls and education." Washington, DC: American Association of University Women Foundation.

American Association of University Women. (1995) "Achieving gender equity in the classroom and the campus: The next step." Washington, DC: American Association of University Women Foundation.

Apple, M. W. (1988) *Teachers and Texts: A Political Economy of Class and Gender Relations in Education.* New York: Routledge & Kegan Paul.

Apple, M. W. (2000) *Official Knowledge: Democratic Education in a Conservative Age.* New York: C. R. & Routledge Ashbaugh.

Apple, M. W. (2001) *Educating the "Right" Way: Markets, Standards, God, and Inequality.* New York: Routledge Falmer.

Apple, M. W. (2003) *The State and the Politics of Knowledge.* New York: Routledge Falmer.

Astuto, T. A., Clark, D. L., and Read, A. M. (eds.) (1994) *Roots of Reform: Challenging the Assumptions that Control Education.* Bloomington, IN: Phi Delta Kappa Education Foundation.

Bakhtin, M. (1981) *The Dialogic Imagination.* Austin, TX: University of Texas Press.

Banks, J. A. (2001) *Cultural Diversity and Education: Foundations, Curriculum and Teaching* (4th ed.). Boston: Allyn & Bacon.

Barth, R. J. (1990) *Improving Schools from Within: Teachers, Parents, and Principals Can Make the Difference.* San Francisco: Jossey-Bass.

Beauchamp, T. L., and Childress, J. F. (1984) "Morality, ethics and ethical theories." In P. Sola (ed.), *Ethics, Education, and Administrative Decisions: A Book of Readings.* New York: Peter Lang.

Beck, L. G. (1994) *Reclaiming Educational Administration as a Caring Profession.* New York: Teachers' College Press.

Beck, L. G., and Murphy, J. (1994a) *Ethics in Educational Leadership Programs: An Expanding Role.* Thousand Oaks, CA: Corwin Press.

Beck L. G., and Murphy, J. (1994b) "A deeper analysis: Examining courses devoted to ethics." Paper presented at the annual meeting of the American Educational Research Association, New Orleans, April 6.

Beck, L. G., Murphy, J., and Associates (1997) *Ethics in Educational Leadership Programs: Emerging Models.* Columbia, MO: The University Council for Educational Administration.

Beckner, W. (2004) *Ethics for Educational Leaders.* Boston: Pearson Education.

Begley, P. T. (ed.) (1999) *Values and Educational Leadership.* Albany, NY: State University of New York Press.

Begley, P. T., and Johansson, O. (1998) "The values of school administration: Preferences, ethics, and conflicts." *Journal of School Leadership,* July 9(4); 399–422.

Begley, P. T., and Johansson, O. (eds.) (2003) *The Ethical Dimensions of School Leadership.* Boston: Kluwer Academic Publishers.

Begley, P. T., and Zaretsky, L. (2004) "Democratic school leadership in Canada's public school systems: Professional value and social ethic." *Journal of Educational Administration,* 42(6).

Belenky, M. F., Clinchy, B. M., Goldberger, N. R., and Tarule, J. M. (1986) *Women's Ways of Knowing.* New York: Basic Books.

Blackburn, S. (2001) *Being Good: A Short Introduction to Ethics.* Oxford: Oxford University Press.

Blackburn, S. (2006) Personal communication, February 1.

Board of Education, Island Trees Union Free School District No. 26 v. Pico, 457 U.S. 853 (1981).

Bolman, L. G., and Deal, T. E. (1991) *Reframing Organizations: Artistry, Choice, and Leadership.* San Francisco: Jossey-Bass.

Bourdieu, P. (1977) "Cultural reproduction and social reproduction." In J. Karabel and A. H. Halsey (eds.), *Power and Ideology in Education.* New York: Oxford.

Bourdieu, P. (2001) *Masculine Domination.* Stanford, CA: Stanford University Press.

Bowles, S., and Gintis, H. (1988) *Democracy and Capitalism.* New York: Basic Books.

Boyd, W. L. (2000) "The r's of school reform and the politics of reforming or replacing public schools." *Journal of Educational Change*, 1(3); 225–252.

Braybrook, R. (1985) *The Aircraft Encyclopedia*. New York: Simon and Schuster.

Brown, G. T. (2000) "Dempsey concerned that escalating athletics costs contradict educational mission." *NCAA News Online*. http://www.ncaa.org/news/2000/20001023/active/3722n06.html

Burford, C. (2004) "Ethical dilemmas and the lives of leaders: An Australian perspective on the search for the moral." 9th Annual Values and Leadership Conference. Christ Church, Barbardos, October.

Buber, M. (1965) "Education." In M. Buber (ed.), *Between Man and Man*. New York: Macmillan.

Cambron-McCabe, N. H., and Foster, W. (1994) "A paradigm shift: Implications for the preparation of school leaders." In T. Mulkeen, N. H. Cambron-McCabe, and B. Anderson (eds.), *Democratic Leadership: The Changing Context of Administrative Preparation*. Norwood, NJ: Ablex.

Campbell, E. (2004) *The Ethical Teacher*. Maidenhead, UK: Open University Press.

Camus, A. (1957) *The Fall*. New York: Knopf.

Capper, C. A. (1993) "Educational administration in a pluralistic society: A multiparadigm approach." In C. A. Capper (ed.), *Educational Administration in a Pluralistic Society*. Albany, NY: State University of New York Press.

Carnoy, M., and Levin, H. (1985) *Schooling and Work in the Democratic State*. Stanford, CA: Stanford University Press.

Cate, J. (2005) "A democratic principled leader." Paper presented at the annual convention of the University Council of Educational Administration, Nashville, November.

Collins, P. H. (1997) "Comment on Hedeman's 'The truth and method: Feminist standpoint theory revisited:' Where's the power?" *Signs*, (22)2; 375–381.

Counts, G. S. (1932) *Dare the Schools Build a New Social Order?* Carbondale, IL: Southern Illinois University Press.

Crow, G. (2006) "Democracy and educational work in an age of complexity." *UCEA Review*, XLVIII(1); 1–5.

Cushner, K., McClelland, A., and Safford, P. (1992) *Human Diversity in Education: An Integrative Approach*. New York: McGraw-Hill.

Dantley, M. E. (2005) "Moral leadership: Shifting the management paradigm." In F. W. English (ed.), *The Sage Handbook of Educational Leadership: Advances in Theory, Research, and Practice*. Thousand Oaks, CA: Sage Publications.

Darling-Hammond, L. (2000) "How teacher education matters." *Journal of Teacher Education*, 51(3); 166–173.

Darling-Hammond, L., Chung, R., and Frelow, F. (2002) "Variation in teacher preparation." *Journal of Teacher Education*, 53(4); 286–302.

Darling-Hammond, L., and Snyder, J. (1992) "Reframing accountability: Creating learner-centered schools." In A. Lieberman (ed.), *The Changing Contexts of Teaching*. 91st Yearbook of the National Society for the Study of Education, Pt. 1. Chicago: National Society for the Study of Education.

Davis, J. E. (2000) "Mothering for manhood: The (Re)production of a black son's gendered self." In M. C. Brown II and J. E. Davis (eds.), *Black Sons to Mothers: Compliments, Critiques, and Challenges for Cultural Workers in Education*. New York: Peter Lang.

Davis, J. E. (2001) "Transgressing the masculine: African American boys and the failure of schools." In W. Martino and B. Meyenn (eds.), *What About the Boys?* Philadelphia: Open University Press.

Delgado, R. (1995) *Critical Race Theory: The Cutting Edge*. Philadelphia: Temple University Press.

Dewey, J. (1902) *The School and Society*. Chicago: University of Chicago Press.

Dewey, J. (1903) *Democracy and Education*. New York: The Free Press.

Dewey, J. (1916) *Democracy and Education: An Introduction to the Philosophy of Education*. New York: The Macmillan Company.

Dewey, J., and Dewey, E. (1962) *Schools of Tomorrow*. New York: E. P. Dutton & Company.

Donaldson, G. A. (2001) *Cultivating Leadership in Schools: Connecting People, Purpose, and Practice*. New York: Teachers College Press.

Driscoll, M. E. (2001) "The sense of place and the neighborhood school: Implications for building social capital and for community development." In R. Crowson (ed.), *Community Development and School Reform*. New York: JAI/Elsevier.

Duke, D., and Grogan, M. (1997) "The moral and ethical dimensions of leadership." In L. G. Beck, J. Murphy, and Associates (eds.), *Ethics in Educational Leadership Programs: Emerging Models*. Columbia, MO: University Council for Educational Administration.

Elmore, R. F. (2000) *Building a New Structure for School Leadership*. Washington, DC: Albert Shanker Institute.

Emerson, R. W. (1993) *Self-Reliance and Other Essays*. New York: Dover Publications.

Foster, W. (1986) *Paradigms and Promises: New Approaches to Educational Administration*. Buffalo, NY: Prometheus Books.

Foucault, M. (1983) "On the genealogy of ethics: An overview of work in progress." In H. L. Dreyfus and P. Rabinow (eds.), *Michel Foucault: Beyond Structuralism and Hermeneutics* (2nd ed.). Chicago: University of Chicago Press.

Freire, P. (1970) *Pedagogy of the Oppressed* (M. B. Ramos, trans.). New York: Continuum.

Friedman, I. A. (2003) "School organizational values: The driving force for effectiveness and change." In P. T. Begley and O. Johansson (eds.), *The Ethical Dimensions of School Leadership.* (pp.161–179.) Boston: Kluwer Academic Press.

Fullan, M. G. (2001) *Leading in a Culture of Change.* San Francisco: Jossey-Bass.

Furman, G. C. (2003a) "The 2002 UCEA presidential address: Toward a new scholarship of educational leadership." *UCEA Review,* 45(1); 1–6.

Furman, G. (2003b) "Moral leadership and the ethic of the community." *Values and Ethics in Educational Administration,* 2(1): 1–8.

Furman, G. C. (2004) "The ethic of community." *Journal of Educational Administration,* 42; 215–235.

Furman-Brown, G. (ed.) (2002) *School as Community: From Promise to Practice.* New York: SUNY Press.

Gardner, H. (1993) *Frames of Mind: The Theory of Multiple Intelligences.* New York: Basic Books.

Gilligan, C. (1982) *In a Different Voice.* Cambridge, MA: Harvard University Press.

Gilligan, C., Ward, J., and Taylor, J. (1988) *Mapping the Moral Domain: A Contribution of Women's Thinking to Psychology and Education.* Cambridge, MA: Harvard University Graduate School of Education.

Ginsberg, A. E., Shapiro, J. P., and Brown, S. P. (2004) *Gender in Urban Education: Strategies for Student Achievement.* Portsmouth, NH: Heinemann.

Giroux, H. A. (1988) *Schooling and the Struggle for Public Life: Critical Pedagogy in the Modern Age.* Minneapolis, MN: University of Minnesota Press.

Giroux, H. A. (ed.) (1991) *Postmodernism, Feminism, and Cultural Politics: Redrawing Educational Boundaries.* Albany, NY: State University of New York Press.

Giroux, H. A. (1994) "Educational leadership and school administrators: Rethinking the meaning of democratic public culture." In T. Mulkeen, N. H. Cambron-McCabe, and B. Anderson (eds.), *Democratic Leadership: The Changing Context of Administrative Preparation.* Norwood, NJ: Ablex.

Giroux, H. A. (2000) *Stealing Innocence: Youth, Corporate Power, and the Politics of Culture.* New York: St. Martin's Press.

Giroux, H. A. (2003) *The Abandoned Generation: Democracy beyond the Culture of Fear.* New York: Palgrave MacMillan.

Giroux, H. A., and Aronowitz, S. (1985) *Education under Siege.* South Hadley, MA: Bergin & Garvey.

Glaser, B. G., and Strauss, A. L. (1967) *The Discovery of Grounded Theory: Strategies for Qualitative Research.* Chicago: Aldine Publishing Company.

Glickman, C. D. (2002) *Leadership for Learning: How to Help Teachers Succeed.* Alexandria, VA: Association of Supervision and Curriculum Development.

Goals 2000: Educate America Act. (1993) Washington, DC: U.S. Government Printing Office.

Gold, E., and Simon, E. (2004) "Public accountability: School improvement efforts need the active involvement of communities to succeed." *Education Week,* XXIII(11), January 14.

Goldberger, N., Tarule, J., Clinchy, B., and Belenky, M. (eds.) (1996) *Knowledge, Difference and Power.* New York: Basic Books.

Goldman, E. (1970) *My Disillusionment in Russia.* New York: Thomas Y. Crowell Company.

Goldring, E., and Greenfield, W. (2002) "Understanding the evolving concept of leadership in education: Roles, expectations, and dilemmas." In J. Murphy (ed.), *The Educational Leadership Challenge: Redefining Leadership for the 21st Century.* 101st Yearbook of the National Society for the Study of Education. Chicago: University of Chicago Press.

Goleman, D. (1995) *Emotional Intelligence: Why It Can Matter More than IQ.* New York: Bantam.

Gollnick, D. M. and Chinn, P. C. (1998). *Multicultural Education in a Pluralistic Society* (5th ed.). Columbus, OH: Merrill.

Goodlad, J. I., Soder, R., and Sirotnik, K. A. (eds.) (1990) *The Moral Dimension of Teaching.* San Francisco: Jossey-Bass.

Greene, M. (1988) *The Dialectic of Freedom.* New York: Teachers College Press.

Greenfield, W. D. (1991) "The micropolitics of leadership in an urban elementary school." In J. Blasé (ed.), *The Politics of Life in Schools: Power, Conflict, and Cooperation.* (pp.161–184). Newbury Park, CA: Sage.

Greenfield, W. D. (1993) "Articulating values and ethics in administrator preparation." In C. Capper (ed.), *Educational Administration in a Pluralistic Society.* Albany, NY: State University of New York Press.

Greenfield, W. D. (1995) "Toward a theory of school administration: The centrality of leadership." *Educational Administration Quarterly,* 31(1); 61–85.

Greenfield, W.D. (2004) "Moral leadership in schools." *Journal of Educational Administration,* 42(2); 174–196.

Grogan, M. (1996) *Voices of Women Aspiring to the Superintendency.* Albany, NY: State University of New York Press.

Gronn, P. (1999) "Leadership from a distance: Institutionalizing values and forming character at Timbertop." In P. T. Begley and P. Leonard (eds.), *The Values of Educational Administration.* (pp. 140–167). London: Falmer Press.

Gross, S. J. (1998) *Staying Centered: Curriculum Leadership in a Turbulent Era.* Alexandria, VA: Association for Supervision and Curriculum Development.

Gross, S. J. (2000) "From turbulence to tidal wave: Understanding the unraveling of reform at one innovative and diverse urban elementary school for children at risk." Northeast Educational Research Association Annual Conference, Ellenville, NY, October.

Gross, S. J. (2004) *Promises Kept: Sustaining Innovative Curriculum Leadership.* Alexandria, VA: Association of Supervision and Curriculum Development.

Gross, S. J. (2005a) "Building the case for a New DEEL: Democratic-ethical educational leadership and the future of our profession." Paper presented at the UCEA Convention 2005, Nashville, TN, November 12.

Gross, S. J. (2005b) "New DEEL leadership at the district level: Taking responsibility to create greater local, state and national democracy from the superintendent's office." Paper presented at the annual convention of the University Council of Educational Administration, Nashville, TN, November.

Gross, S. J. (2006) *Leadership Mentoring: Maintaining School Improvement in Turbulent Times.* Lanham, MA: Rowman & Littlefield.

Gross, S. J., and Shapiro, J. P. (2002) "Towards ethically responsible leadership in a new era of high stakes accountability." In G. Perrault and F. Lunenberg (eds.), *The Changing World of School Administration.* Lanham, MD: Scarecrow Press.

Gross, S. J., and Shapiro, J. P. (2005) "Our new era requires a New DEEL: Towards democratic ethical educational leadership." *UCEA Review,* 1–4.

Gross, S. J., Shaw, K., and Shapiro, J. P. (2003) "Deconstructing accountability through the lens of democratic philosophies: Toward a new analytic framework." *Journal of Research for Educational Leadership,* 1(3); 5–27.

Gryskiewicz, S. S. (1999) *Positive Turbulence: Developing Climates for Creativity, Innovation, and Renewal.* San Francisco: Jossey-Bass.

Guiney, E. (2001) "Coaching isn't just for athletes: The role of teacher leaders." *Phi Delta Kappan,* 82(10); 740–743.

Guthrie, J. W. (1990) "The evolution of educational management: Eroding myths and emerging models." In B. Mitchell & L. Cunningham (eds.), *Educational Leadership and Changing Contexts of Families, Communities, and Schools: Eighty-ninth Yearbook of the National Society for the Study of Education* (pp. 210–231). Chicago: University of Chicago Press.

Gutmann, A. (1999) *Democratic Education.* Princeton, NJ: Princeton University Press.

Gutmann, A., and Thompson, D. (2004) *Why Deliberative Democracy?* Princeton, NJ: Princeton University Press.

Ha, J. (2002) *The Crazed.* New York: Pantheon Books.

Haladyna, T. M., Nolen, S. B., and Haas, N. C. (1991) "Raising standardized achievement test scores and the origins of test score pollution." *Educational Researcher*, 20(5); 2–7.

Hansen, D. T. (2001) "Teaching as a moral activity." In V. Richardson (ed.), *Handbook of Research on Teaching* (4th ed.). Washington, DC: American Educational Research Association.

Hart, A. W. (1994a) "Creating teacher leadership roles." *Educational Administration Quarterly*, 30(4); 472–479.

Hart, A. W. (1994b) "Work feature values of today's and tomorrow's teachers: Work redesign as an incentive and school improvement policy." *Educational Evaluation and Policy Analysis*. 16(4); 458–473.

Hauser, M. E. (1997) "How do we really work? A response to 'Locked in uneasy sisterhood: Reflections on feminist methodology and research relationships.'" *Anthropology & Education Quarterly*. (28)1; 123–126.

Hazelwood School District et al. v. Kuhlmeier et al. (No. 86-836) Supreme Court of the United States, 484 U.S. 260, January 13 (1988), Decided.

Hegel, G. W. F. (1892) *The Logic of Hegel*. Oxford: Clarendon

Hersh, R. H., Paolitto, D. P., and Reimer, J. (1979) *Promoting Moral Growth: From Piaget to Kohlberg*. New York: Longman.

Holm, L., and Horn, C. (2003) "Priming schools of education for today's teachers." *Education Digest*, 68(7); 25–32.

Homer-Dixon, T. (2000) *The Ingenuity Gap*. New York: Knopf.

Hostetler, K. D. (1997) *Ethical Judgment in Teaching*. Boston: Allyn & Bacon.

Hyman, I. A., and Snook, P. A. (1999) *Dangerous Schools: What We Can Do about the Physical and Emotional Abuse of Our Children*. San Francisco: Jossey-Bass.

Interstate School Leaders Licensure Consortium (ISLLC). (1996) *Standards for School Leaders*. Washington, DC: ISLLC.

Jacquelin, N. (2002) "What in God's name?" Paper presented at The Toronto Conference, the 7th Annual Values and Leadership Conference, OISE/University of Toronto, October 3–5.

Katzenmeyer, M., and Moller, G. (2001) *Awakening the Sleeping Giant: Helping Teachers Develop as Leaders* (2nd ed.). Thousand Oaks, CA: Corwin.

Keith, N. Z. (1999) "Whose community schools? Discourses, old patterns." *Theory into Practice*, 38(4); 225–234.

Keith, N. Z. (2005) "Community service learning in the face of globalization: Rethinking theory and practice." *Michigan Journal of Community Service Learning*, 11(2); 5–24, Spring.

Keller, B. (2003) "Snapshot of 'highly qualified' teachers is fuzzy." *Education Week*, 23(2); 24–26.

Kennedy, J. F. (1956) *Profiles in Courage*. New York: Harper Perennial.

Kezar, A. (2000) "Pluralistic leadership: Incorporating diverse voices." *Journal of Higher Education*, 71(6); 722–743.

Kliebard, H. M. (1987) *The Struggle for the American Curriculum: 1893–1958*. New York: Routledge & Kegan Paul.

Kochan, F. K., and Reed, C. J. (2005) "Collaborative leadership, community building, and democracy in public education." In F. W. English (ed.), *The Sage Handbook of Educational Leadership: Advances in Theory, Research, and Practice*. Thousand Oaks, CA: Sage Publications.

Koetsier, C. P., and Wubbels, J. T. (1995) "Bridging the gap between initial teacher training and teacher induction." *Journal of Education for Teaching*, 21(3); 13–23.

Kohl, H. (1991) *I Won't Learn from You: The Role of Assent in Learning*. Minneapolis, MN: Milkweed Editions.

Kohlberg, L. (1981) *The Philosophy of Moral Development: Moral Stages and the Idea of Justice* (Vol. 1). San Francisco: Harper & Row.

Koopman, O., Miel, A., and Misner, P. (1943) *Democracy in School Administration*. New York: Appleton-Century.

Kruse, S. D., and Louis, K. S. (1997) "Teachers' reflective work: School based support structures." *Educational Administration Quarterly*, 33(3); 261–289.

Kurlansky, M. (2004) *1968: The Year that Rocked the World*. New York: Ballantine Books.

Lareau, A. (1987) "Social class differences in family school relationships: The importance of cultural capital." *Sociology of Education*, 60; 73–85.

Lareau, A. (2003) *Unequal Childhoods: Class, Race and Family Life*. Berkeley, CA: University of California Press.

Larson, C., and Murtadha, K. (2002) "Leadership for social justice." In J. Murphy (ed.), *The Educational Leadership Challenge: Redefining Leadership for the 21st Century*. Chicago: University of Chicago Press.

Lebacqz, K. (1985) *Professional Ethics: Power and Paradox*. Nashville, TN: Abingdon.

Leithwood, K. (2001) "School leadership in the context of accountability policies." *International Journal of Leadership in Education*, 4(3); 217–236.

Lester, P. F. (1994) *Turbulence: A New Perspective for Pilots*. Englewood, CO: Jeppesen.

Lewin, K. (1947) "Frontiers in group dynamics II." *Human Relations*, Vol. 1; 443–453.

Marshall, C. (1992) "School administrator's values: A focus on 'atypicals'." *Educational Administration Quarterly*, 28(3); 368–386.

Marshall, C., Patterson, J. A., Rogers, D. L. and Steele, J. R. (1996) "Caring as career: An alternative perspective for educational administration." *Educational Administration Quarterly*, 32(2); 271–294.

McKee, A. (1982) *Dresden 1945: The Devil's Tinderbox.* New York: E. P. Duffon.

McNeil, L. M. (2000) *Contradictions of School Reform: Educational Costs of Standardized Testing.* New York: Routledge.

Maher, F.A., and Tetreault, M. K. (1993) "Frames of positionality: Meaningful dialogues about gender and race." *Anthropological Quarterly*, 62(3); 118–126.

Maher, F. A., and Tetreault, M. K. T. (1994) *The Feminist Classroom.* New York: Basic Books.

Marshall, C. (1995) "Imagining leadership." *Educational Administration Quarterly*, 31(3); 484–492.

Mertz, N. T. (1997) "Knowing and doing: Exploring the ethical life of educational leaders." In L. G. Beck, J. Murphy, and Associates (eds.), *Ethics in Educational Leadership Programs: Emerging Models.* Columbia, MO: University Council for Educational Administration.

Mezirow, J. (1991) *Transformative Dimensions of Adult Learning.* San Francisco: Jossey-Bass.

Mitra, D. L. (2004) "The significance of students: Can increasing 'student voice' in schools lead to gains in youth development?" *Teachers College Record*, 106(4); 651–688.

Morgan, G. (1997) *Images of Organization* (2nd ed.). Thousand Oaks, CA: Sage Publications.

Nash, R. J. (1996) *"Real World" Ethics: Frameworks for Educators and Human Service Professionals.* New York: Teachers College Press.

National Commission on Excellence in Education (1983). *A Nation at Risk: The Imperative for Educational Reform.* Washington, DC: U.S. Government Printing Office.

Neufeld, B., and Roper, D. (2003) *Coaching: A Strategy for Developing Instructional Capacity.* Aspen, CO: Aspen Institute Program on Education.

No Child Left Behind Act of 2001. Pub. L. No. 107-110, 115 Stat. 1425, codified as amended at 20 U.S.C. 6301 et. seq. (2002).

Noddings, N. (1984) *Caring: A Feminine Approach to Ethics and Moral Education.* Berkeley: University of California Press.

Noddings, N. (1992) *The Challenge to Care in Schools: An Alternative Approach to Education*. New York: Teachers College Press.

Noddings, N. (1999) "Care, justice and equity." In M. S. Katz, N. Noddings, and K. A. Strike (eds.), *Justice and Caring: The Search for Common Ground in Education*. New York: Teachers College Press.

Noddings, N. (2002) *Educating Moral People: A Caring Alternative to Character Education*. New York: Teachers College Press.

Noddings, N. (2003) *Caring: A Feminine Approach to Ethics and Moral Education* (2nd ed.). Berkeley, CA: University of California Press.

Normore, A. H. (2004) "Ethics and values in leadership preparation programs: Finding the North Star in the dust storm." *Values and Ethics in Educational Administration*, 2(2); 1–8.

Oakes, J. (1993) "Tracking, inequality, and the rhetoric of reform: Why schools don't change." In S. H. Shapiro and D. E. Purpel (eds.), *Critical Social Issues in American Education: Toward the 21st Century*. White Plains, NY: Longman.

O'Hair, M. J., McLaughlin, H. J., and Reitzug, U. C. (2000) *Foundations of Democratic Education*. Cambridge, MA: Thomson Wadsworth.

O'Keefe, J. (1997) "Preparing ethical leaders for equitable schools." In L. G. Beck, J. Murphy, and Associates (eds.), *Ethics in Educational Leadership Programs: Emerging Models*. Columbia, MO: University Council for Educational Administration.

Orwell, G. (1992) *1984*. New York: Signet.

Paige, R. (2003) "Guidance on constitutionally protected prayer in public elementary and secondary schools," *ERIC*, February, #ED475823, 3.

Parker, L., and Shapiro, J. P. (1993) "The context of educational administration and social class." In C. A. Capper (ed.), *Educational Administration in a Pluralistic Society*. Albany, NY: State University of New York Press.

Pennsylvania Code of Professional Practice and Conduct for Educators, 22 Pa.Code, §§ 235.1–235.11 (1992).

People v. Dukes, 580 N.Y.S. 2d 850, New York Criminal Court (1992).

Poglinco, S. M., Bach, A. J., Hovde, K., Rosenblum, S., Saunders, M., and Supovitz, J. A. (2003) *The Heart of the Matter: The Coaching Model in America's Choice Schools*. Philadelphia: CPRE.

Purpel, D. E. (1989) *The Moral and Spiritual Crisis in Education: A Curriculum for Justice and Compassion in Education*. New York: Bergin & Garvey.

Purpel, D. E. (2004) *Reflections on the Moral and Spiritual Crisis of Education*. New York: Peter Lang.

Purpel, D. E., and Shapiro, S. (1995) *Beyond Liberation and Excellence: Reconstructing the Public Discourse on Education*. Westport, CT: Bergin & Garvey.

Rapp, D. (2002) "Social justice and the importance of rebellious oppositional imaginations." *Journal of School Leadership*, 12; 226–245.

Rawls, J. (1971) *A Theory of Justice*. Cambridge, MA: Harvard University Press.

Reitzug, U. C. (1994) "A case study of empowering principal behavior." *American Educational Research Journal*, 31(2); 283–307.

Reitzug, U. C., and O'Hair, M. J. (2002) "From conventional school to democratic school community: The dilemmas of teaching and leading." In G. Furman-Brown (ed.), *School as Community: From Promise to Practice*. New York: SUNY Press.

Riesman, D. (1953) *The Lonely Crowd: A Study of Changing American Culture*. Garden City, NY: Doubleday.

Roland Martin, J. (1993) "Becoming educated: A journey of alienation or integration?" In S. H. Shapiro and D. E. Purpel (eds.), *Critical Social Issues in American Education: Toward the 21st Century*. White Plains, NY: Longman.

Roosevelt, A. E. (1963) *Tomorrow Is Now*. New York: Harper & Row.

Sarason, S. B. (1990) *The Predictable Failure of Educational Reform: Can We Change Course before It's Too Late?* San Francisco: Jossey-Bass

Scheurich, J. J., Skrla, L., and Johnson, J. F. (2000) "Thinking carefully about equity and accountability." *Phi Delta Kappan*, 82(4); 293–299.

Schlesinger, A. (1991) *The Disuniting of America: Reflections on a Multicultural Society*. New York: W. W. Norton & Company.

Senge, P. (1990) *The Fifth Discipline*. New York: Doubleday.

Sergiovanni, T. J. (1992) *Moral Leadership: Getting to the Heart of School Improvement*. San Francisco: Jossey-Bass.

Sernak, K. (1998) *School Leadership—Balancing Power with Caring*. New York: Teachers College Press.

Sernak, K. (2005) "The realities and risks of democratic ethical leadership: Toward Dewey's creative democracy." Paper presented at the annual convention of the University Council of Educational Administration, Nashville, TN, November.

Sewell, T. E., DuCette, J. P., and Shapiro, J. P. (1998) "Educational assessment and diversity." In N. M. Lambert and B. L. McCombs (eds.), *How Students Learn: Reforming Schools through Learner-Centered Education*. Washington, DC: American Psychological Association.

Shapiro, H. S. (2006) *Losing Heart: The Moral and Spiritual Miseducation of America's Children*. Mahwah, NJ: Lawrence Erlbaum.

Shapiro, H. S., and Purpel, D. E. (eds.) (1993) *Critical Social Issues in American Education: Toward the 21st Century.* New York: Longman.

Shapiro, H. S., and Purpel, D. E. (eds.) (1998) *Social Issues in American Education: Transformation in a Postmodern World.* Mahwah, NJ: Erlbaum Associates.

Shapiro, H. S., and Purpel, D. E. (eds.) (2004) *Critical Social Issues in American Education: Democracy and Meaning in a Globalizing World* (3rd ed.). Mahwah, NJ: Lawrence Erlbaum.

Shapiro, J. P. (1979) "Accountability—A Contagious Disease?" *Forum: For the Discussion of New Trends in Education,* 22(1); 16–18.

Shapiro, J. P. (2005) "Control versus democracy: A paradox at the center of democratic ethical educational leadership (New DEEL)." Paper presented at the UCEA Convention, Nashville, TN, November.

Shapiro, J. P. (2006) "Ethical decision making in turbulent time: Bridging theory with practice to prepare authentic educational leaders." *Values and Ethics in Educational Administration,* 4(2); 1–8.

Shapiro, J. P., Ginsberg, A. E. and Brown, S. P. (2003). "The ethic of care in urban schools: Family and community involvement." *Leading & Managing,* 9(2); 45–50.

Shapiro, J. P. and Gross, S. J. (2002) "Understanding educational leadership in a time of turbulence." The University Council of Educational Administration Annual Convention, Pittsburgh, PA, October.

Shapiro, J. P., Sewell, T. E., and DuCette, J. P. (2002) *Reframing Diversity in Education.* Lanham, MD: Rowman & Littlefield.

Shapiro, J. P., Sewell, T. E., DuCette, J., and Myrick, H. (1997) "Socio-cultural and school factors in achievement: Lessons from tuition guarantee programs." Paper presented at the annual meeting of the American Educational Research Association, Chicago, March.

Shapiro, J. P., and Smith-Rosenberg, C. (1989) "The 'other voices' in contemporary ethical dilemmas: The value of the new scholarship on women in the teaching of ethics." *Women's Studies International Forum,* 12(2); 199–211.

Shapiro, J. P., and Stefkovich, J. A. (1997) "The ethics of justice, critique and care: Preparing educational administrators to lead democratic and diverse schools." In J. Murphy, L. G. Beck, and Associates (eds.), *Ethics in Educational Administration: Emerging Models.* Columbia, MO: University Council for Educational Administration.

Shapiro, J. P., and Stefkovich, J. A. (1998) "Dealing with dilemmas in a morally polarized era: The conflicting ethical codes of educational leaders." *Journal for a Just and Caring Education,* 4(2); 117–141.

Shapiro, J. P., and Stefkovich, J. A. (2001) *Ethical Leadership and Decision Making in Education: Applying Theoretical Perspectives to Complex Dilemmas.* Mahwah, NJ: Lawrence Erlbaum Associates.

Shapiro, J. P., and Stefkovich, J. A. (2005) *Ethical Leadership and Decision Making in Education: Applying Theoretical Perspectives to Complex Dilemmas* (2nd ed.). Mahwah, NJ: Lawrence Erlbaum Associates.

Shapiro, S. (1999) *Pedagogy and the Politics of the Body.* New York: Garland.

Shen, J. (2002) "Student teaching in the context of a school university partnership: A case study of a student teacher." *Education,* 122(3); 564–580.

Skrla, L., Scheurich, J. J., and Johnson, J. F. (2000) *Equity-Driven, Achievement-Focused School Districts.* Austin, TX: Charles A. Dana Center.

Sleeter, C. E., and Grant, C. A. (2003) *Making Choices for Multicultural Education: Five Approaches to Race, Class, and Gender* (4th ed.). New York: J. Wiley & Sons.

Spady, W. G. (1988) "Organizing for results: The basis of authentic restructuring and reform." *Educational Leadership,* 46(2); 4–8.

Spillane, J., Halverson, R., and Diamond, J. B. (2001) "Investigating school leadership practice: A distributed perspective." *Educational Researcher,* 30(3); 23–28.

Starratt, R. J. (1991) "Building an ethical school: A theory for practice in educational leadership." *Educational Administration Quarterly,* 27(2); 185–202.

Starratt, R. J. (1994a) *Building an Ethical School.* London: Falmer Press.

Starratt, R. J. (1994b) "Afterword." In L. G. Beck and J. Murphy (eds.), *Ethics in Educational Leadership Programs: An Expanding Role.* Thousand Oaks, CA: Corwin Press.

Starratt, R. J. (1994c) "Preparing administrators for ethical practice: State of the art." Paper presented at the annual meeting of the American Educational Research Association, New Orleans, April.

Starratt, R. J. (2003) *Centering Educational Administration: Cultivating Meaning, Community, Responsibility.* Mahwah, NJ: Lawrence Erlbaum Associates.

Starratt, R. J. (2004) *Ethical Leadership.* San Francisco: Jossey-Bass.

Stefkovich, J. A. (2006) *Applying Ethical Constructs to Legal Cases: The Best Interests of the Student.* Mahwah, NJ: Lawrence Erlbaum Associates.

Stefkovich, J. A., and Guba, G. J. (1998) "School violence, school reform, and the Fourth Amendment in public schools." *International Journal of Educational Reform,* 7(3); 217–225.

Stefkovich, J. A., and O'Brien, G. J. (2000) "Students' Fourth Amendment rights and school officials' responsibilities: Implications for law and practice." *Thresholds in Education,* 20.

Stefkovich, J. A., and O'Brien, G. M. (2004) "Best interests of the student: An ethical model." *Journal of Educational Administration*, 42(2); 197–214.

Stefkovich, J. A., O'Brien, G. M., and Moore, J. (2002) "School leaders ethical decision making and the 'best interests of students.'" Paper presented at the 7th Annual Values and Leadership Conference, Toronto, Canada, October.

Stefkovich, J. A., and Shapiro, J. P. (1994) "Personal and professional ethics for educational administrators." *Review Journal of Philosophy and Social Science*, 20(1–2); 157–186.

Stefkovich, J. A., and Shapiro, J. P. (2003) "Deconstructing communities: Educational leaders and their ethical decision-making processes." In P. Begley and O. Johansson (eds.), *The Ethical Dimensions of School Leadership*. Dordrecht, The Netherlands: Kluwer Academic Publishers.

Strike, K. A. (1991) "The moral role of schooling in liberal democratic society." In G. Grant (ed.), *Review of Research in Education*. Washington, DC: American Educational Research Association.

Strike, K. A. (1999) "Justice, caring, and universality: In defense of moral pluralism." In M. S. Katz, N. Noddings, and K. A. Strike (eds.), *Justice and Caring: The Search for Common Ground in Education*. New York: Teachers College Press.

Strike, K. A., Haller, E. J., and Soltis, J. F. (1998) *The Ethics of School Administration* (2nd ed.). New York: Teachers College Press.

Strike, K. A., Haller, E. J., and Soltis, J. F. (2005) *The Ethics of School Administration* (3rd ed.). New York: Teachers College Press.

Strike, K. A., and Ternasky, P. L. (eds.) (1993) *Ethics for Professionals in Education: Perspectives for Preparation and Practice*. New York: Teachers College Press.

Suggs, W. (2000) "Knight commission asks, have conditions in college sports gotten better, or worse?" *Chronicle of Higher Education*, posted with permission on http://www.collegevalues.org, September.

Texas Administrative Code, Title 19, § 177.1 (1998).

Thoreau, H. D. (1964) *Walden and On the Duty of Civil Disobedience*. New York: Holt, Rinehart, & Winston.

Tigchelaar, A., and Korthagen, F. (2004) "Deepening the exchange of student teaching experiences: Implications for the pedagogy of teacher education of recent insights into teacher behavior." *Teaching and Teacher Education*, 20(7); 665–679.

Tilly, C. (2004) *Social Movements 1768–2004*. Boulder, CO: Paradigm Publishers.

Tooms, A., and Alston, J. (2005) "What's democracy and ethics got to do with them?: Administrative aspirants' attitudes towards the gay community." Paper presented at the UCEA Annual Convention, Nashville, TN, November.

Tutu, D. (2004) *God Has a Dream*. New York: Random House.

Vallance, E. (1973) "Hiding the hidden curriculum: An interpretation of the language of justification in nineteenth-century educational reform." *Curriculum Theory Network* 4:1; 5–21.

Walker, K. (1995) "The kids' best interests." *Canadian School Executive*, 15(5); 2–8.

Walker, K. (1998) "Jurisprudential and ethical perspectives on 'the best interests of children.'" *Interchange*, 29(3); 283–304.

Webb, L., and McCarthy, M. C. (1998) "Ella Flagg Young: Pioneer of democratic school administration." *Educational Administration Quarterly*, 34(2); 223–242.

Weis, L., and Fine, M. (1993) *Beyond Silenced Voices: Class, Race, and Gender in U.S. Schools*. Albany, NY: State University of New York Press.

Welch, S. (1991) "An ethic of solidarity and difference." In H. Giroux (ed.), *Postmodernism, Feminism, and Cultural Politics: Redrawing Educational Boundaries*. Albany, NY: State University of New York Press.

Whyte, W. H. (1956) *The Organization Man*. New York: Simon & Schuster.

Willower, D. J. (1999) "Work on values in educational administration: Some observations." Paper presented at the annual meeting of the University Council for Educational Administration Center for the Study of Ethnics and Leadership, Charlottesville, VA, October.

Willower, D. J., and Licata, J. W. (1997) *Values and Valuation in the Practice of Education Administration*. Thousand Oaks, CA: Corwin Press.

Wraga, W. (2006) "The heightened significance of *Brown v. Board of Education* in our own time." *Phi Delta Kappan*, 87(6); 424–428.

Young, I. M. (1990) *Justice and the Politics of Difference*. Princeton, NJ: Princeton University Press.

Young, M. D, Petersen, G. J., and Short P. M. (2002) "The complexity of substantive reform: A call for interdependence among key stakeholders." *Educational Administration Quarterly*, 38(2); 136–175.

Yudof, M., Kirp, D., and Levin, B. (1992) *Educational Policy and the Law* (3rd ed.). St. Paul, MN: West Publishing Company.

Zaretsky, L. (2005) "Moving beyond the 'talk' toward the 'enactment' of democratic ethical educational leadership: A conversation between two principals." Paper presented at the annual convention of the University Council of Educational Administration, Nashville, TN, November.

AUTHORS

Joan Poliner Shapiro is professor of educational administration in the Department of Educational Leadership and Policy Studies at Temple University's College of Education. At Temple, she previously served as an associate dean for research and development and as a chair of her department. She also has been the co-director of the Women's Studies Program and a supervisor of intern teachers at the University of Pennsylvania. In addition, she taught middle school and high school in the United States and the United Kingdom. Currently, she serves as a trustee of the University Council of Educational Administration's Center for Values and Leadership, as a board member of Research for Action, and is on the review board of the *Journal of School Leadership*. Dr. Shapiro holds a doctorate in educational administration from the University of Pennsylvania and completed a postdoctoral year at the University of London's Institute of Education. She has co-authored the books *Reframing Diversity in Education* (Rowman & Littlefield, 2002), *Gender in Urban Education: Strategies forStudent Achievement* (Heinemann, 2004), and *Ethical Leadership and Decision Making in Education: Applying Theoretical Perspectives to Complex Dilemmas* (Erlbaum, 2005, 2nd ed), and has written 50 articles in refereed journals or edited books.

Steven Jay Gross is associate professor of educational leadership and policy studies at Temple University, Philadelphia, Pennsylvania. His research interests center on initiating and sustaining democratic ethical innovations in schools and on Turbulence Theory. His books include *Leadership Mentoring: Maintaining School Success in Turbulent Times* (2006), *Staying Centered: Curriculum Leadership in a Turbulent Era* (1998) and *Promises Kept: Sustaining School and District Leadership in a Turbulent Era* (2004). Dr. Gross served as editor of ASCD's curriculum handbook series and is a senior fellow at the Vermont Society for the Study of Education. His previous professional experience includes serving as associate professor of education at Trinity College of Vermont, chief of curriculum and instruction for the State of Vermont, executive director of the China Project Consortium, curriculum and staff development director for the Rutland Northeast Supervisory Union, and high school social studies teacher in Philadelphia. Dr. Gross earned his undergraduate degree in history at Temple University, a masters' degree in modern Chinese history at the University of Wisconsin, Madison, a doctorate in educational leadership at the University of Pennsylvania, and was a Klingenstein fellow at Teachers College, Columbia University. Gross also studied Mandarin Chinese at the Chinese University of Hong Kong.

CONTRIBUTORS

Stacey L. Aronow holds an EdD in educational administration and policy studies from Temple University. Dr. Aronow's dissertation "Education's Middle Managers: High School Perceptions of Distributive Leadership" examined perceptions of high school department leaders in relation to how they perceived their roles within their department and the school. The study also sought to determine how department leaders resolved administrative and collegial tensions while still completing their various responsibilities. A two-time presenter for the University Council for Educational Administration, Dr. Aronow holds a BA in English and an MS in education from the University of Pennsylvania. Presently, Dr. Aronow teaches English and journalism at a Montgomery County, Pennsylvania high school, where she also advises the high school's nationally award-winning school newspaper.

Rita M. Becker, EdD, earned an MS in curriculum and instruction from Western Maryland College and a DEA from Temple University. She has held positions as an elementary school teacher, as both an elementary and secondary school principal, and as a director of elementary education before becoming an assistant superintendent of a school district in south-central Pennsylvania. Dr. Becker is also an adjunct professor in the Educational Leadership Program at Temple University.

Sara M. Becker earned her undergraduate degree in biology from LaSalle University in 1998. She was an Americorps volunteer in Philadelphia before beginning her graduate studies in educational psychology at Temple University. While at Temple, she earned a state teaching certificate in elementary education and then went on to become a literacy intern and early childhood educator in the Head Start program in the Philadelphia school district. She is examining the components of the student-teaching experience for her doctoral dissertation. She currently serves as the associate director of the Teacher Preparation Program (TPP) on the Camden Campus of Rutgers University. Additionally, she is a part-time lecturer for the TPP.

Corrinne A. Caldwell has spent more than 30 years in educational administration from community colleges to research universities. For the past five years, Dr. Caldwell has served as a professor and coordinator of the Educational Administration program at Temple University. Prior to assuming her faculty responsibilities, she held a wide variety of administrative posts, including director of career programs at Fraser Valley College; dean of mathematics, physical sciences, and technology at Community College of Philadelphia; campus executive officer of Penn State, Mont Alto; and most recently vice president, dean of Temple University, Ambler, and acting provost of Temple University. She has continued her research interests throughout her academic career, writing on access and opportunity for under-represented groups in higher education, faculty careers and development, women's leadership, science-related curriculum, and accreditation. Dr. Caldwell earned a BA and MSW from the University of British Columbia and a PhD in higher education leadership from the University of Pennsylvania.

Albert F. Catarro, Jr. is a business education teacher and internship program coordinator at William Tennent High School in Warminster, Pennsylvania. Catarro entered education after 20 years in the business community. As internship program coordinator, he works closely with local businesses to expand educational opportunities for many students. Mr. Catarro has a leadership position in the Centennial Education Association and is currently president-elect. He is a doctoral student in the educational leadership and policies studies at Temple University in Philadelphia, Pennsylvania. He has an MS in education, also from Temple University. He successfully completed the teacher certification program at Rider University, Lawrenceville, New Jersey. He earned his undergraduate degree in business from Thomas Edison State College in New Jersey. He earned an associates degree in mortuary science from Mercer County Community College. Mr. Catarro's educational pursuits, combined with his entrepreneurial endeavors, have fueled his passion in the area of career development for high school students.

Joseph P. DuCette is a professor of educational psychology and chairperson of the Department of Psychological Studies in Education (PSE) in the College of Education at Temple University. Dr. DuCette received his bachelor's degree from the University of Wisconsin, Eau Claire, in psychology and economics and his PhD in experimental psychology from Cornell University. His research interests include attribution theory, the evaluation of teaching, program evaluation, and learning styles. He recently published a book (with Dr. Vincent Anfara) on middle school principals. A central theme in his research is the effect of diversity on teaching and learning.

Mary M. Figura is the principal of Belmont Hills Elementary School in the Bensalem Township School District in Bucks County, Pennsylvania. Prior to becoming principal, she was an assistant principal, reading specialist, and fifth grade teacher. She received her bachelor's degree from Bloomsburg University, her masters of education in reading from Kutztown University, and principal certification from Pennsylvania State University. She is currently pursuing a doctorate in educational administration at Temple University. Along with presenting at the Seventh Annual Toronto Leadership Conference, she has conducted staff development workshops in various school districts in Pennsylvania and Delaware.

David X. Fitt is a clinical assistant professor in the Department of Curriculum, Instruction, and Technology in Education at Temple University's College of Education. He previously served as the director of field placements for pre-service teachers and he also served as a supervisor of student teachers. In addition, he holds certification as a school psychologist in the State of Pennsylvania. Dr. Fitt holds a doctorate in measurements, evaluation, testing, and research from the University of Pennsylvania. His research interests include assessment of classroom learning and program evaluation. He is currently co-authoring an e-textbook focusing on the preparation of pre-service teachers to use technology in the classroom.

Kendall L. Glouner earned a bachelors degree in elementary education from Millersville University and a masters degree in educational administration from Temple University. Formerly an elementary teacher and principal, she is currently the director of curriculum in the school district of Hatboro-Horsham in Horsham, Pennsylvania. She lives with her husband and son in suburban Philadelphia.

Emily L. Gross is from Middlebury, Vermont, and is completing her undergraduate degree work in public communications at the University of Vermont (UVM). Emily has also lived in Beijing, China, where she studied Mandarin and Chinese culture. She is continuing her Chinese studies in the United States. Most recently, she interned at a social justice non-governmental organization in Sydney, Australia. Emily briefly went to college in New Orleans.

Kelly D. Harbaugh has been involved in education for 20 years as a teacher and administrator. She earned her masters from Pennsylvania State University and her doctorate in educational administration from Temple University. Dr. Harbaugh's research interest is in the area of school violence, and in particular, bomb threats. She is currently an administrator in the Palmyra Area School District of Pennsylvania.

Ellen Henderson Brown received her doctorate in the Education Leadership and Policy Studies Department at Temple University with a focus in higher educational administration. She received her bachelors degree in communication from the College of New Jersey and her masters degree in school counseling from Oregon State University. After working for several years as an academic counselor for student athletes at two athletically competitive institutions, she served as the ombudsperson for the College of Education at Temple University and teaches psychology courses at Delaware County Community College. Dr. Henderson's dissertation focused on faculty perceptions of and responses to academic dishonesty, utilizing an ethical perspective.

Noelle Jacquelin is a director of curriculum at the Dennis Township School District in Cape May County, New Jersey. She holds a BA in English, an MEd in educational leadership, an MEd in curriculum, and she has completed her doctoral courses. She is currently an advanced doctoral candidate at Temple University. She is the single mother of four children aged 12, 10, 23 months, and 5 months.

Christopher J. Lake is the principal at St. Aloysius' School in Wilkes-Barre, Pennsylvania. He earned his BS and MS degrees from the University of Scranton and his doctorate in educational administration from Temple University. Dr. Lake has been a classroom English teacher for 19 years and is a language arts National Board certified teacher. His in-depth studies include arts in education and teacher self-reflection to improve instruction.

Maureen F. Linton is a doctoral candidate in the Higher Education Administration program at Temple University. She works as a coordinator of transfer students in the office of undergraduate admissions at Temple University. Prior to working at Temple University, Ms. Linton taught mathematics and science at William Sayre Middle School in Philadelphia. Her research interests include transfer students' perceptions of adjustment strategies offered by four-year colleges. She also explores resilience theory and adult learning theories, as well as the impact of social reproduction on transfer students. Ms. Linton presented a paper focusing on an ethical dilemma with the application of Turbulence Theory at the 10th Annual Values and Leadership Conference held at Pennsylvania State University.

Shaun Little has been a classroom teacher for the past six years. He currently teaches seventh grade geography at Abington Junior High School in Pennsylvania. Previously, he taught seventh grade world civilizations at Marlboro Middle School in New Jersey. He received his bachelor of arts from LaSalle University and his masters and doctoral degrees from Temple University. Currently, he is pursuing his doctoral degree in school administration at Temple University. His dissertation focused on the impact that performance-related pay has on teacher retention.

Terry M. McDonald is a high school counselor at Bridgewater-Raritan High School in Bridgewater, New Jersey, where she has counseled for 16 years. She received her BS in the area of teacher of health and physical education from Montclair State University in New Jersey and her MA in student personnel services from Kean University in New Jersey. Currently, she is a doctoral candidate in the Department of Educational Leadership and Policy Studies at Temple University. Her dissertation will provide a critical analysis of how school counselors make ethical decisions in their work.

Robert J. Murphy is the administrative director of the Department of Pathology and Laboratory Medicine at Temple University Hospital and the Temple University School of Medicine. He has served as an adjunct lecturer in the Graduate Health Administrative Services program at St. Joseph's University in Philadelphia for over 23 years. Mr. Murphy received both his MBA and EdM degrees from Temple University and is currently a doctoral student in Temple's Department of Educational Leadership and Policy Studies. His research interests are in the curricular design of ethics teaching in medical and nursing professional undergraduate schools in the United States and Canada.

Yvonnette J. Marshall has been involved in public education in the Caribbean island of Jamaica for 31 years. As a science educator, she has been involved in teaching, curriculum development, testing and evaluation, and teacher training. Her work as an administrator has involved secondary schools supervision, strategic planning, and policy development for higher education in Jamaica. She received her bachelors degree in chemistry from the University of the West Indies, Mona, and her masters degree in science education from the State University of New York (SUNY) at Buffalo. Most recently Dr. Marshall received her Ed.D. in educational administration from Temple University. Her research interests include quality assurance in higher education, educational policy, and change theory.

James M. O'Connor has been a professional educator for 32 years, beginning his career in a semi-rural secondary high school as a teacher of technology education. He is currently a middle school administrator and school board member. He has taught as an adjunct instructor at the college level and frequently conducts teacher training sessions. O'Connor earned his doctorate in 2007 from Temple University with a research concentration in experiential education.

Cynthia L. Renehan is currently serving as an elementary school principal in an urban Pennsylvania setting. Renehan holds a bachelors degree in early childhood, elementary, and special education from Millersville University, a masters degree from Western Maryland College, and her principal certification from Shippensburg University. Renehan is pursuing a doctoral degree from the Educational Leadership and Policy Studies Department at Temple University. Her research centers on discovering the ethic of the profession demonstrated through the work of teacher leaders. Renehan intends to model for her faculty, staff, and students the joy of continued academic pursuit, as well as the implementation of best practice designed to bring about Margaret Mead's vision: "Never doubt that a small group of thoughtful, committed citizens can change the world. Indeed, it is the only thing that ever has."

Susan H. Shapiro is the director of a child-care center in New York City. Prior to this position, she was a teacher director and before that, a teacher in a preschool classroom. Dr. Shapiro earned her bachelors degree from the New School for Social Research, Eugene Lang College, and a masters degree from Bank Street College of Education. She received her doctoral degree at New York University in the Educational Leadership Program, where she wrote a dissertation on the effects of September 11, 2001, on early childhood directors.

Jamie R. Shuda is the co-founder and current director of a university-based education outreach program that targets underserved students. She earned her BS in psychology and a masters in education with an elementary certification from Drexel University. She holds a doctoral degree in the Department of Education Leadership and Policy Studies at Temple University. Her dissertation, "A qualitative analysis of an institute on disabilities embedded in a research institution," focused on the sustainability and institutionalization of university-based community service programs. Dr. Shuda's research interests include university–community partnerships, service learning, and the role of strategic planning in higher education. She has co-authored an article appearing in the journal *Public Library of Science.*

Alison J. Staplin is dean of admissions and academics for the Rock Academic Program Alliance (RAPA), an on-site academic program for the conservatory level pre-professional high school students at the Rock School for Dance

Education in Philadelphia. Ms. Staplin was a dancer for 20 years prior to assisting in the creation of the RAPA program and becoming dean of the Rock School. She is currently an advanced doctoral student in the Department of Educational Leadership and Policy Studies at Temple University. Her research and writing encompass a wide range of topics surrounding arts and education, including the ability for dancers to complete high school diplomas and pursue higher education degrees while dancing professionally to ensure smoother career transition.

Melissa Sterba is currently an administrator at New York University. She is a practicing attorney advocating for students and families in crisis. She was previously a faculty member at Temple University, where she taught school law. She earned her JD from Villanova University and a PhD in education policy from the University of Pennsylvania. Her research focuses on gender equity, ethics, and students' First Amendment rights.

Lisa Marie Waller graduated in the top 10% of her high school class in Harrisburg, Pennsylvania, and attended Pennsylvania State University. At the university, she fine-tuned her teaching abilities, gained a broader perspective on the world, and graduated on the Dean's List in 1990 with a BS in social studies education. Ms. Waller was a high school teacher for the next six years. During that period she won numerous awards, including Teacher of the Year. Leaving the teaching ranks, Ms. Waller served as an assistant principal for four years while she pursued her masters degree in educational administration from Temple University. One of the initial pioneers in the development of a new high school, Waller became the director of SciTech High School, where she served in this capacity for a number of years. She was working on her doctorate from Temple University in educational administration. Sadly, Ms. Waller passed away in 2007.

Troy L. Wiestling is currently an elementary principal in the Dover Area school district, where he has been an administrator for seven years. Throughout his career, he has held positions as a certified athletic trainer, health teacher, at-risk program coordinator, dean of students, assistant middle school principal, and elementary principal. He earned his BS degree in biology from Shippensburg University and his MEd in health education and his administration certification from Pennsylvania State University. Wiestling is currently enrolled as a doctoral candidate in educational administration at Temple University.

W. Douglas Zander is a student at Temple University, where he is pursuing his doctor of education in educational leadership and policy studies. His dissertation is tentatively entitled, "Identification and analysis of successful persistence strategies for urban, African-American students enrolled at predominantly rural, white campuses." Mr. Zander has worked in the field of higher education administration for more than 20 years. He has held positions in both the public and private sector and has focused on student services, campus life, and enrollment management.

INDEX

A

Academic jeopardy, student placed in, 108
Accommodation
  flexibility demanded by, 68
  power versus, 67–85
    authentic education or
      organizational threat, 75–77
    culturally sensitive teaching
      approach, 78–82
    elite versus appropriate curriculum,
      82–85
    who should teach unwanted class,
      71–74
  school assessment, 69
Accountability, 167, *see also* Responsibility,
    accountability versus
  diverse forms of, 175
  forms of, 87
  measurement of, 91
  national reports on, 87
  NCLB and, 87, 89, 90
ACLU
  attorney, 80
  case, 11
Action research, organizational, 43
Administrator requirements, 30
Affirmative action, 121
  African-American student and, 128–133
  benefits of, 133
African-American student(s)
  affirmative action and, 128–133
  impact of student teacher on, 158
Anger management classes, 64
Apprentice model, student teacher, 152
Asian students, 146
Authority
  disobedience to, 137
  embracing of inauthentic duality, 138
  personal vision versus, 137–150
    revenue or integrity, 145–146

  school friend or foe, 141–144
  storm warnings, 147–150
  student wishes versus faculty advice,
    139–141

B

Bay of Pigs invasion, 138
Bible belt, school district in, 75
Bomb threat(s), 62
  media sharks and, 61
  questions for discussion, 62
  real or hoax, 60–62
BPE, *see* Buttonwood Proficiency Exam
Brown v. Board of Education decision, 105
Building an Ethical School, 20
Bureaucracy, democratic principles and, 55
Buttonwood Proficiency Exam (BPE), 65

C

Career-training workshops, 127
Caring
  foundational ethic of, 27
  types of, 28
Cascading
  effect of, 46
  example of heightened turbulence
    through, 47
  metaphor of, 46
Censorship, student, 109–111
Chain of command, repercussions for
    breaking, 124–125
Change
  agents, business leaders trained to be, 79
  opposition to, 39
  teacher's background emphasizing, 76
Chaos, avoidance of, 61

Chaos Theory, Turbulence Theory and,
47–48
Cheating, 139, 143
Children
frightened, 58–59
unlawful absence of, 96
Children and Youth Services agency, 96
CIA triangle, *see* Curriculum–Instruction–
Assessment triangle
Civil disobedience, moral foundation for, 137
Civil liberties, security versus, 55–66
bomb threat, 60–62
disciplinarian or intimidator, 62–64
protection of children in terrifying times,
57–59
questions for discussion
bomb threat, 62
disciplinarian or intimidator, 64–65
protection of children in terrifying
times, 59–60
student incident, 66
student incident, 65–66
Classroom
discipline, 161
management problems, student teacher,
156
management skills, teacher's problem
with, 112
organized chaos in, 76
safe space of, 18
uncontrolled, 76
College admission(s)
standards, bending of, 134–136
volatility of issue of, 121
College program audit, 134
Color codes, labeling of threatening
situations with, 55
Community
-based curriculum, 83–84
building, 104
democratic-ethical, 176
New DEEL skills of, 171
disjointed, 40
fundraising by, 83
outreach center, university, 121
problems, 12
separate ethic of, 33
severe turbulence experienced by, 41

standards, *see* Individual rights,
community standards versus
tension between individual and, 103
university involvement with, 125, 126
values
questioning of, 15
values incompatible with, 5
Community Outreach Center, 126
Competition, need to deemphasize, 28
Control, *see* Democracy, control versus
Crisis Management Plan, 61
Curriculum
accommodation in, 69, 70
career-level, 72
community-based, 83–84
controversial, 50, 70
design, 171
elite versus appropriate, 82
emphasis of on liberal studies, 67
honors, 140
improved delivery of, 60
instruction and, 68
Curriculum–Instruction–Assessment (CIA)
triangle, 68

D

Dare the Schools Build a New Social Order?
169
D-Day invasion, 37
Decision(s)
ethical
three Rs of, 35
Turbulence Theory and, 9–10
making
students at center of, 35
values involved in, 4
moral
educational leaders facing, 3
ethic of care in making, 27
Deliberate democracy, 169
Democracy
control versus, 167–176
democracy and public schooling,
168–169
empirical studies, 174
ethical leadership, 171–173, 173–174

moving educational leadership forward, 170–171
New DEEL, 169–170, 174–175
deliberate, 169
need for moral leaders to be concerned with, 25
school as laboratory of, 167
tension in, 6, 103
Democratic citizenship, complex task of, 170
Democratic Education, 168
Democratic Ethical Educational Leadership (New DEEL), 5, 169
community building under, 171
comparison of traditional behaviors with, 172
control versus democracy, 174
forward movement of, 171
mission of, 170
promotion of ethical reasoning, 171
Democratic school administration movement, 170
Dilemma(s)
contradictory value systems, 154, 157–158
educational, turbulence and, 18
ethical
example of, 10–13
moderate turbulence of, 15–17
multiple ethical paradigms approach to, 13–15
principal's, 91
special education, 120
turbulence gauge for, 16
use of as teaching vehicles, 20
moral, complexity of confrontations with, 34
Distinguished Flying Cross, 37
Distributive leadership, caveat concerning, 4
District, *see* School district
Disturbance, emotional strength of, 39
Diversity goals, post-secondary institution, 121
Double-loop learning, 69

E

Educate America Act, 87
Education
authentic, 75
basic principle driving, 34
caring in, 27
political theory of, central question of, 168
reason and emotion in, 27
recent trends in, 174
service, 167–168
special, ethical dilemma of, 120
Educational administration moral obligation of, 29
Educational debate, queries of, 67
Educational leader(s), *see also* Teacher
list of positions of, 4
moral decisions of, 3
onion model of, 173
student protection expected of, 56
tactics in dealing with violent students, 57, 62–64
Educational leadership, definition of, 4
Educational program, severe disruption of, 93–94
Education Amendments of 1972, Title IX of, 120
Emotional/rational dichotomy, 5
Emotional support students, 99
Equal consideration, 119
Equality, *see* Equity, equality versus
Equal treatment, definition of, 119
Equity, equality versus, 119–136
affirmative action, 128–133
bending of college admission standards, 134–136
mission or money bound, 125–128
paradox of, 120
rigor or rhetoric, 122–125
Ethical codes
definition of, 30
discussion of at union meetings, 32
paradox regarding, 31
Ethical Leadership and Decision Making in Education: Applying Theoretical Perspectives to Complex Dilemmas, 6
Ethic of care, 14
articulation of my feminist scholars, 7
ethic of justice and, 26
public forum of, 27
question for discussion, 17
teacher's, 114, 123
utilitarianism and, 27

Ethic of critique, 6, 14
 aim of, 25
 critical theory and, 23, 25
 language of possibility, 24
 question for discussion, 17
 social class and, 24, 25
Ethic of justice, 6, 13
 ethic of care and, 26
 feminist challenge to, 26
 incrementalism and, 21
 issues of, 22
 legal principles and, 22
 question for discussion, 17
 traditions and, 21
Ethic of the profession, 7, 15
 development of, 33
 for educational administration, 29
 ethical codes, 30–32
 question for discussion, 17
Ethics
 codes of, professional and personal, 32
 community, 33
 definition of, 20
 merging of, 19
 professional, development of, 33
Experiential learning, teacher's emphasis on, 76

F

Faculty
 advice, student wishes versus, 139
 betrayed, 84
 emergency meeting, 82
 evaluation committee, 84
Fears, re-awakening of following trauma, 39
Feminist scholars, challenge of to ethic of justice, 26
Fighter-pilot exploits, heroism for, 37
First Amendment, 13
Frankfurt school, 25
Freedom of speech, student, 106
Fundraising, soft-money, 127

G

Galloping Gertie, 48, 50
God Has a Dream, 104
Great Depression, progressive education movement during, 169
Greater good, sacrifice for, 145
Grounded Theory, 44
Group think, 138
Guest teacher, emergency certified, 99
Guidance counselor
 attendance report provided to, 95
 phone call to parent, 97
 requirements of, 89

H

Harvard Business School, 79
Harvard in the Mountains, 83
Head learners, 28
Health care
 administration, graduate program in, 78
 delivery, globalization of, 79
High Schools That Work model, 122
Human resources management instructor, 80
Hurricane Katrina
 college student caught in pathway of, 139, 147–150
 danger of, 149
 student decisions following, 150
 turbulence of, 52

I

IEP, see Individualized Education Plan
Indian Ocean tsunamis, turbulence of, 52
In a Different Voice, 26
Individualized Education Plan (IEP), 100, 124
Individual rights, community standards versus, 103–117
 coaching in intercollegiate athletics, 115–116
 intoxicated teacher, 111–114
 paradox, 56
 student newspaper censorship, 109–111
 troublemaker, 107–108

"In God We Trust" signs, 11
   philosophical debate about, 12
   putting up and tearing down, 15
Inner-city youth, types of caring of, 28
In-service meetings, 8
In-service training, 122
Instruction, organization of, 105
Instructional innovations, 69
Interactive learning, 77
Intercollegiate athletics, coaching in, 115
Internet, student mastery of, 107
Interstate School Leaders Licensure
         Consortium (ISLLC), 7, 30, 175
ISLLC, *see* Interstate School Leaders
         Licensure Consortium
I Won't Learn from You!, 105

J

Just-community concept, 22
Justice paradigm, professional ethics as
         subset of, 30

K

Kindergarten program, attendance in, 95
Knowing, diverse ways of, 19

L

Language of possibility, 24
Law training, 20
Leadership
   distributive, caveat concerning, 4
   educational
      ethic of the profession and, 29
      forward movement of, 171
   ethical, 171, 173
   moral, 174
   style emphasizing relationships, 28
   turnover, 98
Learning
   double-loop, 69
   experiential, teacher's emphasis on, 76
   interactive, 77

service, 168
Legal principles, ethic of justice in, 22
Liberal studies, curriculum emphasizing, 67
*Lonely Crowd: A Study of Changing
      American Culture, The*, 138
Lorenz Attractor, 48

M

Manifesto, The, 73
Media sharks, bomb threats and, 61
Medicine, emerging business model in, 79
Metaphor(s)
   cascading as, 46
   limited, 42
   machine, 68
   organizations, 68–69
   significance of, 49
   Turbulence Theory as, 48
Minority recruitment plan, 129, 131
Model
   apprentice, student teacher, 152
   business, in medicine, 79
   Multiple Ethical Paradigms, 6, 19
   onion, of educational leaders, 173
Moral codes, winning versus, 115
Moral decisions
   educational leaders facing, 3
   ethic of care in making, 27
Morality, American, triumvirate of, 12
Moral leadership, 174
Moral problems, way to respond to, 28
Multiple Ethical Paradigms, 5, 6–7, 19–35
   approach to ethical dilemma, 13–15
   diagram of, 7
   ethic of care, 7, 26–29
   ethic of critique, 6, 23–25
   ethic of justice, 6, 21–23
   ethic of the profession, 7, 29–35
   model development, 19–21
   Turbulence Theory and, 10, 11

N

NASA science awards, 145

National Association of Basketball Coaches, 115
National identity, preservation of, 67
National Policy Board for Educational Administration (NPBEA), 30
Nazi war criminals, 137
NCAA
    Division I "Character University", 115
    violations, 116
NCLB, *see* No Child Left Behind Act of 2001
New DEEL, *see* Democratic Ethical Educational Leadership
New School for Social Research, 25
No Child Left Behind Act of 2001 (NCLB), 4, 69, 87
    accountability and, 87, 89, 90
    implementation of, 88
    paperwork, 93, 94
    power under, 68
    state testing requirements, 122
NPBEA, *see* National Policy Board for Educational Administration

O

OBE, *see* Outcomes-based education
Once-and-for-all answers, 3–4
Onion model, educational leadership, 173
Organization(s)
    action research in, 43
    threat to, 75
    volatility of, 50
Organizational theory, positive feedback loops in, 47
Organizational turbulence, 44
Organization Man, 138
Organized chaos, classroom, 76
Outcomes-based education (OBE), 41
Outreach program, minority population of, 133

P

Paradoxes, decisions dealing with, 3
Parent(s)
    access to children, 59
    angry, 39, 112
    grievances aired on public radio talk shows, 135
    information on school test scores transferred to, 89
    notification of child's failing in class, 124
    phone call to, 97, 159
    principal's meeting with, 124
    threats from, 113
Participatory planning system, commitment to, 83
Pennsylvania Code of Professional Practice and Conduct for Educators, The, 30
Personal vision, *see* Authority, personal vision versus
Plagiarism, 143, 146
Positionality
    definition of functional groups, 50
    demographics of, 51
    organizational turbulence and, 44
    questions illuminating, 46
    Theory, Standpoint Theory and, 45
Poverty, challenges of, 42
Power, *see* Accommodation, power versus
PRAXIS tests, student teaching, 155
Principal(s)
    decision to tear down "In God We Trust" sign, 15
    disturbing comment made by, 75
    ethical dilemma of, 91
    new, student resistance to, 98
    parent meeting with, 124
    post-observation conference with, 77
    rookie, 56, 60
    safety measures demanded of, 108
    student-teaching program feedback from, 163
    teacher schedule e-mailed from, 71
Private schools, scholarships offered by, 130
Productive processes, reproductive processes versus, 26
Professional ethical codes, definition of, 30
Professional organizations, education-related, ethical codes of, 30
Promises Kept: Sustaining School and District Leadership in Turbulent Times, 8
Public radio talk shows, grievances aired on, 135

Q

Questions for discussion
affirmative action, 133–134
authentic education or organizational
threat, 78
balancing responsibility, 97–98
bending of college admission standards,
136
bomb threat, 62
coaching in intercollegiate athletics, 117
competence versus ineptitude, 94
culturally sensitive teaching approach, 82
disciplinarian or intimidator, 64–65
elite versus appropriate curriculum, 85
ethic of care, 17
ethic of critique, 17
ethic of justice, 17
ethic of the profession, 17
family level of turbulence, 60
intoxicated teacher, 114
leadership turnover, 101–102
mission or money bound, 128
reduction of turbulence, 85
revenue or integrity, 146
rhetoric versus reality, 91–92
rigor or rhetoric, 125
school friend or foe, 144–145
storm warnings, 150
student incident, 66
student newspaper censorship, 111
student teaching
cooperating teachers, 162
deficits, 157
ethically compromising demands, 164
principles meeting reality, 160
values, 158–159
student wishes versus faculty advice, 141
terrifying times, 59
troublemaker, 108–109
Turbulence Theory, 17
who should teach unwanted class, 75

R

Responsibility, accountability versus, 87–102
balancing responsibility, 95–97

competence versus ineptitude, 92–94
leadership turnover, 98–101
rhetoric versus reality, 90–91
Responsibility, perception of, 88

S

SAT scores, 132
School(s)
accountability, 90
administration, democratic, 170
administrators
disciplinary letters from, 63
personal values influencing, 32
assessment, accommodation in, 69
attendance
hearing, 96
policies, 88
reporting requirements, 89
state requirements for, 95
attitude of toward students, 105
block schedule, transition to, 74
building lockdown, 65
community boundaries, 106
competitive, 115
curriculum, well-organized, 42
equality of educational opportunity in, 21
financial audit, 11
innovating
challenges facing, 42
destabilizing blows facing, 46
just-community concept, 22
as laboratory of democracy, 167
leaders, comparison of New DEEL vision
with traditional behaviors of, 172
legislation, mandatory, 89
mentor, 144
on need-to-improve list, 42
organizations, change in leadership in,
102
prayer in, 13
private, scholarships offered by, 130
reform
agenda, 40
angry parents and, 39
destruction of, 42
resource officers (SRO), 65, 66
schedule, block format of, 71

-sponsored publication, freedom of
    speech in, 106
superintendent, first woman, 104
test scores, decrease in, 90
troublemaker, 107
urban, student transferred from, 90
violence, zero-tolerance policy toward, 57
virtuous, design of, 22
vocational technical, 72
year, anxiety for upcoming, 122
School district
    assessment, 92
    avoidance of litigation threats, 123
    bible belt, 75
    budgetary constraints of, 101
    personnel meetings, 89, 92
    potentially volatile, 16
    severe turbulence experienced by, 41
    on state empowerment list, 65
Schools of Tomorrow, 104
Security, *see* Civil liberties, security versus
Security tape, review of incident from, 64
Selfdetermination
    conflict with, 167
    right of, 55
Separation of church and state, 13, 18
September 11 (2001)
    evacuation of preschool, 57–59
    turbulence of, 52
Service education, 167–168
SES, *see* Socioeconomic status
Sex discrimination, 120
Smooth-as-glass flying, 40
Social class analysis, ethic of critique and,
    24, 25
Social policy, 119
Socioeconomic status (SES), 45, 51
Socio-political culture, East Asian, 81
Soft-money fundraising, 127
Southfield program
    business practices taught by, 81
    distinguishing characteristics of, 78
Special education
    department, imposed guidelines of, 100
    ethical dilemma of, 120
SRO, *see* School resource officers
Standardized codes, deficit of, 31
Standardized tests, school ranking on, 88
Standpoint Theory, 45

State empowerment list, school district on, 65
*Staying Centered: Curriculum Leadership in
    a Turbulent Era*, 8, 41, 67–68
Step Up program
    disadvantaged students and, 129
    minority population of, 133
Struggle for the American Curriculum, The,
    67
Student(s)
    activities, teacher's involvement in, 76
    African-American
        affirmative action and, 128–133
        impact of student teacher on, 158
    anxiety, 140
    Asian, 146
    assaulted, 65, 66
    attitude of school toward, 105
    best interests of, 34
    buddy system, 41
    censorship, 109–111
    cheating, 139
    competition among, 142
    detention, 65
    disadvantaged, Step Up program for, 129
    disciplining of, 146
    emotional support, 99
    fights, 66
    freedom of speech, 106
    frustration, 107
    graduate
        critical thinking promoted in, 81
        educational experiences of, 19–20
        levels of turbulence of, 49
        moral compasses of, 32
    grievances aired on public radio talk
        shows, 135
    learning styles of, 161
    minority, recruitment of, 131
    nervous, 142
    new, consequences of not
        accommodating, 40
    overwhelmed, internal conflict facing, 139
    pressures, understanding of, 144
    protests, 47
    resistance to new principal, 98
    self-reflection, 19
    special education, 120
    transfer, attending to, 91
    unfriendly, 149

unlawful absence of, 96
violence, teacher's tactics in dealing with,
    57, 62–64
writing skills of, 145
Student teacher(s)
    classroom management problems, 156
    director of, 158
    inadequate, 155
    possibility of failure of, 152
    preference of, 155
    supervisor of, 157
    training, field-based, 153
Student teaching, 151–164
    cooperating teachers, 161–162
    deficits, 155–156
    ethically compromising demands,
        162–164
    field experiences, 153–155
    model, 152
    placements, coordination of, 162
    PRAXIS tests, 155
    principles meeting reality, 159–160
    program
        focus group feedback about, 163
        mismanaged, 163
    training, 151–153
    unsatisfactory grade in, 156
    values, 157–158
Summer internships, 126
Superintendent certification, alternate route
    for, 12

T

Tardy-to-school letters, 95
Teacher(s), see also Educational leader
    accused of being selfish, 72
    alternate schedule, 73
    assessment tools of, 152
    background emphasizing change, 76
    betrayed, 74
    cooperating, 161–162
    course preferences of, 71
    decision to stay, 101
    draining of emotional energy, 101
    emphasis on experiential learning, 76
    ethic of care employed by, 123
    first-year, scheduling of, 74

guest, emergency certified, 99
half-time, 71–72
immoral, 113
intoxicated, 111–114
involvement in student activities, 76
network, unauthorized access to, 144
new, accommodation and, 70
overt threat made at, 108
personal lives of, 114
potential stress level of, 71
preparation programs,
    government-mandated, 154
schedule satisfaction, 72
scheduling philosophy, 74
school community boundaries affecting,
    106
student
    classroom management problems, 156
    director of, 158
    inadequate, 155
    possibility of failure of, 152
    preference of, 155
    supervisor of, 157
    training, field-based, 153
students feared by, 107
tenured, 160
training process, 151
transformation of role of student to role
    of, 152
union, 160
unprofessional behavior of, 73
unsatisfactory evaluation of, 112
Teaching
    approach
        collective faculty, 79
        culturally sensitive, 78
    certificate, denial of recommendation for,
        156
    profession, gatekeeper for, 161
    revised philosophy of, 77
    vehicles, ethical dilemmas used as, 20
Technology committee, power of, 84
Test(s)
    PRAXIS, 155
    scores
        decrease in, 90
        meeting of standards through raising
            of, 167
    standardized, school ranking on, 88

Testing
    high-stakes, 88, 168
    requirements, NCLB, 122
Texas' Ethics, Standards, and Practices, 30
Tracking, inequities related to, 24
Transfer students, attending to, 91
Truth telling, 162
Turbulence
    contradictory values and, 159
    definition of, 9
    extreme, 40, 42
    gauge, 10, 16, 48, 51
    level, change in, 51
    light, 8, 40
    metaphor of, 42
    moderate, 8, 9, 15–17, 40
    organizational, 44
    questions illuminating positionality
        during, 46
    severe, 8, 9, 40
        community experience of, 41
        first experience with, 38
    understood, 43
Turbulence Theory, 5, 8–9, 37–52
    application of, 49–52
        consequences of changing levels of
            turbulence, 51–52
        contextual forces, 50
        establishment of current level of
            turbulence, 51
        positionality, 50–51
    cascading, 46–47
    Chaos Theory and, 47–48
    ethical decision making and, 9–10
    example, 37–42
    hope of, 52
    intention of, 49
    metaphor, 48–49
    moderate turbulence, 8
    Multiple Ethical Paradigms and, 10, 11
    natural phenomena and, 48
    positionality, 44, 45–46
    positive aspects, 43–44
    questions for discussion, 17
    severe turbulence, 8–9

Tutoring, 140, 141
Two minds, 5

U

UCEA, *see* University Council of
            Educational Administration
Union meetings, discussion of ethical codes
        at, 32
University
    outreach work of, 121, 126
    recruiting strategies, 145
    teacher preparation programs, 154
University Council of Educational
        Administration (UCEA), 43, 170
Urban school, student transferred from, 90
USA PATRIOT Act, 55
U.S. News and World Report, 131
Utilitarianism, ethic of care and, 27

V

Value-less society, 12
Value systems, contradictory, 154, 157–158
Violence
    school, zero-tolerance policy toward, 57
    visual representation of, 108
Violin competition, 141
Virtuous schools, design of, 22
Vocational technical school, 72

W

War on Terror, student questioning of, 77
Western thought, traits associated with
        females, 26
Whistle-blowers, 138
Winning, moral codes versus, 115
Women's rights movement, 137
Women's studies course, 20
World Trade Center (WTC), 56, 57–59
World War II, massive bombing in, 46
WTC, *see* World Trade Center